Hockey
NOW!
SIXTH EDITION

FLYERS
29
Business

Hockey NOW!

SIXTH EDITION

MIKE LEONETTI

FIREFLY BOOKS

A Firefly Book

Published by Firefly Books Ltd. 2010

First printing

Publisher Cataloging-in-Publication Data (U.S.)
Leonetti, Mike, 1958-
Hockey now! / Mike Leonetti.
6th ed.
[ ] p. : col. ill. ; cm.
Includes index.
ISBN-13: 978-1-55407-639-0 (pbk.)
ISBN-10: 1-55407-639-0 (pbk.)
1. National Hockey League -- Biography. 2. Hockey players -- Biography. I. Title.
796.962/092 B dc22 GV848.5.A1L45 2010

Library and Archives Canada Cataloguing in Publication
Leonetti, Mike, 1958-
Hockey now! / Mike Leonetti. -- 6th ed.
Includes index.
ISBN-13: 978-1-55407-639-0 (pbk.)
ISBN-10: 1-55407-639-0 (pbk.)
1. Hockey players--Biography. 2. National Hockey League--Biography. 3. Hockey players--Pictorial works. 4. National Hockey League--Pictorial works. I. Title.
GV848.5.A1L455 2010 796.962092'2 C2010-901194-5

Published in the United States by
Firefly Books (U.S.) Inc.
P.O. Box 1338, Ellicott Station
Buffalo, New York 14205

Published in Canada by
Firefly Books Ltd.
66 Leek Crescent
Richmond Hill, Ontario L4B 1H1

Cover and interior design by Kimberley Young
Printed in Canada

The publisher gratefully acknowledges the financial support for our publishing program by the Government of Canada through the Canada Book Fund as administered by the Department of Canadian Heritage.

PHOTO CREDITS

Getty Images:

Graig Abel/NHLI: 85, 130, 142; Abelimages: 18, 36, 40, 71, 102, 104, 110, 131, 170; Scott Audette/NHLI: 8, 27, 34, 72, 112, 137, 163; Joel Auerbach: 20, 126, 157, 168; Brian Babineau/NHLI: 9, 12, 76, 105, 138; Al Bello: 33; Bruce Bennett: 23, 31, 56, 143, 156, 172; Mark Buckner/NHLI: 69, 148; Scott Cunningham/NHLI: 53, 107, 139; Kevin C. Cox: 11, 13; Jonathan Daniel: 47, 92, 108; Greg Fiume/NHLI: 16, 19, 38, 86, 116, 117; Gregg Forwerck/NHLI: 158; Tom Gannam/NHLI: 173; Noah Graham/NHLI: 59, 79, 161; Jeff Gross: 42; Norm Hall/NHLI: 136; Harry How: 6–7, 61, 154, 175; Bruce Kluckhohn/NHLI: 91; Francois Lacasse/NHLI: 17, 21, 39, 103, 113, 145; Mitchell Layton/NHLI: 80, 88, 162; Scott Levy/NHLI: 77, 97; Phillip MacCallum: 8, 28, 81, 144; Michael Martin/NHLI: 43, 49, 70, 119, 164, 165; Ronald Martinez: 52, 106; Jim McIsaac: 22, 25, 29, 41, 68, 84, 96, 121, 151, 169; Christopher Pasatieri/NHLI: 94, 114, 146; Christian Petersen: 24, 118, 127; Len Redkoles/NHLI: 30, 46, 50, 54, 120; Dave Reginek/NHLI: 32, 123, 149, 154, 166; Andre Ringuette/NHLI: 5, 60, 87, 114, 134; Debora Robinson/NHLI: 174; John Russell/NHLI: 10, 14, 62, 64, 74, 109, 124, 140, 160; Jamie Sabau/NHLI: 35, 51, 63, 89, 152; Dave Sandford/NHLI: 2–3, 93, 125; Joe Sargent/NHLU: 37, 111; Eliot J. Schechter/NHLI: 115; Gregory Shamus/NHLI: 82, 83, 153; Ezra Shaw: 58; Bill Smith/NHLI: 65, 132; Don Smith/NHLI: 45, 55, 57, 66, 67, 128, 129, 133, 167; Mike Stobe/NHLI: 73, 135, 147; Rebecca Taylor/NHLI: 159; Gerry Thomas/NHLI: 40, 44, 72, 78; Jeff Vinnick/NHLI: 26, 141, 150; Bill Wippert/NHLI: 15, 75, 122, 155, 171; Richard Wolowicz: 48.

Front Cover: G Fiume (Alex Ovechkin); Jim McIsaac (Sidney Crosby).

Back Cover: Len Redkoles/NHLI (Nicklas Lidstrom); Dave Reginek/NHLI (Brent Seabrook); John Russell/NHLI (Ryan Miller).

DEDICATION

The sixth edition of Hockey Now! is dedicated to all the members of the Chicago Blackhawks organization for ending one of longest championship droughts — 49 years — with their Stanley Cup win 2009–10.

CONTENTS

Introduction **6**

Eastern Conference Team Stars **8**

Western Conference Team Stars **40**

Impact Players **72**

Game Breakers **114**

On the Rise **154**

Acknowledgments/Profile Index **176**

INTRODUCTION

When 22-year-old Jonathan Toews of the Chicago Blackhawks raised the Stanley Cup to end the 2009–10 season, it marked the fourth time in five years that a team with a youthful core won the championship. In 2005–06, it was 21-year-old Eric Staal who led Carolina to their first-ever title, while in 2006–07 Ryan Getzlaf and Corey Perry were part of the reason the Cup went to the Anaheim Ducks. In 2009, Sidney Crosby and Evgeni Malkin led the Pittsburgh Penguins to their first title since 1992. The only championship team largely made up of veterans was the 2007–08 Detroit Red Wings, but even two of their key players, Pavel Datsyuk and Henrik Zetterberg, are still in their prime. The trend is clear: young players are likely to lead a team to the championship.

It has been said that the Stanley Cup is the hardest professional championship to win: four grueling best-of-seven rounds of playoff hockey means teams need fresh, young legs to survive. The Blackhawks won with the likes of Toews, Patrick Kane, Duncan Keith and Brent Seabrook leading a group of young Chicago stars. Washington hopes to capitalize on having Alex Ovechkin and Mike Green. The Los Angeles Kings have built their championship hopes around superstar defender Drew Doughty, while the Islanders hope to regain some of their old status with John Tavares showing the way.

Tampa Bay has Steven Stamkos as their new superstar, while Toronto wants Dion Phaneuf and a group of youngsters like Tyler Bozak and Phil Kessel to lead the Maple Leafs back to respectability. Colorado pins their hopes on Paul Stastny and Matt Duchene, while the Penguins hope to regain their championship status with Jordan Staal and Marc-Andre Fleury who are both still young enough to take the team deep into the playoffs. Other young players building great careers include David Backes, Jeff Carter, Evander Kane, Anze Kopitar, Tyler Myers, James Neal and Bobby Ryan.

The salary cap imposed on the NHL is a restraint many teams have a difficult time dealing with, but it is proving to be a great equalizer. The potential for more players changing teams is growing every year — even a championship club like Chicago had to move many of its players to clear cap space. With so much turnover, each season promises plenty of excitement.

All of the young players mentioned here are profiled in this edition of *Hockey Now!* alongside many veteran superstars, including award-winners like Martin St-Louis, Henrik Sedin, Ryan Miller and Shane Doan. It is our hope that *Hockey Now!* provides all hockey fans a great lead into next season when we again wait to see who will capture and raise the most coveted team trophy in all of sport — the Stanley Cup!

10 Atlanta Thrashers: Nik Antropov
12 Boston Bruins: Zdeno Chara
14 Buffalo Sabres: Ryan Miller
16 Carolina Hurricanes: Eric Staal
18 Florida Panthers: Stephen Weiss
20 Montreal Canadiens: Mike Cammalleri
22 New Jersey Devils: Martin Brodeur
24 New York Islanders: John Tavares
26 New York Rangers: Marian Gaborik
28 Ottawa Senators: Daniel Alfredsson
30 Philadelphia Flyers: Mike Richards
32 Pittsburgh Penguins: Sidney Crosby
34 Tampa Bay Lightning: Steven Stamkos
36 Toronto Maple Leafs: Phil Kessel
38 Washington Capitals: Alex Ovechkin

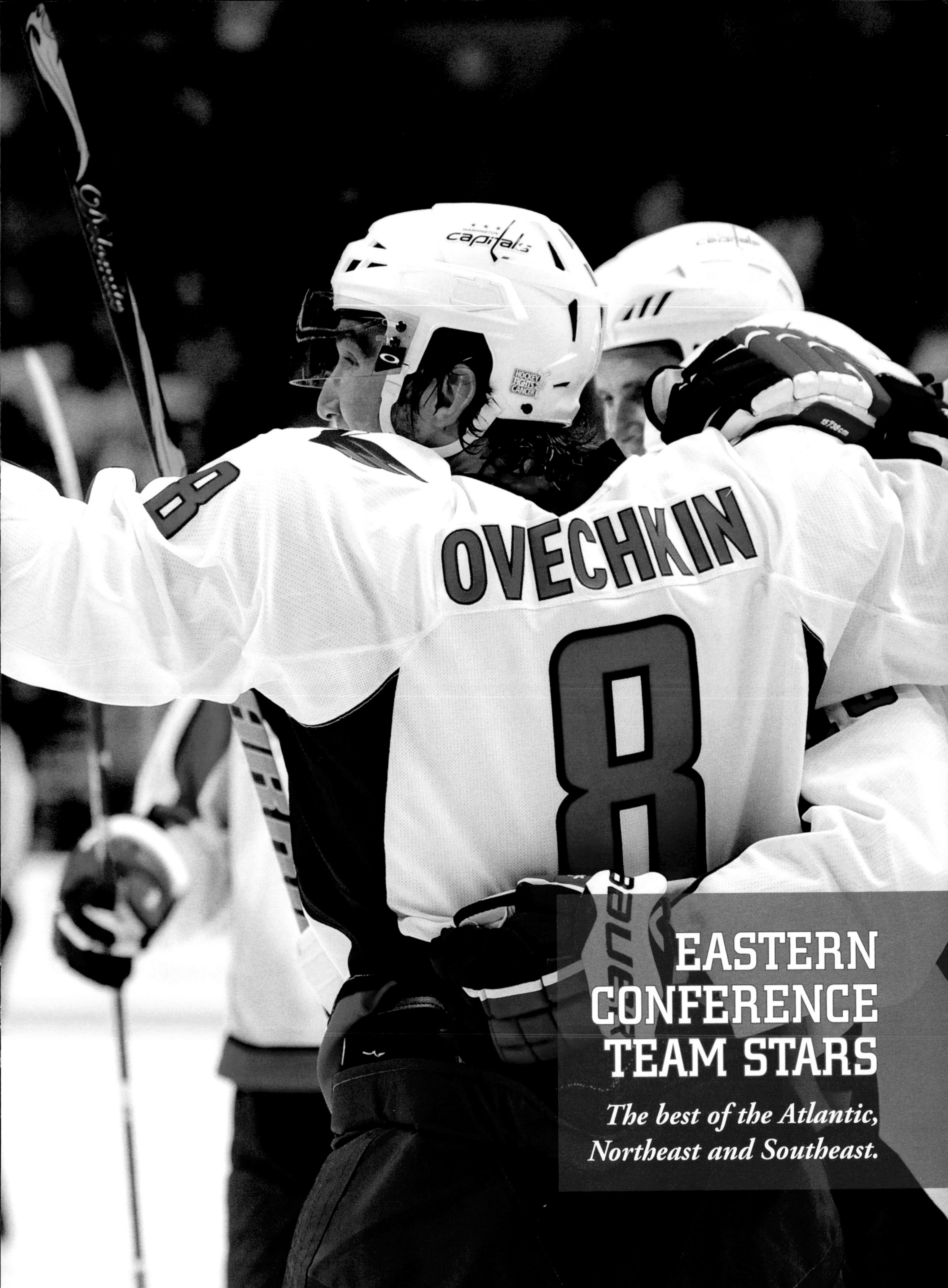

EASTERN CONFERENCE TEAM STARS

The best of the Atlantic, Northeast and Southeast.

When the Toronto Maple Leafs drafted center Nik Antropov back in 1998, they were quite happy to snag what everyone considered a 'sleeper pick' at the time. Many teams had the 6-foot-6, 230-pounder from Kazakhstan on their radar, but no one anticipated he would go as high as 10th overall. Like the other teams interested in Antropov, the Leafs saw great potential despite a prospect whose skating was somewhere between poor and average. Fast forward 10 years and it seemed the Maple Leafs could not wait to get rid of someone who had played 509 games in a blue and white uniform, while recording a very respectable 291 points. Those career numbers in Toronto were by no means outstanding, especially for a player drafted so high, but Antropov was a solid hockey player who was not yet 30 years of age. New management in Toronto decided Antropov did not produce enough to warrant a new contract and dealt him to the New York Rangers at the 2009 trade deadline for a second round draft choice (the Leafs took Kenny Ryan with the pick). Not loved as a Ranger despite seven goals and 13 points in 18 games, he was forced to look for work via the free agent market.

When someone like Ilya Kovalchuk calls to make a pitch, it is no wonder Antropov was listening carefully. The Atlanta Thrashers superstar talked about how the franchise was going in the right direction and how the team was very close to a playoff spot. The Thrashers were able to complete a deal with Antropov, thanks to Kovalchuk's help and a four-year contract worth roughly $4 million annually. At the start of the 2009–10 season, Antropov and Kovalchuk played on the same line and the team posted a respectable 14 wins through two months. The lanky Antropov was looking to set up Kovalchuk so much that he did not shoot enough — a criticism he often heard in Toronto — and as a result did not score a goal until the 18th game of the year. He did have 16 assists over the same time frame, but eventually the Thrashers started to lag behind in the hunt for a playoff spot and soon all talk turned to Kovalchuk, who was eligible to become an unrestricted free agent in the summer of 2010. Unable to sign their star to a new deal, Kovalchuk soon found his way to New Jersey in return for young prospects and a draft choice. Antropov could easily have become bitter at the turn of events, but he kept up his strong play for the Thrashers, finishing the year with 24 goals and a team-high 67 points. He also led the team with a plus-13 mark. That's not entirely surprising given Antropov is a career plus-66 and has finished the season as a minus player only twice, a fact often overlooked in discussions about his worth. All things considered, Antropov put in a great year with the Thrashers and his 76 games played represent the most he's seen with one team in a single season.

The Thrashers did not get going again until the last 20 games of the season and nearly pulled into a playoff spot with a 35–34–7 record, but too many losses at the end kept them out of the post-season by five points. Antropov had an especially satisfying game at the end of the year when he scored the winning goal and assisted on another at the Air Canada Centre versus the Maple Leafs. He had failed to record a point against his old team in three previous games, but he came through that night as Atlanta won an important game by a 3–2 score. He was especially pleased that game officially knocked the Leafs out of playoff contention and did not mind being booed by the same crowd that once hoped he would become a dominating player. Coach John Anderson noted Antropov was the rock of the team all year long and that he had played some wonderful hockey for the Thrashers — something rarely, if ever, said about him in his Toronto days.

Missing the playoffs ultimately cost Anderson his job and GM Don Waddell was replaced by Rick Dudley. The management and coaching moves mean Antropov will have prove himself all over again, but he has more confidence now that he put together such an outstanding year. It is unlikely Antropov will ever reach the heights expected when he was a teenager, but he has become a solid performer and if his most recent season is any indicator, a team leader.

BY THE NUMBERS Led the Atlanta Thrashers in scoring in 2009–10 with a career-high 67 points

- Scored a career-high 28 goals in 81 combined games with the Toronto Maple Leafs and New York Rangers in 2008–09
- Represented Kazakhstan in the 2006 Olympics
- Originally drafted 10th overall by Toronto in 1998
- Ranked fourth in the NHL with a 19.0 shooting percentage in 2009–10

CAREER HIGHLIGHTS

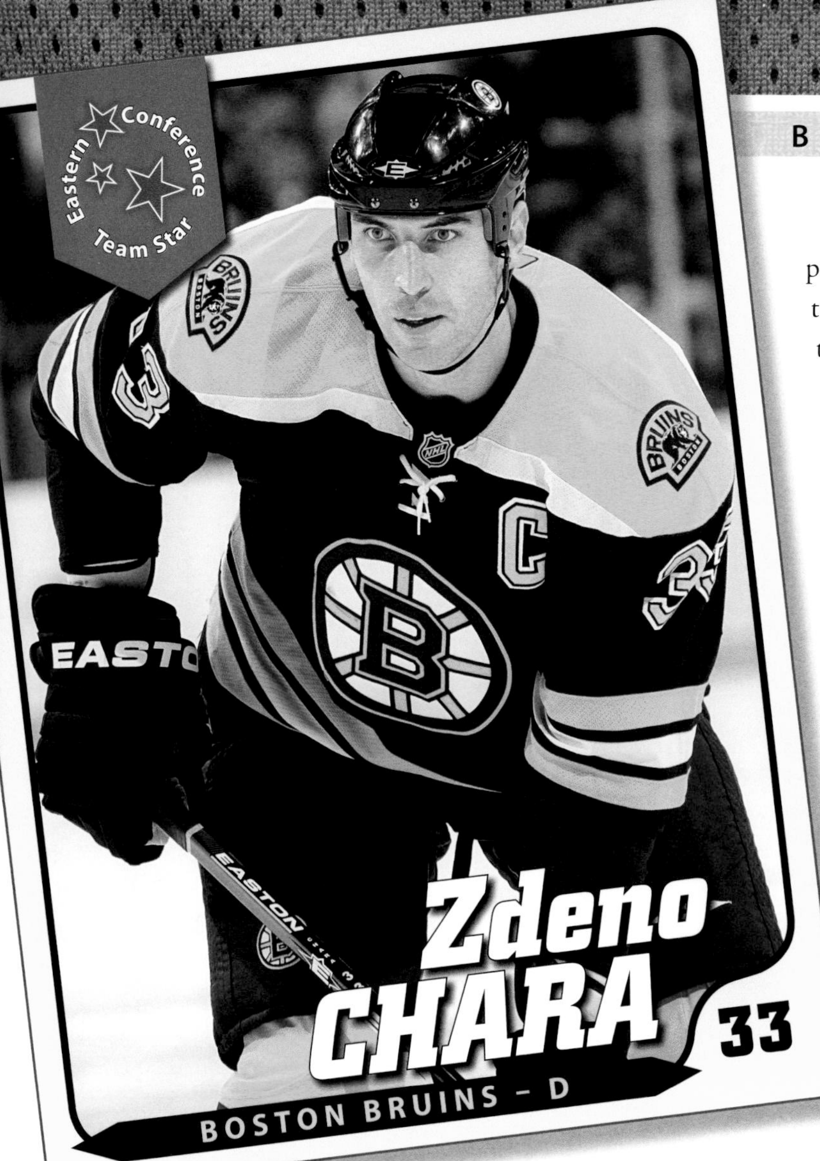

Zdeno Chara is the tallest player in the NHL at 6-foot-9 and one of the heaviest at 255 pounds. He is also the captain and leader of the Boston Bruins and on some nights, he never seems to leave the ice. Chara can certainly contribute on offense, but he is best known as a bruising defenseman who will battle with any opponent to gain an advantage. He is very physical — perhaps overly so at times, as his 1,297 career penalty minutes indicate — and is willing to drop the gloves whenever someone is foolish enough to challenge him. Chara has a decorated resume, including the 2009 Norris Trophy to go along with First Team All-Star selections in '09 and '04, as well as Second Team honors in '06 and '08. One thing he has yet to do, however, is lead a team to the Stanley Cup final. The 2010 playoffs provided another golden opportunity for Chara to take his team further into the post-season, but instead the Bruins were staring at a long summer after blowing a 3–0 series lead against the Philadelphia Flyers in the second round.

When Chara first suited up for Boston at the start of the 2006–07 season, great things were expected from the huge blueliner. He signed a $37.5 million deal with the Bruins as a free agent leaving the Ottawa Senators in the summer of 2006. His first year in Beantown was a huge disappointment, with the Bruins finishing last in the NHL's Northeast Division. Chara was a horrific minus-21 on the season and Boston ended up firing coach Dave Lewis. It was suggested Chara was trying too hard and that he was not exactly comfortable in his new role as Bruins captain. Adjustments were made for the next season, including consulting senior Boston players about team issues, and Chara scored 17 times and had 51 points in 77 games, earning a second nomination for the Norris after being a finalist with Ottawa in 2004.

His third year in Boston was the best of his career with 19 goals and 50 points in 80 games. The Bruins surged to top spot in the Eastern Conference during the regular season, then knocked off the Montreal Canadiens easily in the first round before falling short in seven games against a Carolina Hurricanes team they were favored to beat.

Both the team and Chara took a step back the following campaign in 2009–10. A nagging finger injury he didn't want to surgically repair during the season hampered the big Slovak for most of the year and then a broken nose had to be covered up with a full cage. He scored only nine times and totaled 44 points in 80 games. He was plus-19 and Boston played a stout defensive style, gaining a playoff spot late in the year with 91 points in a rather weak Eastern Conference. Chara was very strong in the final games of the regular season and during the Bruins' defeat of the Buffalo Sabres in the first round of the playoffs. However, the ignominy of losing like the Bruins did to the Flyers is a scar that will take a long time to heal. The last two playoff losses by the Bruins exposed weaknesses in Chara's game that teams like Carolina and Philadelphia were able to exploit. Chara plays too much and too physically to last four rounds in the playoffs. Twenty-nine penalty minutes in 13 2010 post-season games indicate he is easily riled and smaller forwards tend to buzz around him when they are able to get into the Bruins' zone unimpeded. Boston needs to support Chara with more reliable defensemen who can move the puck quickly and keep opponents off his large back.

While he must be nasty at times to be truly effective, Chara needs to understand he is of more value on the ice than in the penalty box. Since he has developed a stellar reputation as one of the NHL's elite defensemen, Chara gets the benefit of many referees looking the other way, but he would be smarter trying to unload his booming slapshot at the opposition net and creating more scoring for a team that struggled badly to find the net in 2009–10.

Chara needs to change his game somewhat if he is to be the leader the Bruins imagined when he had the 'C' sewn on his black and gold sweater.

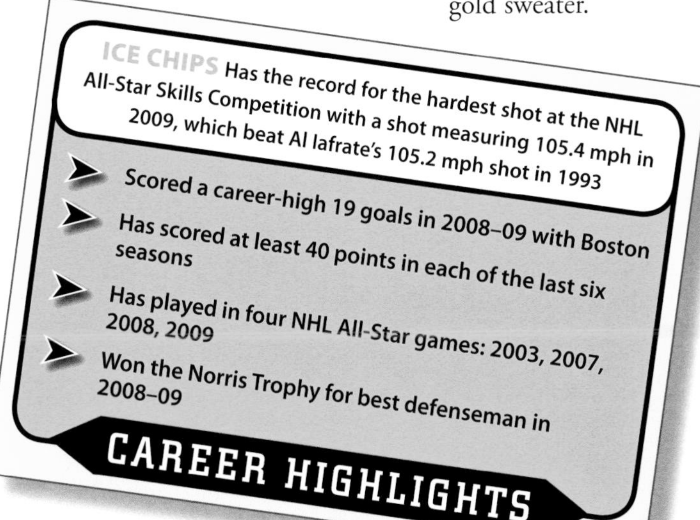

ICE CHIPS Has the record for the hardest shot at the NHL All-Star Skills Competition with a shot measuring 105.4 mph in 2009, which beat Al Iafrate's 105.2 mph shot in 1993

- Scored a career-high 19 goals in 2008–09 with Boston
- Has scored at least 40 points in each of the last six seasons
- Has played in four NHL All-Star games: 2003, 2007, 2008, 2009
- Won the Norris Trophy for best defenseman in 2008–09

CAREER HIGHLIGHTS

A long-time hockey scout named Paul Henry was one of the first to spot and tout goaltender Ryan Miller as a potential NHL player. Working for Florida at the time, Henry tried to get the Panthers to select Miller during the 1999 NHL draft, but they did not heed his advice. Instead Miller was selected by the Buffalo Sabres 138th overall. Miller has never forgotten Henry's efforts on his behalf and after the 2010 Winter Olympics, Henry received a Miller-signed puck in the mail. It was one of 139 such pucks sent out by Miller (one for every save he made during the Games for Team U.S.A.) to people he said helped fulfill his dream of playing in the Olympics. It was an honest appreciation for those whom Miller knew did the most for him. His regret was that it was not 140 pucks stopped — that would have meant a save on Sidney Crosby's overtime-winning shot, the one that secured gold for Team Canada.

Miller was determined to be a goalie by the age of eight, when he told his father, Dean, that he wanted netminding equipment. He made the declaration right in the middle of a game and his father, who was coaching Miller's team, had to promise his son to get him back out on the ice — he could be a goalie if he went out and did something to help his team right then. The youngster was motivated. He scored three goals and never played as a forward again. The incident showed just how intense and determined Miller can be, and that he was certain playing goalie was going to be how he left his mark on the game. His intensity has never waned and is still evident before he plays today. Prior to the pre-game warm-up, Miller will stand alone at the Buffalo bench, lean on his goal stick and prepare his mind for the task at hand that evening. Miller is the last player to leave the ice after the pre-game skate and he leads his team out for the contest, ready to do whatever it takes to keep his team in the game.

Since Miller arrived in Buffalo full-time in 2005–06, the Sabres have had up-and-down results. They have been the best team in the league (in 2006–07 when they won 53 games) and have been to the Eastern Conference final on two occasions. They have also missed the playoffs twice, for two straight seasons in 2007–08 and 2008–09 when Miller missed 13 games due to an ankle injury. The Sabres were determined to make it back to the playoffs in 2009–10 and it was Miller's fine performance that got them there. He was generally acknowledged as the top netminder in the league, winning 41 games, recording five shutouts and posting a .929 save percentage. In fact many insisted Miller was the most valuable player in the entire NHL, because without him in goal, Buffalo's low-scoring roster (no Buffalo player hit the 30-goal mark in 2009–10) had no chance of making the playoffs. He didn't win the Hart Trophy, but did take home the Vezina for top goaltender. Miller's performance was even more surprising when Buffalo's ordinary defense is taken into account. There were some decent veterans along the blueline such as captain Craig Rivet, and some talented youngsters such as Tyler Myers, but the Sabres defense would be very ordinary if Miller were absent.

Miller has now won 30 or more games for five consecutive seasons and his goals-against average has never hit the 3.00 mark, with his best coming in 2009–10 at a stellar 2.22. Although he looks fairly large in net, Miller is actually a rather thin 170 pounds on a 6-foot-2 frame. He works hard to keep his body square to the shooter at all times and his quick reflexes do most of the work for him. Miller's anticipation may be his biggest asset and he thrives on all the playing time since there has been virtually no faith in any backup the Sabres have had behind him. He moves very well post-to-post and has a terrific glove hand. Miller is very competitive and studious, giving the media thoughtful, opinionated answers when asked questions.

Miller has become an NHL star in every sense of the word.

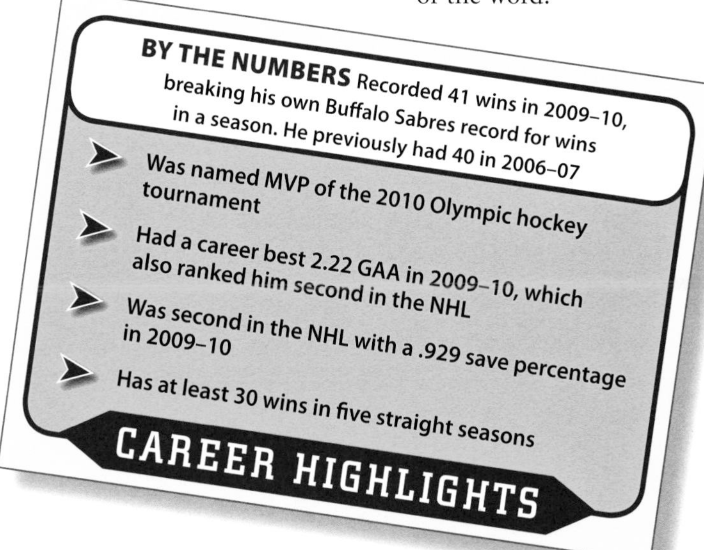

BY THE NUMBERS Recorded 41 wins in 2009–10, breaking his own Buffalo Sabres record for wins in a season. He previously had 40 in 2006–07

- Was named MVP of the 2010 Olympic hockey tournament
- Had a career best 2.22 GAA in 2009–10, which also ranked him second in the NHL
- Was second in the NHL with a .929 save percentage in 2009–10
- Has at least 30 wins in five straight seasons

CAREER HIGHLIGHTS

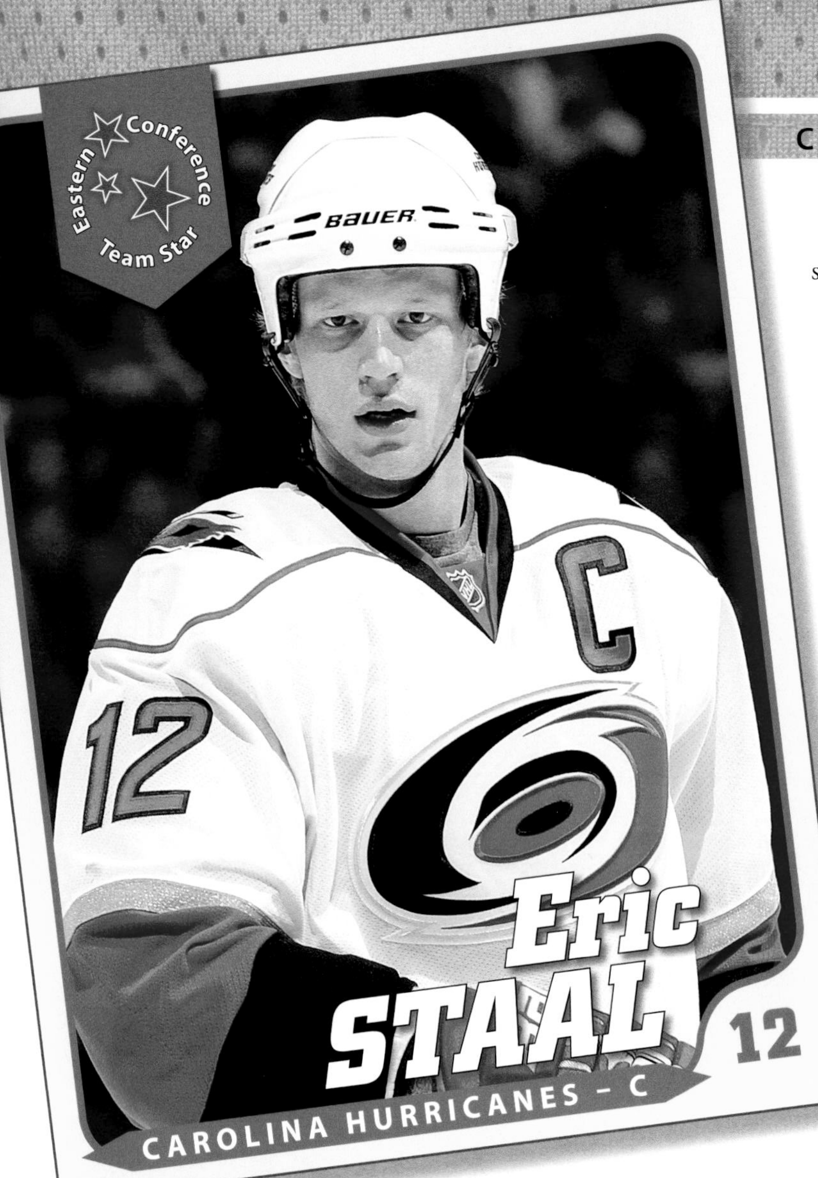

To put it simply, Carolina Hurricanes center Eric Staal is a winner. In February 2010, Staal recorded one goal and six points in seven games for the Canadian Olympic team that won the gold medal at the Vancouver Games. He also won the Stanley Cup with Carolina in 2006, scoring nine goals and 28 points in 25 games, and a gold medal with Team Canada at the 2007 World Championship, notching five goals and 10 points in 10 games. Those three titles gained Staal entry to the exclusive 'Triple Gold Club' at the ripe old age of 25. Just 23 other players and one coach are members of the club, including sure-fire Hall of Famers Joe Sakic, Scott Niedermayer, Chris Pronger and Nicklas Lidstrom. For Staal, it was quite an honor to be included with such elite players, but it should really be of no surprise to anyone who has followed his career.

Staal came out of the Ontario Hockey League development factory known as the Peterborough Petes. He spent three seasons with the Petes, scoring 39 goals and 98 points in 66 games in 2002–03, his draft year. Staal's name was bandied about as the potential No. 1 overall pick, but Pittsburgh selected goaltender Marc-Andre Fleury from the Quebec Major Junior Hockey League's Cape Breton Screaming Eagles first. However, Staal did not have to wait too long; the Hurricanes called his name with the second overall selection. Despite being a high pick, it was no sure thing Staal would make Carolina right out of junior, but he impressed enough to stay the entire 2003–04 season, tallying 11 goals and 31 points in 81 games. The NHL's lockout season followed and proved very beneficial to Staal. He spent the entire season with the American Hockey League's Lowell Lock Monsters, producing 26 goals and 77 points in 77 games. Playing in the AHL better prepared Staal for the NHL and he responded with 45 goals and 100 points the next season as an NHL sophomore. Then came his superb postseason, as Carolina won the Stanley Cup. For his efforts, Staal was named to the NHL's Second All-Star Team.

Playing all 82 regular season games has become fairly routine for Staal, who accomplished the feat in four consecutive campaigns from 2005 to 2009. The Hurricanes have not yet matched the success they achieved in 2006, but Staal has been very productive with seasons of 30, 38, 40 and 29 goals while totaling at least 70 points every year since his 100-point season. Staal's most dramatic goal since the Stanley Cup year came on the road in the final minute of Game 7 against Martin Brodeur and the New Jersey Devils to steal a 2009 first round playoff series which Carolina was supposed to lose. The Canes then bested Boston in seven games to get to the Eastern Conference final, where they were swept by the eventual Cup-champion Pittsburgh Penguins. The Canes hoped to keep the momentum of that surprise run going in 2009–10, but failed largely because Staal was limited by a groin injury and played just 70 games after goaltender Cam Ward missed time early in the year. The team did make a playoff charge, but fell short, finishing with 80 points — eight behind the final playoff position in the East.

When Rod Brind'Amour struggled badly during the 2009–10 season, it was decided the captaincy would be transfered to Staal — a natural progression Brind'Amour agreed with. The 6-foot-4, 205-pound Staal has a terrific all-around game and is a true No. 1 center, the kind any team can build around. His excellent shot and nose for the net make him deadly in close and Staal never seems to get down no matter what the score is; he battles to the final whistle. He is not overly aggressive, despite his large body, but he never backs down from a challenge and is willing to battle physically for any loose puck. Staal's play has all the ingredients needed in a leader and he serves as a great example to his teammates.

The Hurricanes need to add more talent to the team if they are to get the most out of Staal's abilities (he has 193 goals and 428 points in 479 games to date). If the Hurricanes want to return to their former glory, it is imperative Staal continue to play like the winner he has always been.

BY THE NUMBERS

Has 43 points in 43 career playoff games

- Has played in three NHL All-Star games: 2007, 2008, 2009
- Scored 100 points in his sophomore season (2005–06)
- Oldest of the four hockey-playing Staal brothers
- Won a gold medal with the Canadian Men's Hockey Team at the 2010 Olympics in Vancouver
- Was the All-Star Game MVP in 2008

CAREER HIGHLIGHTS

The Florida Panthers have some very good hockey players on their team. David Booth is a highly skilled player, while winger Michael Frolik scored 21 times in 2009–10 and others such as Kamil Kreps, Shawn Matthias and Rostislav Olesz have a great deal of promise. On defense the Panthers believe Dmitry Kulikov will be a very good player in the future, although they rely on capable veterans Bryan McCabe and Bryan Allen to protect Tomas Vokoun, who has manned the Florida net for the past three seasons.

However, their best player in 2009–10 was Stephen Weiss, a center drafted fourth overall in 2001 who is just starting to reach his prime as an NHL player. The Panthers set a dubious NHL record by missing the playoffs for a ninth consecutive year and if that is not going to be stretched to a 10th season of futility, Weiss will have to continue to develop and be more productive in 2010–11.

A native of Toronto, Ontario, Weiss played minor hockey in his hometown for a club known as the Young Nationals and had 51 goals and 109 points in just 48 games in 1997–98. He played another season in the Toronto area before he went to the Plymouth Whalers of the Ontario Hockey League to begin his junior hockey career in 1999. The 5-foot-11, 185-pound Weiss had an excellent first year with the Whalers, recording 66 points in 64 games before scoring 40 times and totaling 87 points in 62 games the next season, his draft year. Ilya Kovalchuk (to Atlanta) and Jason Spezza (to Ottawa) were the first two picks of a mostly average, with the benefit of hindsight, opening round of the 2001 NHL draft. The Panthers got a lucky break when Tampa Bay selected Alexander Svitov third, which allowed Florida to snap up Weiss with the fourth choice. Weiss went back to junior for one more year, scoring 25 goals and 70 points in 46 games, but made the Florida roster for the 2002–03 season, playing in 77 games and recording 21 points. He spent the lockout season in the American Hockey League with a somewhat disappointing total of 38 points in 62 games for the San Antonio Rampage. His subpar performance led to more grooming in the minors for most of the 2005–06 season, but Weiss was a full-time Panther, scoring 20 goals, in 2006–07.

Weiss slipped back somewhat in 2007–08, but got better when Florida hired coach Peter DeBoer, Weiss' bench boss in Plymouth. In 2008–09, Weiss scored only 14 times, but had a career-high 47 assists and a team-leading 61 points to go along with an impressive plus-19 rating. He followed that up with a better year in 2009–10: 28 goals, including his 100th career tally, and another team scoring title with 60 points. Weiss is primarily a finesse player who displays smooth skills in all areas of

the game. He still needs to shoot more, but he is now using his speed to get into better scoring positions. A good passer with excellent vision on the ice, Weiss' main strength is his playmaking ability. Playing on a line with Booth and now former teammate Nathan Horton, the trio was very effective and dangerous on the attack, but injuries meant the Panthers' top line was rarely together.

Weiss signed a six-year deal with the Panthers in 2007 and has now played 481 games without a playoff appearance, a mark that challenges some of the other players who did not make the postseason with the Panthers in the recent past. Former Florida players Robert Svehla, Olli Jokinen and Jay Bouwmeester are names that come to mind for this unwanted distinction.

There is no limit to what Weiss can accomplish now that he has evolved into Florida's No. 1 center and has proven he can make other players around him better. The Panthers missed the playoffs in 2010 by 11 points, so there is plenty of work to be done, but Weiss appears ready for that monumental challenge.

BY THE NUMBERS
Scored a career-high 28 goals in 2009–10

- Was drafted fourth overall by the Florida Panthers in the 2001 NHL draft
- Scored a career-high 61 points in 2008–09
- Played in his first NHL game when he was only 18 years old
- Led the Panthers with 60 points in 2009–10

CAREER HIGHLIGHTS

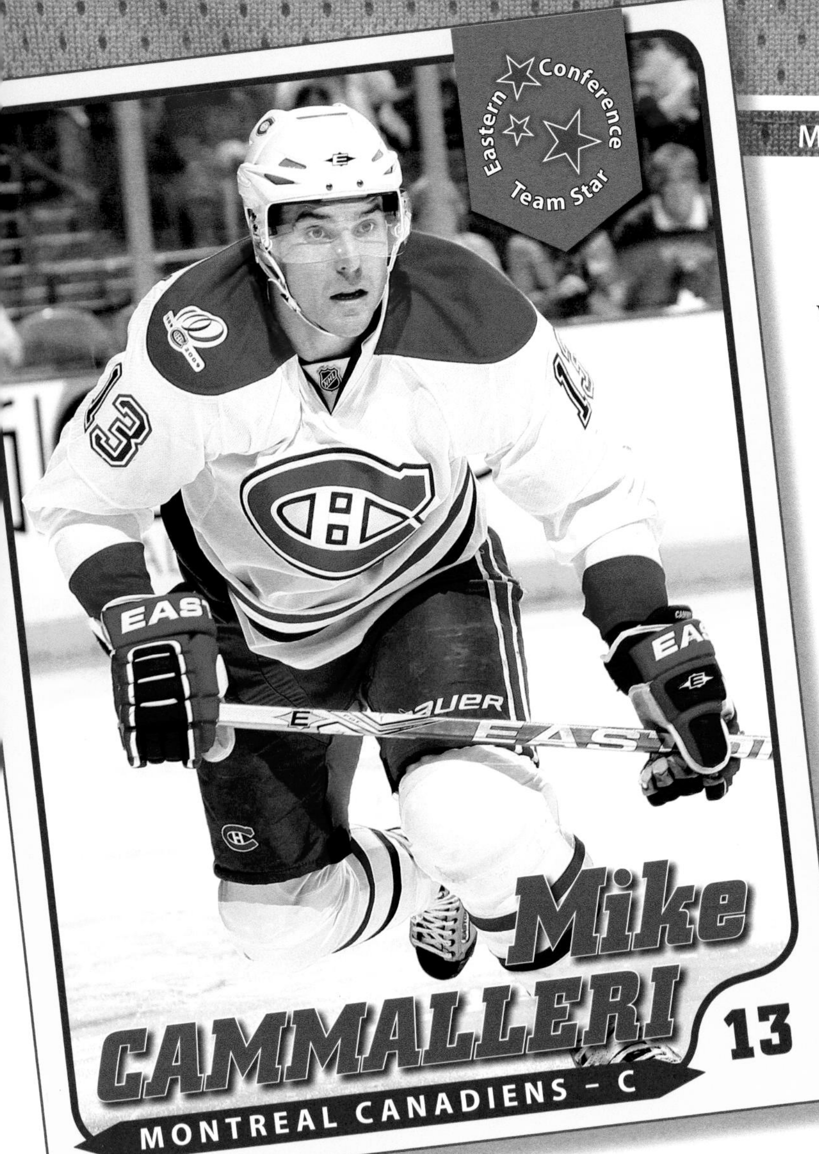

Calgary Flames fans must wonder why Mike Cammalleri was not re-signed by the team after his club-leading 39 goals in 2008–09. Instead, Flames management let the creative and diverse Cammalleri become an unrestricted free agent and watched one of their best players, a guy who can play both center and wing, skate away to the Montreal Canadiens. The decision to let him walk hurt the Flames in a couple of ways: First of all, the team missed the playoffs in 2009–10 with Cammalleri gone and captain Jarome Iginla, who produced 89 points playing largely alongside Cammalleri in 2008–09, saw his output drop to 69 points. Meanwhile, not only did the Canadiens make the playoffs, they had one of the more memorable runs in recent years with Cammalleri leading the way.

A native of Richmond Hill, Ontario, Cammalleri was involved in many sports growing up, including softball, soccer and track, showing great athleticism in each sport. However, hockey was where he excelled most and he played on many great minor hockey teams in the Greater Toronto Area. Cammalleri was often captain of his squads, but always emphasized team play over individual glory. Many tournaments saw Cammalleri-led entries do very well, but it was usually his wingers who would get named MVP — a strong illustration Cammalleri made others better. He was a very focused individual who always achieved what he put his mind to. Although he doesn't have great size, generously listed at 5-foot-9 and 182 pounds even now, Cammalleri would practice his shot in the basement of his home. He would turn up the radio and fire pucks until it was time for some other activity.

Cammalleri's family also believed in education, so he took accelerated courses when he played Jr. A hockey for the Bramalea Blues of the Ontario Provincial League. He hoped that would make him ready to attend an American college. He scored 67 goals and 191 points in 87 games over two seasons for the Blues and that got him into the University of Michigan. After a couple of years there, he was selected 49th overall by the Los Angeles Kings in 2001. He did not turn pro until 2002–03, when the Kings assigned him to their farm team, the American Hockey League's Manchester Monarchs. His final year in Manchester saw him record 46 goals and 109 points in 79 games. He played 59 games for L.A. in the two seasons leading up to that campaign, but was not a full-time King until 2005–06. He proved he belonged in the big league by scoring 26 times and followed up with seasons of 34 and 19 goals. Fearing they would not be able to sign him to a new contract, the Kings dealt Cammalleri to Calgary in June 2008 and he scored a career-high 39 goals in his one and only year as a Flame.

Montreal was looking to completely retool its team for

BY THE NUMBERS Has had at least 200 shots on net in each of the past five seasons

- Had a career-high 39 goals and 82 points in 2008–09 with the Calgary Flames
- Was second in the NHL with 19 power play goals in 2008–09
- Won gold with Canada at the 2007 World Championship
- Originally drafted 49th overall by Los Angeles in 2001

CAREER HIGHLIGHTS

the 2009–10 season and made Cammalleri the centerpiece of its new direction. He loved the idea of playing for the most historic franchise in hockey and liked that his new teammates would include ex-New Jersey Devils players Scott Gomez and Brian Gionta. What Montreal's top trio lacked in size they made up for in gumption and only a serious ankle injury kept Cammalleri from adding to his impressive totals of 26 goals and 50 points in 65 games. The Habs struggled to make the playoffs, but they secured a spot during their last regular season game and then had to face the high-powered Washington Capitals as their reward. Undaunted by the challenge, the Canadiens charged back from a 3–1 series deficit to beat the Caps in seven games, then knocked off the defending Stanley Cup-champion Pittsburgh Penguins in another seven-game shocker. Cammalleri's superb goal-scoring was a huge factor in Montreal's success as his 13 tallies would end up leading the entire playoffs in goals, even though the Canadiens were bounced in the Eastern Conference final by Philadelphia. He displayed an uncanny ability to get himself open and when he fired a drive, it was usually on net and past a startled netminder.

Many will say the Canadiens only made it as far as they did in the playoffs through the great work of Jaroslav Halak. Montreal's former goalie was indeed incredible, but without the goal-scoring exploits of the red-hot Cammalleri, the Habs would have been playing golf much sooner. The Habs would be wise to get Cammalleri some more help, preferably some large forwards who can make life easier for him on the ice.

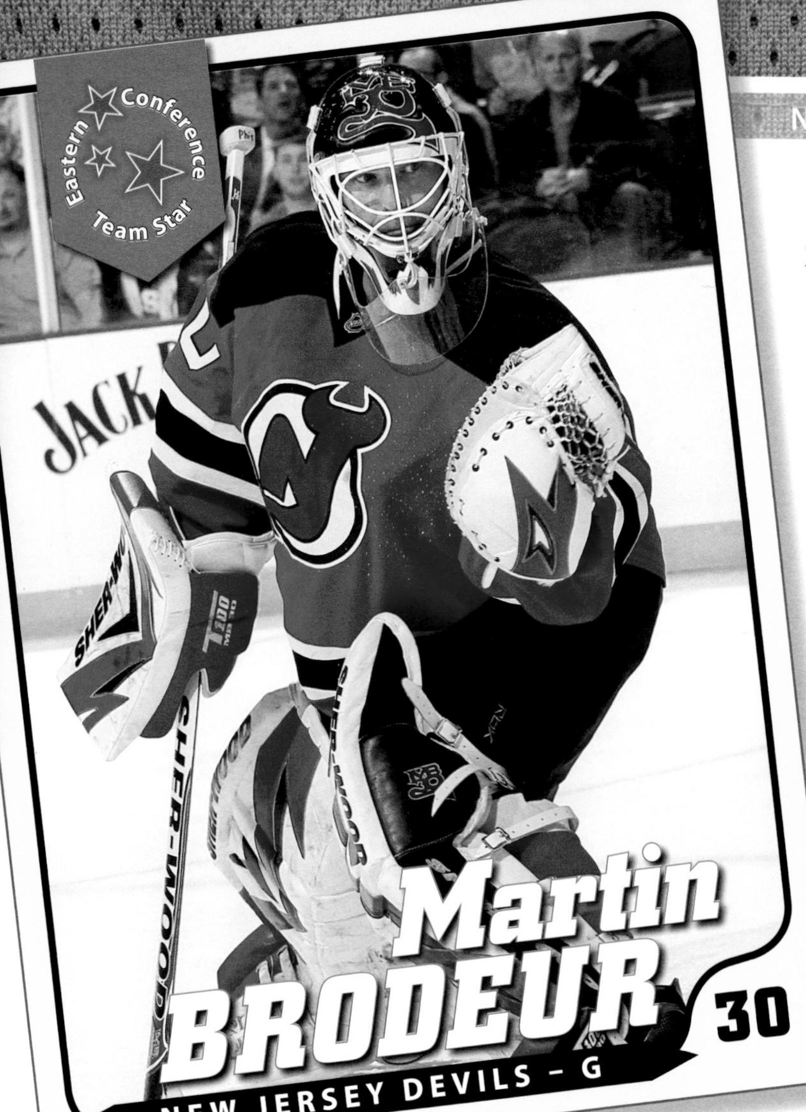

When legendary goaltender Terry Sawchuk recorded his 103rd and final career shutout on February 1, 1970, it was believed the record he established would never be broken. Sawchuk earned most of his shutouts in the 1950s and 1960s when the NHL consisted of just six teams that generally played a more low-scoring brand of hockey. During the super-charged offensive era of the 1970s and 1980s, no one would have dared suggest Sawchuk's total would even be challenged, let alone surpassed. However, the game started to change in the 1990s as the league continued to expand and the quality of play diminished thanks to a blatant disregard for the rulebook. Many teams saw a way to thrive by setting up defensive systems designed around large, rugged players who could protect their end of the ice by interfering with the opposition starting in the neutral zone. Add an outstanding goaltender and you had a winning formula for an era when goals became very scarce. No team did this better than the New Jersey Devils, who, in 1990, drafted a young, Montreal-born netminder named Martin Brodeur.

On the night of December 21, 2009, Brodeur broke Sawchuk's nearly 40-year-old record when the visiting Devils defeated the defending Stanley Cup-champion Pittsburgh Penguins 4–0. He made 35 saves to record his 104th career shutout and take over one of the most coveted marks in all of professional sports. Brodeur established the new benchmark in fine fashion by making big stops on superstars Sidney Crosby and Evgeni Malkin during the contest. Just as he had two weeks earlier when he tied the record with a whitewashing of the Buffalo Sabres, Brodeur went into the third period up 3–0 and his thoughts were focused on keeping the opposition off the board. His teammates were also determined to be a part of history and all the Devils worked to shut down the Penguins. The netminder firmly acknowledged this was a team record and knew he would not have been close to this mark had it not been for the Devils' attention to their own end of the ice. By way of comparison, the next active netminder during 2009–10 on the all-time shutout list was Roberto Luongo of Vancouver and he only had 51.

A three-time Stanley Cup winner, Brodeur has over recent seasons established new marks in just about every goaltending category. He has now appeared in 1,076 games (passing Patrick Roy's previous standard of 1,029), played 63,521 minutes (again eclipsing the mark held by Roy) and has won 602 games (besting another Roy plateau). Brodeur maintained he tried not to focus on all the records, but admitted it was difficult to ignore each historical landmark as it approached. There are myriad reasons why Brodeur has set so many records and most of the explanation can be attributed to the goalie himself. He has loved the game of hockey since he was a child and has worked at getting better every day. His father, Denis, was also a goalie, although he actually made the NHL as the team photographer for the Montreal Canadiens. Brodeur is very respectful of his teammates and, above all, is concerned with winning games, not just focusing on his career numbers. He has been a Devil since he entered the NHL and his cool, calm approach to playing the game has helped define a team with a clear identity. Brodeur also showed the ability to adjust his game as the NHL tried to stress more offense starting in the 2005–06 season.

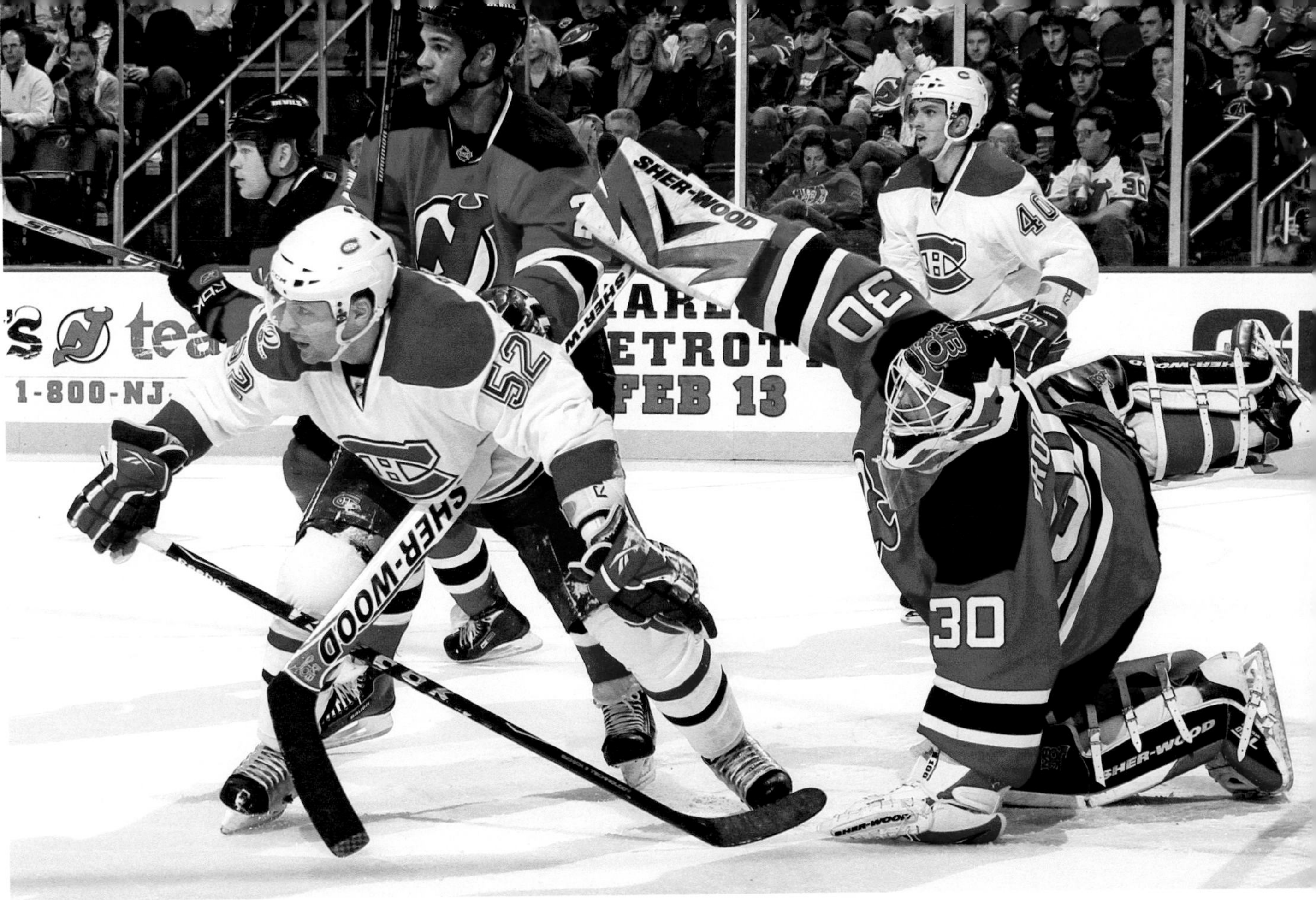

The seven-time league All-Star (three times on the First Team) and four-time Vezina Trophy winner has been an extremely consistent performer, with the exception of being limited to just 31 games in 2008–09 due to injury. However, he is now 38 years old and the last three seasons have been very frustrating for both Brodeur and the Devils, exiting the playoffs far too early. The Devils had another good regular season in 2009–10, with Brodeur posting a league-high 45 wins as the team recorded 103 points. A first round loss to Philadelphia, though, put a damper on what had otherwise been a great year.

Sawchuk was 37 years old when he won his fourth championship by taking the Toronto Maple Leafs to the Stanley Cup title in 1967. The question now becomes, does Brodeur have one more great playoff run in him? There is nothing else left to accomplish since he holds all the major goaltending records, some of which may never be broken.

BY THE NUMBERS Has had at least 40 wins nine times in his NHL career, including a career-high 48 in 2006–07

- Has won three Stanley Cups with New Jersey
- Won Olympic gold with Canada in 2002 and 2010
- Has been named to 10 NHL All-Star games
- Is the NHL all-time leader in wins (602) and shutouts (110)
- Led the league with a 1.88 GAA in 1996–97, which was also a career best

CAREER HIGHLIGHTS

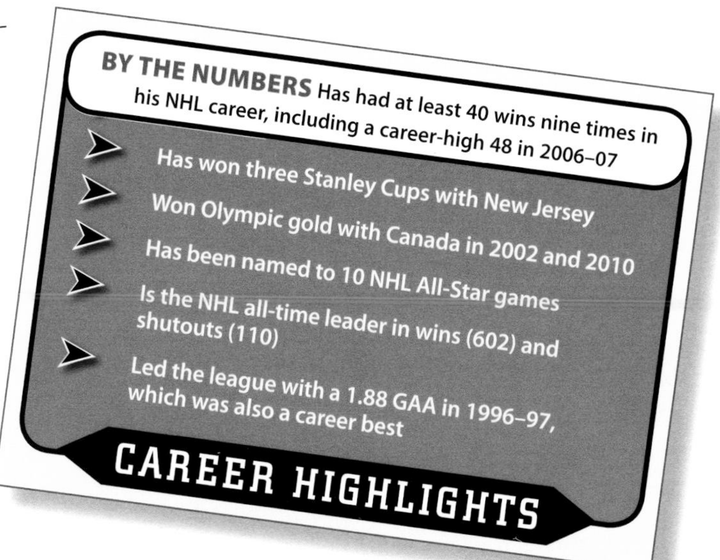

John Tavares has always been a special hockey player, so much so the Ontario Hockey League changed its rules to accommodate his skills. The native of Mississauga, Ontario, was the first player awarded 'exceptional player' status, which allowed him to begin his major junior hockey career one year earlier than is normally allowed. That distinction came after a stellar minor hockey career that included 104 goals and 186 points in 72 games during the 2004–05 season with the Toronto Marlboros and 23 more points in 20 games for the Jr. A Milton Icehawks. That performance convinced the experts Tavares was ready to play against older competition in the OHL and he was drafted first overall by the Oshawa Generals. He played three-and-a-half seasons in Oshawa, scoring 134 points in 2006–07 including 72 goals, which broke Wayne Gretzky's record for goal-scoring by a 16-year-old. His final year of junior was split between Oshawa and London. He scored 58 goals and 104 points, becoming the OHL's all-time leader in goals scored along the way. But a debate began concerning whether or not Tavares would be the first overall selection of the 2009 NHL draft. Fellow OHLer Matt Duchene (who went No. 3 to Colorado) made a late push, but Tavares' only real rival for the coveted No. 1 slot was Swedish defenseman Victor Hedman. However, when they battled head-to-head at the 2009 World Junior Championship it was no contest.

Tavares was named the MVP of the tournament with eight goals and 15 points in six games and made the most memorable play of the tournament during the semifinal against Russia. With time winding down, he corralled a loose puck and fired a backhand drive toward the Russian net. Teammate Jordan Eberle was able to follow it up and grab the rebound, tying the game with just 5.4 seconds to play. Canada scored the winner in overtime and then romped to the gold medal with a 5–1 victory against Sweden. Once seen potentially as equals, Tavares had shown he was able to raise his game to new levels when needed, while Hedman was rather ordinary. If there was any doubt concerning who was No. 1, it was erased by Tavares leading the Canadian team to victory. The New York Islanders held the top pick in the '09 draft. They did not tip their hand until draft day, but it would have been a shock if they had not chosen the 6-foot, 195-pound Tavares, who was by then considered a franchise player. Islanders fans who gathered to watch the draft unfold rejoiced in loud celebration, hopeful that their moribund franchise had found a new face and leader. The 6-foot-6 Hedman went second overall to the Tampa Bay Lightning.

The unique part of Tavares' game is that he isn't the most graceful or speedy of skaters, even though he's able to find an extra gear when the puck nears the

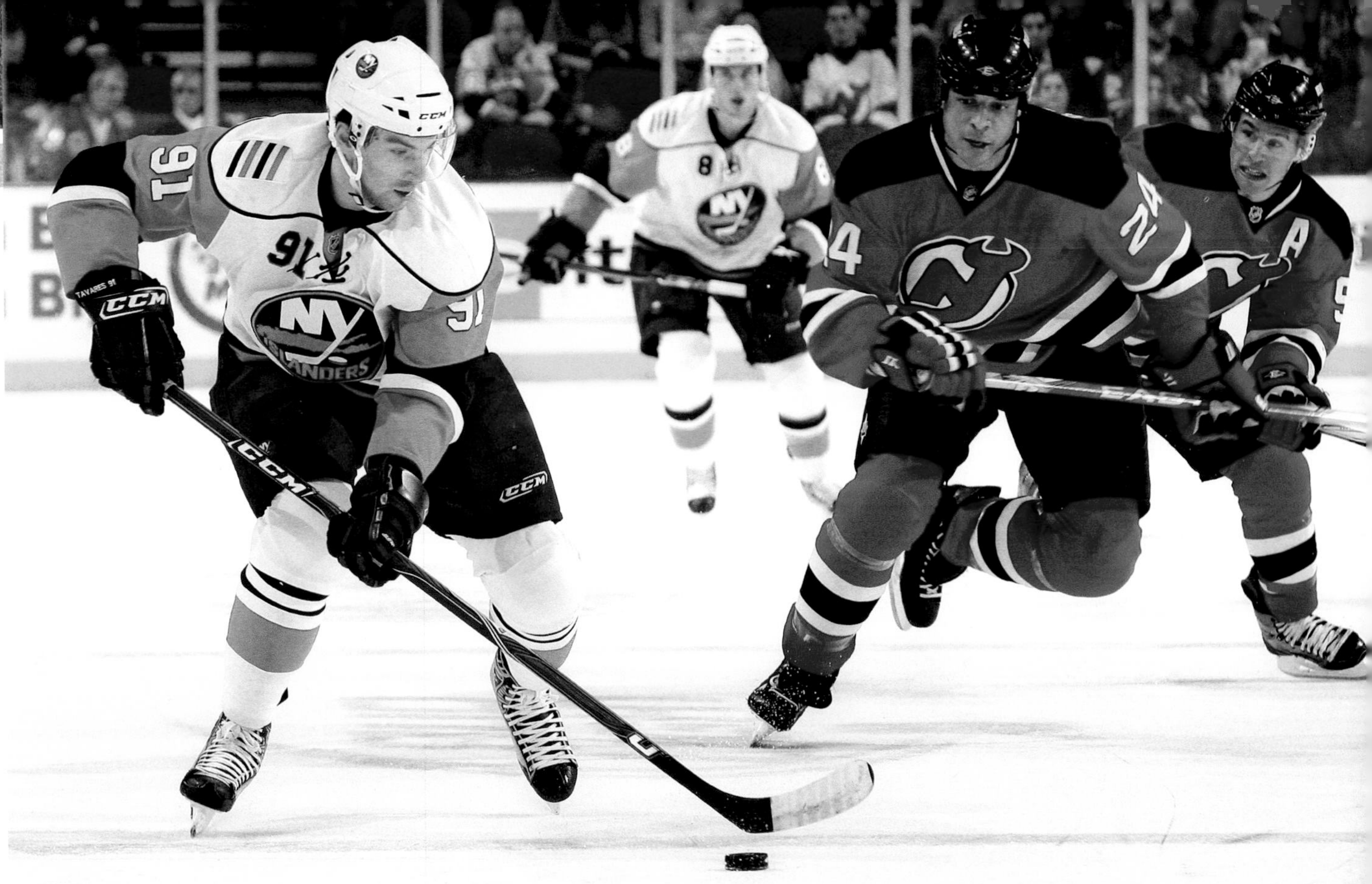

opposing goal. Some critics went as far as to say he was a little on the lazy side, but the opposite is true of the hard-working Tavares. Even at the tender age of 16, he was in the gym after school and also playing lacrosse, while trying to refine his hockey skills at the same time. Tavares' uncle, also named John, is renowned for his lacrosse prowess — some said he was the best to ever play the sport. Tavares watched his uncle John play and thought of him as a role model, someone he could discuss things with because of his experience playing such a high level of sport. Tavares watched how his uncle prepared for games and how he worked at understanding the intricacies of lacrosse. Tavares still corresponds with his uncle and seeks his council as needed.

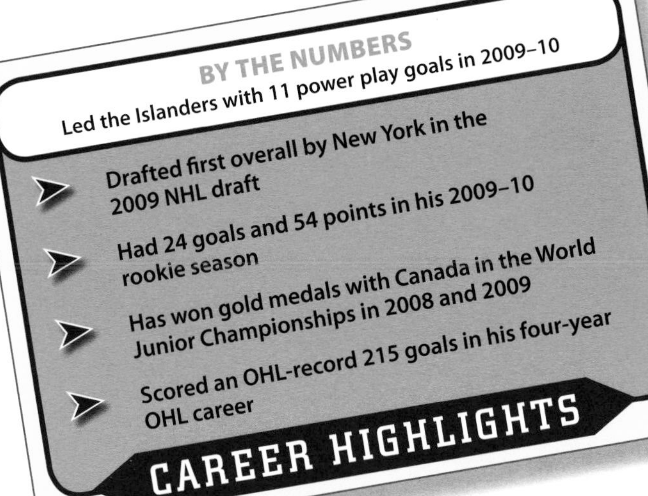

Tavares took time to prepare for each opponent and got off to a fast start with the Islanders as a 19-year-old NHL rookie in 2009. He handled the attention that goes with being a franchise savior in a confident but respectful manner. The Islanders were still a pretty bad team overall, but Tavares did score 24 times, with 11 on the power play, and totaled 54 points to lead the team. Tavares was at times rather ordinary as the season continued, but picked up his game as the campaign closed out. A five-point night (two goals, three assists) during a road game against Vancouver in the middle of March showed Tavares still could come up with a top performance.

The Islanders must continue building their roster and Tavares will have to raise his overall game if the team is to escape the lower echelons of the Eastern Conference. But the team has an abundance of young talent led by 'Johnny T', giving Islanders fans much to look forward to in seasons to come.

BY THE NUMBERS

Led the Islanders with 11 power play goals in 2009–10

- Drafted first overall by New York in the 2009 NHL draft
- Had 24 goals and 54 points in his 2009–10 rookie season
- Has won gold medals with Canada in the World Junior Championships in 2008 and 2009
- Scored an OHL-record 215 goals in his four-year OHL career

CAREER HIGHLIGHTS

Marian Gaborik could have chosen to play just about anywhere in the NHL when he became a free agent in the summer of 2009. His top-level skills would attract any team that had room to sign a big-ticket player and it was only natural the New York Rangers would make a strong pitch. The talented right winger could have spurned the bright lights of Broadway after toiling in relative anonymity for the Minnesota Wild since he joined the league in 2000, but he was not afraid of the spotlight and signed for $7.5 million a year for five seasons with the Blueshirts. From the moment he stepped on the ice at Madison Square Garden, Gaborik excited the always-critical New York crowd with a display of great goal-scoring. He scored 10 times in the Rangers' first 12 games and totaled 18 points in his first month of action. The Rangers do not have the talent of the glamorous New York Yankees, but they now have a talent who can compete with a Derek Jeter or an Alex Rodriguez for the tabloid headlines in the 'Big Apple.'

According to New York coach John Tortorella, Gaborik has innate abilities that cannot be taught and must be allowed the freedom to maximize his skills. He can turn the momentum of a game around with just one drive, most often a howitzer of a wrist shot that hits the back of the net with stunning speed. His greatest asset, however, is his tremendous skating. He is a consistent game-breaker and his 47 career game-winning goals are a testament to that fact. He is also very deadly on the power play because he can exploit the extra space a man advantage provides. Tortorella also recognizes Gaborik's ability to bring out the best in those around him, a trait very few players can claim. The blunt coach was also willing to live with the occasional turnover because Gaborik's ability to see the game is a rare gift.

Gaborik began scoring the moment he came into the NHL, as is evidenced by his six-point night on October 26, 2000, against the Phoenix Coyotes. At 18 years old, he became the youngest player in league history to record that many points in one contest. Gaborik was selected third overall by the expansion Wild during the 2000 draft and the team assumed the young Slovak needed more development time since he had only played in Europe. However, he showed he could play in the NHL by scoring 18 goals, fifth-best among rookies, and adding 18 assists in 71 games in his first year. Gaborik wanted to emulate his hero Peter Bondra, who scored over 500 goals in his NHL career. Bondra, a fellow Slovak, had skated with the youngster and felt Gaborik had all the skills needed to be a top-flight NHL player. Always a focused individual, Gaborik developed his superior shot as a youngster by practicing every day and by playing with other kids in his native town of Trencin. Working on his own was also no trouble for Gaborik, who dreamed of playing against the best in the world.

Gaborik scored 30 goals in each of his second and third campaigns in the league, before slumping to 18 in an injury-shortened 2003–04 season. Watching games from the sideline became an unfortunate trend for Gaborik, who only once played as many as 77 games in four seasons from 2005 through 2009 while battling a series of ailments. He was limited to just 17 contests in his final campaign in Minnesota, but when in the lineup, his all-world skill and ability was undeniable. The Wild wanted to retain their best player and the man who scored the first goal in franchise history, but the lure of New York and a change from the stifling defensive system once played by the Wild proved too much to turn down. Gaborik successfully made the change from the Western Conference to the Eastern Conference and scored a team-best 42 goals, equaling his previous career high. He might have hit the 50-goal mark, but in keeping with a familiar theme, an injury cost him six games and any hope of reaching the magic plateau.

BY THE NUMBERS Tallied a career-high 86 points in 2009–10 with the New York Rangers

- Has scored at least 30 goals in six of his nine NHL seasons
- Was Minnesota's first draft pick ever, third overall in 2000
- Has 261 goals and 523 points in 578 career games
- Played for Slovakia in the 2006 and 2010 Winter Olympic Games

CAREER HIGHLIGHTS

It was interesting to note Tortorella did not use Gaborik as one of his shootout players on the last day of the 2009–10 season — a loss that cost the Rangers a playoff spot. The acerbic coach then made it clear he expected Gaborik to be a more all-around player for the money he was being paid, including getting better at the shootout. It appears health issues will also challenge Gaborik from now to the end of his career, but he will continue to electrify the crowds at MSG and score plenty of goals.

Daniel Alfredsson has been an Ottawa Senator since 1995 and he now owns just about every significant team career mark. Among his franchise-leading totals as of the end of the 2009–10 season are: most games played (1,002), most goals (375), most assists (617), most points (992), most game-winning goals (62), most power play goals (114), most short-handed goals (22), most points in one game (seven) and most seasons (14). The numbers represent an especially strong achievement for a player who was quite happy to be playing in the Swedish Elite League until close to his 23rd birthday. He believed he would log a few years in the NHL before heading back home, but his stellar play has made him the face of an Ottawa team he's captained since 1999 and earned him the appreciation of all Senators fans. At the age of 37, Alfredsson knows he is approaching the end of his career, but because he has such a fondness for both Ottawa and Canada, he's likely to remain in North America after his playing days are over.

Alfredsson grew up in Gothenburg, Sweden, and was one of three children born to Hasse and Margaretta. His father was a carpenter, but at one time was a pretty good athlete himself, playing both soccer and hockey as a youngster. The father would never let his children win just for the sake of it and any victory had to be earned. This approach forced young Daniel to compete hard if he wanted to be labeled a true winner and, if his NHL career is any indication, it's a lesson he has never forgotten. His mother was a hairdresser, but became stricken with multiple sclerosis many years ago and is confined to living life in a wheelchair. His mother's plight is inspirational to Alfredsson, who also has a sister who suffers from anxiety. These family issues have made Alfredsson a worker for charitable causes and no doubt have helped to make him a better leader in his own understated way.

Considering his great success in the NHL, it is hard to believe Alfredsson was selected as low as 133rd overall by Ottawa in 1994 — a year that saw Ed Jovanovski go first overall with Oleg Tverdovsky, Radek Bonk, Jason Bonsignore and Jeff O'Neill rounding out the top five picks. It's safe to say that if the '94 draft was redone, Alfredsson would be a top-five pick ahead of all those listed, with the possible exception of Jovanovski. It also goes to show that selecting at the top of the draft is not necessarily the only way to build a team. In the season leading up to his selection, Alfredsson scored 20 goals and 30 points for Frolunda in the Swedish League.
It was thought Alfredsson would go to the American Hockey League for some pro experience in North America, but he was too good to keep off the Senators. With 26 goals and 61 points in 82 games, there was no doubt the Sens had made the right choice and he was

BY THE NUMBERS

Has at least 70 points in each of the last nine seasons

- Won Olympic gold with Sweden in 2006
- Had career highs of 43 goals, 60 assists and 103 points in 2005–06
- Won the Calder Trophy in 1995–96
- Has played in five NHL All-Star games
- Played in his 1,000th NHL game on April 6, 2010

CAREER HIGHLIGHTS

named winner of the Calder Trophy as the best rookie in the league. The 5-foot-11, 208-pound right winger has produced every season he's been healthy since that time.

Alfredsson's most prolific year came in 2005–06 when he had a career-best 43 goals and 103 points. The next season, Alfredsson scored a playoff-best 14 goals and tied linemates Dany Heatley and Jason Spezza for the post-season scoring lead with 22 points as the Sens advanced all the way to the 2007 Cup final. Though Ottawa lost in five games to the Anaheim Ducks, going that deep in the playoffs removed a lot of the frustration around a franchise that was always in contention, but rarely able to get far in the playoffs. At times — and with some justification — Alfredsson was blamed for Ottawa's playoff failures and his guarantees of success rang hollow. But he refused to quit or get down during that '07 run and scored a key overtime goal to eliminate the Buffalo Sabres from the Eastern Conference final — a moment of sweet revenge for 'Alfie,' who had been the goat during a playoff loss to the Sabres one season prior.

Late in the 2009–10 campaign, Alfredsson played in his 1,000th career game and was honored by the team before a home game for the achievement. It was the highlight of a season that saw Alfredsson lead the team in points for the fourth time in his career, as he popped 71 in just 70 games. It's almost certain Alfredsson will spend his remaining playing days in Ottawa and when he does decide to hang up his skates, there's no doubt his No. 11 will be raised to the rafters.

Mike Richards had one of the most interesting seasons in the 2009–10 NHL campaign. The Philadelphia Flyers captain had more ups and downs than the stock market, but through it all, he was able to keep his focus and lead his team into the Stanley Cup final. At times it looked like the Flyers were about to implode, but coaching and goaltending changes got the ship back on course and when the playoffs were over, the city of Philadelphia could once again be proud of the guys wearing orange and black.

The Flyers were riding high in the early part of the season, recording 12 wins in their first 18 contests, but then Richards got into trouble on the night of October 24 when he hit Florida's David Booth in the head, knocking the Panther player out of the lineup for months. Richards escaped without any retribution from the league, though many felt the blindside hit warranted a lengthy suspension. Even though he escaped punishment from the NHL offices, the incident seemed to affect Richards as the level of his play dipped. If that controversy was not enough, Richards decided to stage a war with the local Philadelphia media regarding off-ice stories written about the team's younger players, himself included. His boycott was a bold move for a young player in just his second season as team captain, but he believed it had to be done in the hopes that some ugly stories about player carousing would stop. Richards quickly learned that fighting the media is a losing battle and if he had consulted veteran teammate Chris Pronger, he might have learned that valuable lesson a little sooner.

One of Richards' main goals was to be selected for the Canadian team that would take part in the Vancouver Olympics. He was thrilled to be chosen and kept the phone message he got from Ken Holland telling him he was on the squad. Team Canada officials liked what they saw from Richards because he was so versatile. They saw him playing an attacking role and were more than comfortable if they had to count on him defensively or to kill penalties. Most of all, executive director Steve Yzerman loved Richards' desire to compete and just about everyone would agree it's the 5-foot-11, 190-pound center's drive to succeed that makes him a very valuable asset. Richards has also done a great deal of winning. In 2005, he captained Team Canada to a gold medal at the World Junior Championship and prior to that, he won a Memorial Cup with the Kitchener Rangers in 2003. He joined the Philadelphia Phantoms in time for the 2005 playoffs and helped the American Hockey League team capture a Calder Cup championship with 14 points in 15 games. It was no surprise that Richards had five points in seven Olympic games and that Canada took the gold medal.

Returning to the Flyers after the high of the Olympics

seemed to rejuvenate Richards, who was getting more comfortable under new coach Peter Laviolette. Richards felt badly when John Stevens was fired as Flyers bench boss early in the season since it was Stevens who first gave him a chance to play on the team and gave him the freedom to go on the attack. Nothing came easy to the Flyers, who had to endure their share of injuries, but a shootout win over the Rangers in the last game of season gave them a playoff spot. Richards finished the season with a team-best 62 points, including a career-high 31 goals.

The Flyers picked up momentum as the playoffs went along and Richards was at his best, scoring key goals and dishing out some devastating bodychecks in each of the four series Philadelphia played. Richards had seven goals and 23 points in 23 games and the Flyers made it back to the final for the first time since 1997. Only the speedier Chicago Blackhawks kept the Flyers from their first Cup win since 1975.

When the series was over, Richards was asked why his team was second best and he quite rightly pointed out that Chicago had four lines going to only three for Philadelphia. Honest reactions like that show Richards is the best team captain since Bobby Clarke and the Flyers will likely soar under his leadership.

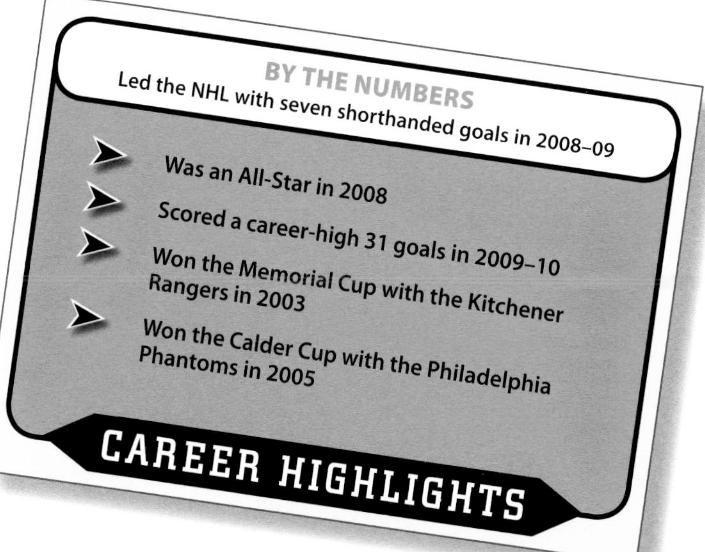
BY THE NUMBERS

Led the NHL with seven shorthanded goals in 2008–09

- Was an All-Star in 2008
- Scored a career-high 31 goals in 2009–10
- Won the Memorial Cup with the Kitchener Rangers in 2003
- Won the Calder Cup with the Philadelphia Phantoms in 2005

CAREER HIGHLIGHTS

Was anyone surprised when Sidney Crosby scored the 'golden goal' at the 2010 Winter Olympic Games? While just about everyone in Canada held their breath as overtime began between Team Canada and the United States, there had to be a certain belief among those wearing the maple leaf on their jersey that somehow 'Sid the Kid' would find a way to score. The Americans had not made it easy, tying the gold medal game in Vancouver 2–2 with less than 30 seconds to play and U.S. goalie Ryan Miller was certainly a formidable obstacle for the Canadian team to overcome in the extra period that would see the teams play four skaters aside. But just past the seven-minute mark of overtime, Crosby yelled for a pass from teammate Jarome Iginla and with one quick swat from his magical stick, the puck was in the net and the conquering hero was mobbed by his teammates and adored once again by all those who live north of the 49th. Teammate Joe Thornton may have expressed it best for every Canadian hockey fan after the game when he said, "You're just happy Crosby is on your team. You're happy he was born in Canada."

The pressure to win gold at the Olympic Games may have produced one of the most tension-filled moments in hockey history, but for Crosby it was just another highlight in a career filled with great opportunities to succeed. Nobody has higher expectations of himself than Crosby and he has had this feeling since the time he first put on skates before his third birthday. His prodigious goal-scoring made him a hockey phenomenon and got him noticed early. The attention this garnered was not always pleasant, but it helped to give the native of Cole Harbour, Nova Scotia, a mental toughness that has enabled him to become hockey's highest achiever. It never bothered him that others might want to see him fail because he was focused on excelling. As he kept rising up the ranks, it became clear he was going to be an NHL star and in 2005, the Pittsburgh Penguins made him the first overall selection at the NHL draft. Crosby responded by recording 39 goals and 102 points as a rookie, and then, to prove he was no fluke, notched a league-leading 120 points in his second year. Comparisons were made to Wayne Gretzky and Mario Lemieux, but those gifted players had the benefit of starting their careers in the 1980s, an era when goals were plentiful. Crosby's 506 career points through 371 games is truly an incredible achievement.

Crosby also knew his career would be measured by how many Stanley Cups he won and in the 2008 playoffs, he missed his first opportunity when the rebuilt Penguins were edged by the Detroit Red Wings in six games during the Stanley Cup final. After that bitter loss, a commercial featuring Crosby had the young Pittsburgh captain stating he would never again want to watch another team skate off with the coveted silver trophy. In the 2009 playoffs, Crosby had a league-leading 15 goals to go with 31 points in 24 post-season games as the Pens got their revenge on Detroit, winning the Cup in a thrilling seven-game series.

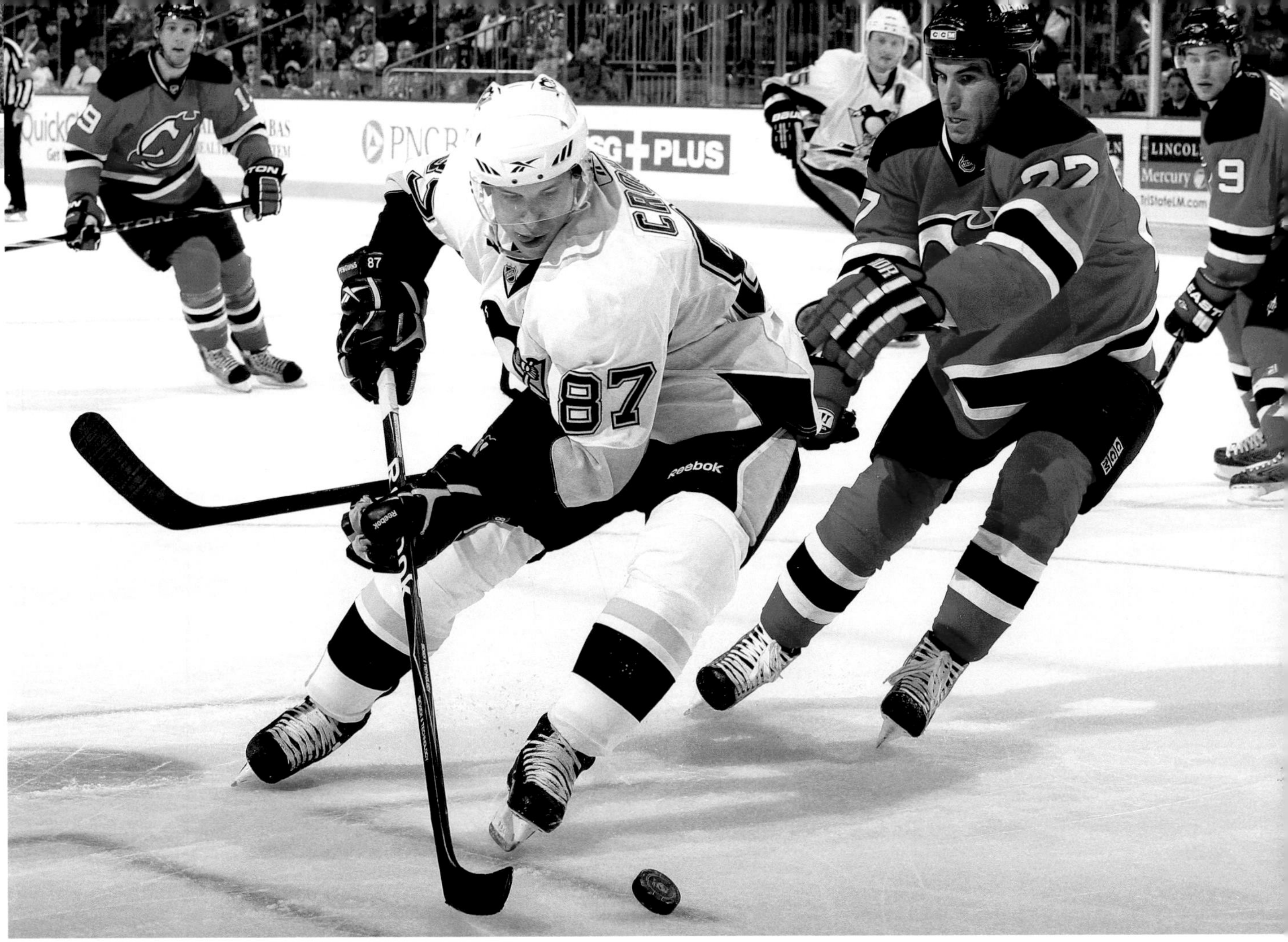

Even though the Penguins won the Cup, Crosby was asked by coach Dan Bylsma to start shooting more in 2009–10 in hopes his regular season goal total would rise. Crosby realized it was good advice and took a career-high 298 shots on goal, which resulted in him setting a new personal goal standard of 51 — a total that tied him with Steven Stamkos for the league lead, one ahead of rival Alex Ovechkin. Pucks started to go in for Crosby from all over the ice and that gave him even more confidence to keep firing at opposition nets. Breaking the 50-goal barrier might have been the last thing he had to prove to critics who favored Ovechkin — an argument that now seems ridiculous. Well mannered, polite and giving with his time, Crosby is everything a great hockey player should be and the best of role models for youngsters. Crosby is now the face of the NHL and that might be the best thing to happen since the days of Gretzky and Lemieux.

The 5-foot-11, 200-pounder is by no means the biggest player in the NHL, but he is pathologically driven to win over and over again. At the age of 23, Crosby has plenty of time to keep adding awards and championships to his ever-growing list of achievements.

BY THE NUMBERS Has scored at least 100 points in four of his five NHL seasons

- Had a career-high 51 goals in 2009-10
- Only teenager to ever win the Art Ross Trophy (120 points in 2006-07)
- Scored the winning goal in the gold medal game at the 2010 Winter Olympic Games
- Second-youngest player to win the Hart Trophy
- Is the youngest NHL captain to win the Stanley Cup

CAREER HIGHLIGHTS

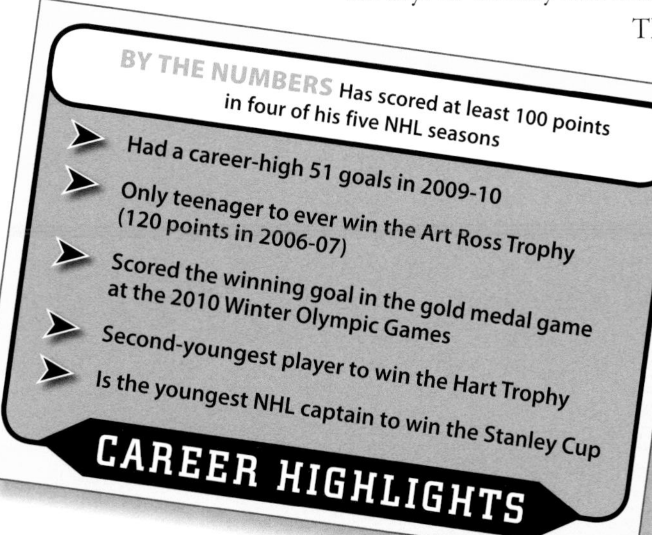

Considering center Steven Stamkos was drafted first overall by the Tampa Bay Lightning in 2008, he got very little respect as an NHL rookie. The Lightning started the 2008–09 season under coach Barry Melrose (who had not coached in the league since the 1990s) and he was quite adamant that Stamkos was simply not strong enough to play in the NHL at the tender age of 18. Melrose lasted all of 16 games before he was sent back to the broadcast booth and replaced with Rick Tocchet, a very accomplished player in his day with six different NHL teams during 19 seasons. Melrose was so convinced Stamkos was not ready that he often kept him on the bench. Tocchet took a different tack and helped Stamkos with extra assistance off the ice, which included some conditioning work. The rookie did not let his travails get him down and responded to his new coach by scoring 16 times during his final 25 games, finishing the 2008–09 season with 23 goals and 46 points — not bad for a first-year player, but not good enough to win the Calder Trophy either. However, he did play for Canada at the World Championship and was tied for the tournament lead in goals with seven as the Canadian side won silver.

The 6-foot-1, 196-pound Stamkos knew he needed to be better physically prepared for his second season and spent the summer of 2009 training with former NHLer and teammate Gary Roberts, a man known for his conditioning fanaticism. Along with the help of friend Lorne Goldberg, who became the fitness trainer for the Montreal Canadiens, Roberts designed a special program for the youngster that emphasized strength development without sacrificing speed. Stamkos pulled 100-pound sleds, ran sprints and completed balancing exercises designed to give him a strong set of core muscles. Stamkos was put through his paces six days a week and it all paid off once the 2009–10 season got underway.

Stamkos was first noticed while playing minor hockey in Markham, Ontario. He scored 105 goals and totaled 197 points while playing for a team known as the Waxers in 2005–06. He then joined the Sarnia Sting of the Ontario Hockey League for two seasons, recording 92 and 105 points, respectively, before the Lightning selected him with the first pick of the '08 draft. His game is built around his great offensive instincts, combining good playmaking skills with a devastating shot that Stamkos can get on net from any angle. He is a smooth skater who can kick it into high gear very quickly, especially when he sees a chance to lead the attack. Being able to work alongside veteran Martin St-Louis has been invaluable to Stamkos and having tough wingers such as Ryan Malone or the unpredictable Steve Downie on the other side never hurts. The goals came pretty regularly for Stamkos during the 2009–10 season, many of them with the extra man as he led the NHL in power play goals with 24. On the final night of the regular season, Stamkos scored his 51st goal into an empty net to tie Sidney Crosby for the league lead and a share of the Rocket Richard Trophy, quite an achievement for a player who was just 20 years and two months old.

But there was a two-fold disappointment to the 2009–10 season for Stamkos. The first was that the Lightning missed the playoffs and the second was that he was not selected to play for Canada at the 2010 Winter Olympics. It looked like his hot start would get him a spot on the squad, but he was passed over mostly because of his youth and his unpolished defensive play. Stamkos coveted a role on the Olympic team as he recalled being a 12-year-old boy when Canada won gold at the 2002 games in Salt Lake City. He wore his Team Canada sweater that day as he watched the gold medal game, making him late for his own game scheduled later that same day. When he got to the arena, Stamkos and his teammates put the Canadian jersey on a couple of sticks and skated around prior to the contest to the cheers of fans gathered to watch their game.

It's safe to say that Stamkos will wear the Team Canada jersey at the Olympics the next time the team is picked.

BY THE NUMBERS

Led the NHL with 24 power play goals in 2009–10

- Tied for the NHL lead in goals with 51 in 2009–10
- Is the third-youngest player to score 50 goals
- Won a gold medal with Canada at the 2008 World Junior Championship
- Selected first overall in the 2008 NHL draft
- Was 5th in the NHL in scoring with 95 points in 2009–10

CAREER HIGHLIGHTS

Toronto Maple Leafs GM Brian Burke knew he was taking a big risk when he traded two first round picks and a second-rounder to the Boston Bruins for winger Phil Kessel. Burke said it was discussed among his management group that one of those draft choices might turn out to be Taylor Hall or Tyler Seguin, the leading contenders for the top selection in the 2010 NHL draft. The Leafs boss has never been long on patience and made it clear quite often that Toronto is not on a five-year rebuilding program as many critics suggest the team should undertake. The deal was completed in September of 2009 and while Kessel was very impressive in scoring 30 goals in an injury-shortened 70-game campaign, the Leafs' 29th overall showing handed Boston the second pick in the 2010 draft, meaning the transaction will be heavily scrutinized for years to come. The Leafs have a history of making regrettable deals with their first pick and this transaction may be no different in the long run, but at least Toronto has a young sniper who will be an impact player for the next decade. Kessel signed a five-year, $27 million contract when the trade was completed.

Kessel has always been able to score goals and that makes him a valuable commodity. He was called the 'Sidney Crosby of the United States' from the time he was 16 years old, which indicates how high opinions were when it came to his talent level. He could never match the sublime skills of Crosby, who plays a more complete game, but he can score goals as well as anyone. In his bantam and midget days he notched 444 points in 157 games and traveled to all parts of the U.S. and Europe to play. The Madison, Wisconsin, native benefited from participating in the U.S. national team development program before going to the University of Minnesota for the 2005–06 season. He was a consistent goal-scorer at every stop, but his stock dropped a little after his time with the Golden Gophers. Once considered a possible first overall selection, Kessel wasn't picked until the Bruins grabbed him with the fifth selection in 2006. Since that time, Kessel has scored more times than other top picks from that draft like Jordan Staal, Jonathan Toews and Nicklas Backstrom with 96 goals in 289 games — a fact not often reported by his critics. Kessel did this despite missing significant time with severe injuries and illness.

Testicular cancer was the first obstacle Kessel had to overcome. The cancer was surgically treated in December of 2006 and he quickly returned to hockey. Kessel was named winner of the 2007 Bill Masterton Memorial Trophy, becoming the first rookie to win the award given to the player who best demonstrates perseverance and dedication to the game. The following season saw Kessel bag 19 goals, but a benching in the playoffs by Boston coach Claude Julien never sat well with the youngster, who wondered what he did to deserve such treatment. He came back stronger in 2008–09 with 36 markers playing alongside center Marc Savard and rugged winger Milan Lucic. It was a good time to score so many goals since his contract was up, but shoulder surgery at the end of the year placed some doubt as to his future.

The Maple Leafs were convinced Kessel would pick up where he left off and made the deal for the flashy 23-year-old. He missed a total of 12 games while recovering from his shoulder problems, but still managed to record 55 points with a fairly weak team. It was obvious his conditioning left a great deal to be desired, but his shot still had a vital snap to it. Kessel's main strength is making defensemen quake as he steams down the wing. Give him the puck at the right moment and it can be past the opposing defender in a blink of an eye. He is also able to pick the top corner of the net with uncanny ease, making more than one goalie look silly.

Kessel vows to be stronger for the future and to be in better shape. He is not likely to challenge anytime soon for the Selke Trophy as the NHL's best defensive forward, but when a player with his ability to score is on the ice, all eyes go to him as soon as he touches the puck. Toronto is never an easy place to play and comparisons to the players the Bruins draft as a result of the trade will always be brought up at the mere mention of Kessel's name. Realistic Maple Leaf fans will understand that a consistent 35- to 40-goal scorer will be very valuable in his own right.

BY THE NUMBERS

Averaged a career-high 19:33 of ice time in 2009–10

- Has recorded at least 30 goals in each of the last two seasons
- Originally drafted fifth overall by Boston in 2006
- Was the first rookie to be awarded the Bill Masterton Trophy for sportsmanship and perseverance
- Had a career-high 36 goals and 60 points in 2008–09

CAREER HIGHLIGHTS

When Alex Ovechkin was asked to replace traded, long time Washington Capital Chris Clark as captain in late December 2009, the Caps superstar first wanted to know if his teammates wanted him in that role. It was assumed by many that Ovechkin would simply take over the official leadership of the Capitals, but coach Bruce Boudreau was pleased to hear his player's response to the issue. Boudreau decided to ask some of his other players about Ovechkin having the 'C' sewn on his sweater. The feedback from everyone was positive and they all recognized No. 8 was the main man in Washington, so there really was no other choice.

The superstar left winger has been his own man since he entered the NHL in 2005–06 and he really doesn't care what others think of his style. Most of the time Ovechkin has a disheveled, scruffy look and a devil-may-care attitude. Many will argue he is the best player in the world and some will argue he is not, but there is no doubt he is definitely not the corporate type — Ovechkin's mother, not an agent, negotiated his 13-year, $124 million contract extension with the Capitals, showing he marches to the beat of his own drum. He does what he likes and dresses the way he feels comfortable and if some don't like it that is of no concern to the native of Moscow, Russia. His command of the English language is improving, although still somewhat tortured, but the smile on his face has never really changed — nor is it likely to in the future.

Ovechkin's approach on the ice is free-wheeling; no one really knows what he will do next. His enthusiastic approach to playing the game is what makes him a special player. Ovechkin will attack any opponent with the puck using a vigor rarely seen in a superstar player. He will also not hesitate to fling his 6-foot-2, 215-pound body around to deliver a crunching check that packs a great deal of intensity. The speedy winger has the ability to appear out of nowhere, able to deliver his rocket-like shot from anywhere on the ice. Ovechkin's explosive nature makes him a very difficult player to defend and he can cause more than one defender to backpeddle himself right out of the play. He will not hesitate to go to the net and can make a spectacular move at the very last second to score a goal. There is a certain amount of recklessness to his game and during the 2009–10 season it cost him a couple of suspensions for dishing out questionable hits to defensemen Tim Gleason of Carolina and Brian Campbell of Chicago. Both caused injuries, but Ovechkin vowed not to play any differently. He also tends to stay on the ice too long at times (a two-minute shift is not uncommon, a discretion Boudreau gives to his best player) when his team is going badly, but such is the competitive nature of Alex Ovechkin.

BY THE NUMBERS Has led the league in shots on net in all five years of his NHL career, including a career-high 528 in 2008–09

- Has scored at least 50 goals in four of his first five seasons in the NHL
- Won the scoring title in 2007–08 with 112 points, which included a career-high 65 goals
- Won the Hart Trophy in 2007–08 and 2008–09
- Won gold with Russia at the 2008 World Championship

CAREER HIGHLIGHTS

Ovechkin has won most of the NHL's major awards including the Calder, Art Ross, Rocket Richard and Hart Trophies, and the Pearson/Ted Lindsay Award since he joined Washington after being selected first overall in 2004. Fans have seen him score many memorable goals and he has netted 50 or more four of his five seasons in the league (he scored 46 as a sophomore). Twice he has led the league in goals scored with 65 in 2007–08 and 56 in 2008–09 and has recorded 100 or more points four times with his best total being 112 in 2007–08. He has earned five-straight First All-Star Team berths and became one of three players in NHL history to record 200 goals and 200 assists in his first four seasons — the only others to do so are Wayne Gretzky and Mario Lemieux, which puts Ovechkin in a very exclusive group.

The 2009–10 season saw the Capitals win their first Presidents' Trophy for having the best record in the regular season. Ovechkin had another superb year leading his team with 50 goals and 109 points. The Washington club has turned itself into an offensive juggernaut with many talented players putting up great numbers. However, it all came apart for the Capitals in the playoffs when the less-talented Montreal Canadiens, the Eastern Conference's No. 8 seed, defeated them in seven games. Appropriate blame was placed upon Ovechkin's shoulders, although he did have 10 points, and now that he is captain, he must lead at the most important time of year. A great playoff performance might see a Conn Smythe Trophy and Stanley Cup added to Ovechkin's ample trophy case.

42 Anaheim Ducks: Corey Perry
44 Calgary Flames: Jarome Iginla
46 Chicago Blackhawks: Jonathan Toews
48 Colorado Avalanche: Paul Stastny
50 Columbus Blue Jackets: Rick Nash
52 Dallas Stars: Brenden Morrow
54 Detroit Red Wings: Nicklas Lidstrom
56 Edmonton Oilers: Dustin Penner
58 Los Angeles Kings: Anze Kopitar
60 Minnesota Wild: Niklas Backstrom
62 Nashville Predators: Shea Weber
64 Phoenix Coyotes: Ilya Bryzgalov
66 San Jose Sharks: Joe Thornton
68 St. Louis Blues: David Backes
70 Vancouver Canucks: Henrik Sedin

WESTERN CONFERENCE TEAM STARS

The best of the Central, Northwest and Pacific.

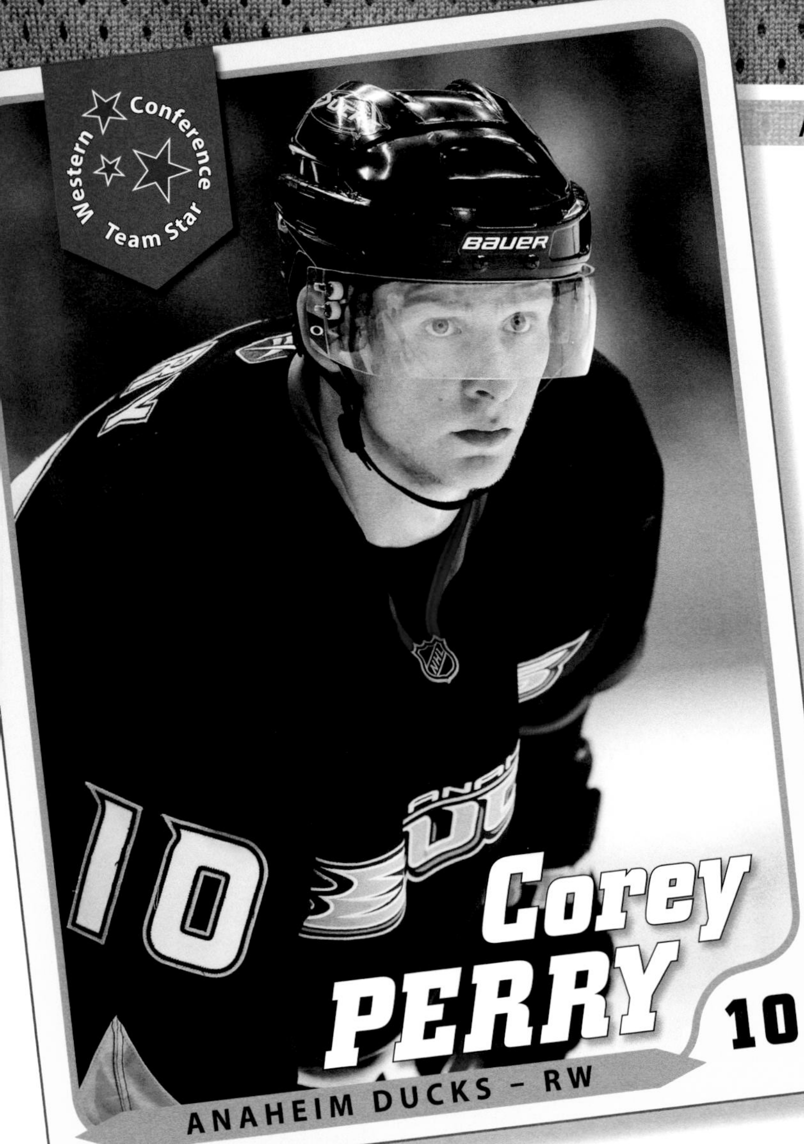

Corey Perry was born in Peterborough, Ontario, May 16, 1985. Life was pretty simple for the youngster, who recalls his youth as hockey in the winter and water activities in the summer. Perry remembers watching hockey on television as a kid and told his mother that one day she would be watching him on TV when he played in the NHL. He was skating by the age of two and playing hockey a couple of years later on local rinks. His father, Geoff, was an Ontario Provincial Police officer and coached his son until he was eight years old (his last year with his father as bench boss, Perry scored 205 goals in 60 games). Young Corey was told to always go all out on the ice and to be careful. Perry certainly goes all out, but he is not exactly careful. A yappy agitator since his minor hockey days, Perry knows how to rattle the opposition and create havoc on the ice. Getting the opposition off its game can be very effective and Perry has created his share of enemies. But he also played for teams that won more often than not, including championships with his midget and bantam squads.

Perry was drafted by the Ontario Hockey League's London Knights and joined the team weighing a mere 160 pounds. His first two years produced seasons of 59 and 78 points and his energizing style got him selected 28th overall in the 2003 NHL draft by the Anaheim Ducks. During his final year of junior, Perry played a major role by scoring 130 points for the powerhouse Knights, considered by many as one of the best junior teams ever assembled. London posted a 59–7–2 record and romped all the way to the 2005 Memorial Cup championship, defeating Sidney Crosby's Rimouski Oceanic in the final. Perry was punched early in the contest — something that inevitably happens to agitators — and remembers little of that game. The Cup win just added to a great year for Perry, who had also won a gold medal for Canada at the 2005 World Junior Championship. It was obvious Perry had learned valuable lessons from the Hunter brothers — Dale and Mark — who ran the Knights and got him ready for the NHL, where they once played.

The Portland Pirates of the American Hockey League had Perry on their team to start the 2005–06 season and it was thought the Ducks would likely leave him there for the entire season. However, 16 goals and 34 points in 19 games forced Ducks management to change its mind about the ready-to-rumble 20-year-old and got him promoted to the big club. He played on the fourth line with Ryan Geztlaf, a player also taken in the first round of the 2003 draft by the Ducks, but still managed 13 goals and 25 points in only 59 games. The right winger was a little better in his second season, scoring 17 goals and 44 points, and played all

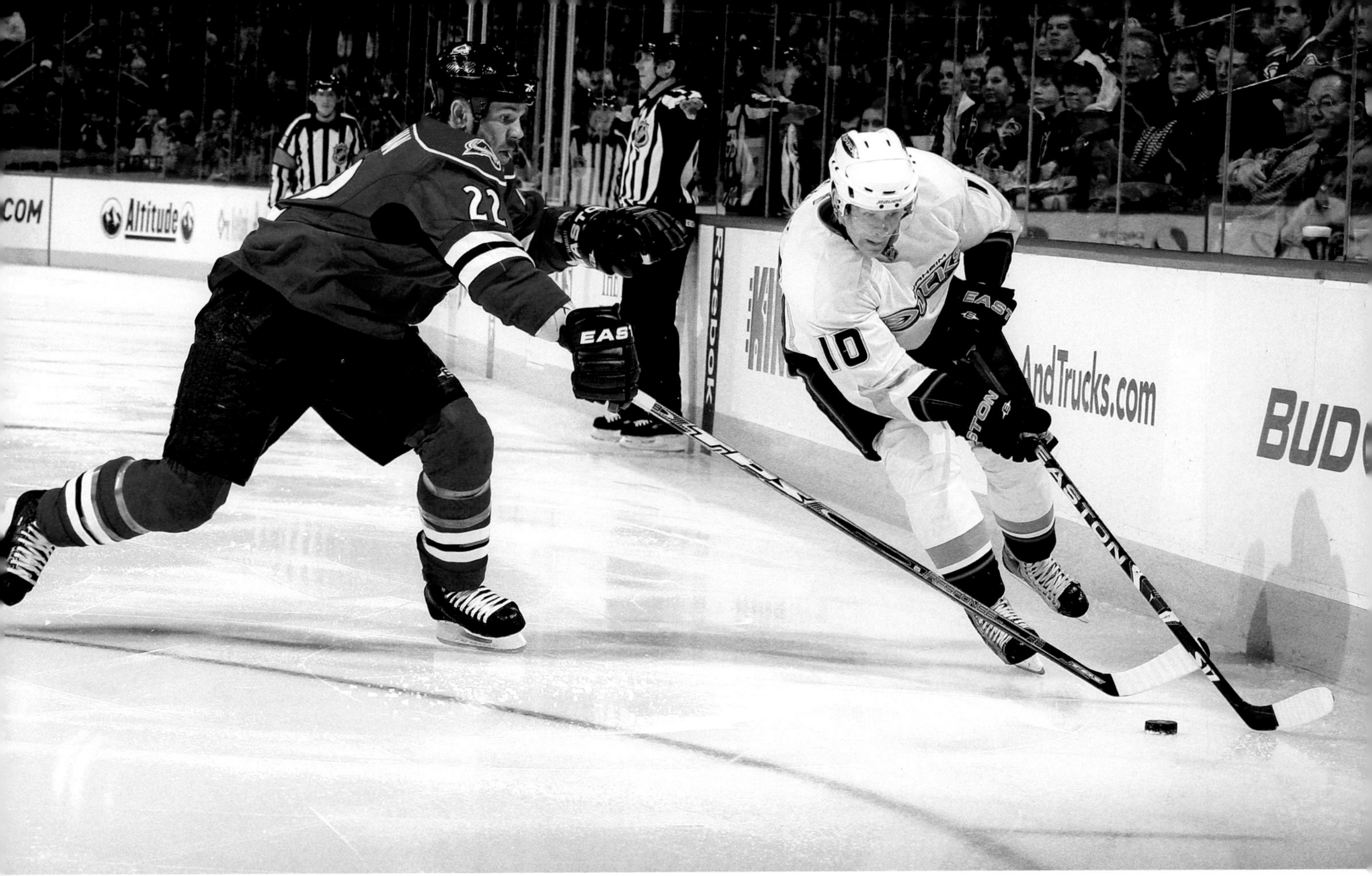

82 games. He was very good in the playoffs, notching 15 points in 21 games when the Ducks surprised just about everyone by winning the Stanley Cup in five games over the Ottawa Senators. At the final buzzer, Perry threw his gloves in the air and waited anxiously to lift the silver trophy over his head. The dream of being seen on TV had become reality as millions across North America watched Perry score the sixth Ducks' goal in a 6–2 Anaheim victory.

Perry has now filled out to 6-foot-3 and 209 pounds and is a much more complete player. He plays a power game and is willing to take whatever the opposition throws at him night after night. Perry still pushes the limits of the rulebook and has paid the price with suspensions, but the Ducks love the fact he is hard to play against. He is at his best when he uses his creativity to manufacture offense as he led the Ducks in scoring in 2009–10 with 76 points in 82 games, including a career-best 49 assists, and his goal-scoring prowess is good for about 30 goals a season (32 is his career high to date). Perry's improvement was noticed by many, including Team Canada management who selected him for the 2010 Winter Olympic Games. He scored four goals in the tournament and the Canadian side took the gold, adding to Perry's long list of great triumphs.

A new five-year contract valued at more than $26 million means the Ducks also believe in what Perry brings to their team, even if it gets him in trouble on occasion.

BY THE NUMBERS

Had six goals, nine assists and 15 points in the 2007 playoffs, the year the Ducks won the Stanley Cup

- **Played in the 2008 NHL All-Star Game**
- **Had a career-high 76 points in 2009–10**
- **Won gold with the Canadian Olympic team in 2010**
- **Was selected 28th overall in the 2003 NHL draft**

CAREER HIGHLIGHTS

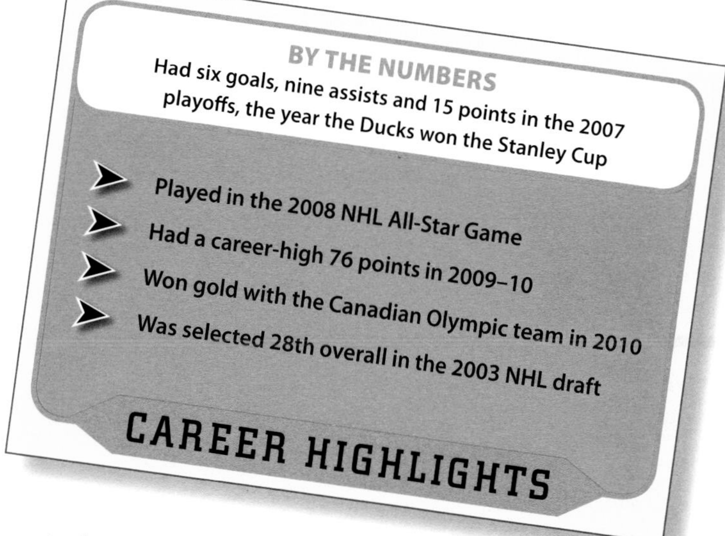

When you make $7 million dollars a year, have led the NHL in goals twice in your career and wear the captain's 'C' on your jersey, a great deal is expected of your on-ice performance. Such is the case for right winger Jarome Iginla, who has now played 1,024 games as a Calgary Flame, the only team he has ever dressed for in his NHL career. He usually gets a good amount of the credit when Calgary wins, but he seems to get all of the blame when the Flames lose, as was the case when a playoff spot was lost to end the 2009–10 season. However, Iginla still led his team in scoring for the ninth straight season — the longest streak of any current player. Yet the questions continue about his value to the Flames as he now enters his mid-30s.

A large part of the problem for the Flames has been trying to find a complementary center to play with the rugged winger. Many have come and gone — including names like Craig Conroy, Steven Reinprecht, Matthew Lombardi and the lamentable Olli Jokinen — but none have been able to click with Iginla long-term. The Flames made major changes to their roster in the middle of the 2009–10 season and one of those additions was former Toronto Maple Leaf pivot Matt Stajan. A solid 50-point player who has signed on to stay in Calgary for the long haul, Stajan may get the greatest benefit from playing with Iginla since he is more likely to pass than shoot, but there is no assurance the two will stay together. It is just as likely Calgary will have to make another deal or sign a free agent to get a true No. 1 center who can play with Iginla. Further change could occur if coach Brent Sutter would give his troops more leeway on the attack and not try to win every game 2–1, but that is not likely to happen. Frustrated by the Flames' inability to make the playoffs, Iginla expressed the thought that he would listen if the Flames wanted him to waive his no-trade clause. Moving a large contract is very difficult in the salary cap era, but even if it were possible, Calgary would be wise to hold onto one of its best-ever players.

Iginla was a largely unknown commodity until the Flames acquired him in a deal with the Dallas Stars in 1995. The trade cost Calgary one of its best players in Joe Nieuwendyk, who was a part of the Flames' only Stanley Cup win in 1989. Iginla was a solid but unspectacular player over his first five years and the Flames always failed to make the playoffs. But then he scored a career-high 52 goals in 2001–02 and was suddenly an All-Star player. Since that time he has been a consistent producer by scoring 35, 41, 35, 39, 50 and 35 times over the next six seasons. The four-time league All-Star has also won major trophies and has represented Canada on the world stage on numerous occasions. He was a member of Team Canada when they won gold at the

Winter Olympics of 2002 and again in 2010, setting up the overtime winner by Sidney Crosby in the latest Olympic effort. Through it all, Iginla has kept up his very classy demeanor and he is a great example of how a hockey player should conduct himself.

Iginla was at his absolute best when he led the Flames to within one game of the Stanley Cup in 2004, as Calgary lost the final in seven games to the Tampa Bay Lightning. He had 13 goals and 22 points in 26 post-season games and did everything a great leader should. The Flames have not won a playoff series since that time, including a rather one-sided series defeat at the hands of the Chicago Blackhawks in 2009. While Iginla is still very productive, his game can be inconsistent over the course of a long season. He is very strong around the opposition net and can swat in loose pucks with some ease. Iginla's shot is very hard and accurate, but if he carries the puck too much he's not in position to unleash it. Having better players on his line would help his game greatly, as would having another teammate who could be counted on for scoring. Given the recent approach of Flames management, that might be wishful thinking.

BY THE NUMBERS

Led the NHL in goals (52) and points (96) in 2001–02

- Has scored at least 30 goals in nine straight seasons
- Originally drafted 11th overall by the Dallas Stars in 1995
- Has 920 points in 1,024 games played
- Had a career-high 98 points in 2007–08
- Traded to Calgary from Dallas for Joe Nieuwendyk

CAREER HIGHLIGHTS

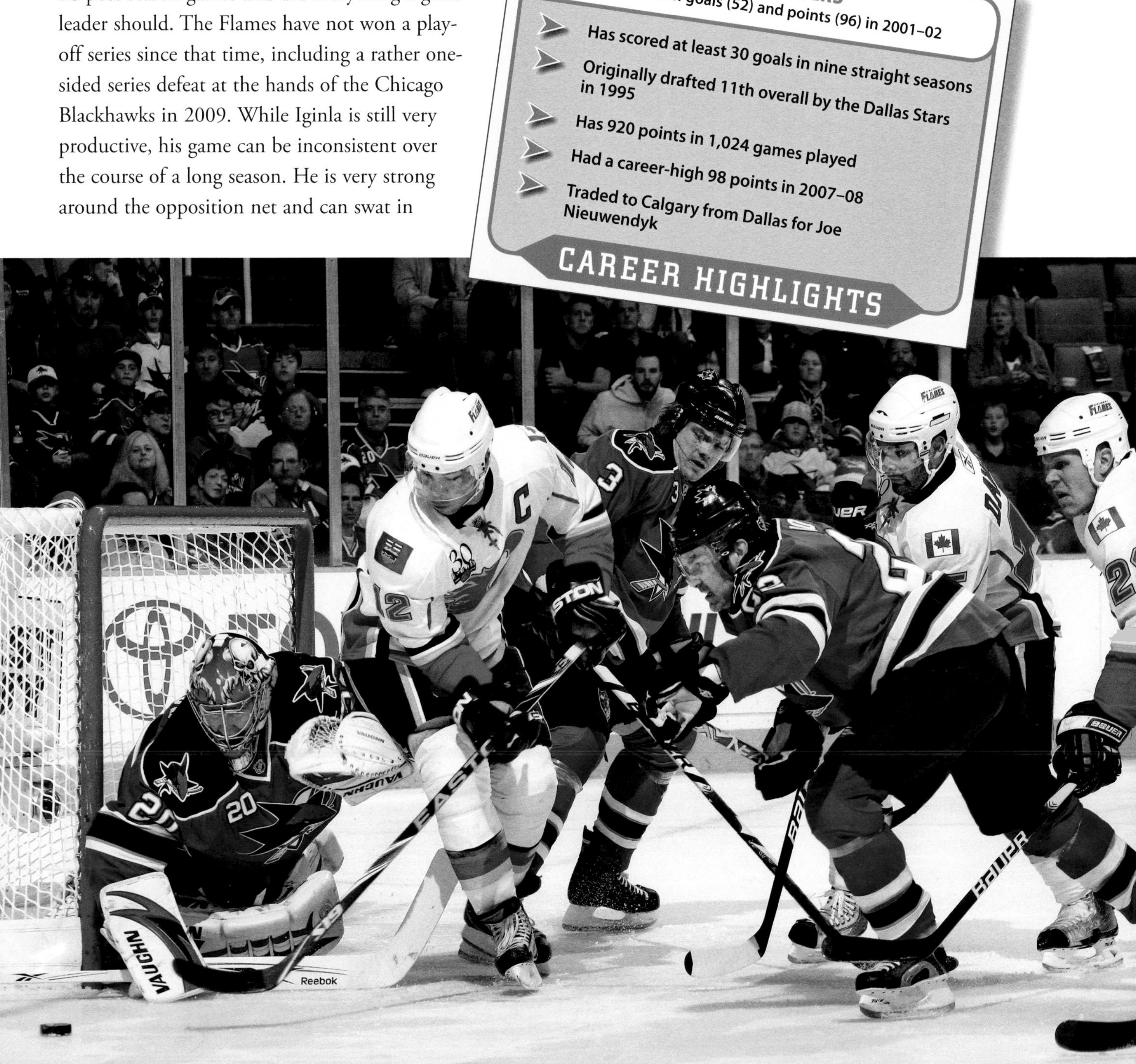

An old family photo taken at Christmas time when Jonathan Toews was about six years old features the youngster wearing a Chicago Blackhawks sweater. The picture shows Toews, his brother, David, his mom, Andree, and dad, Bryan, all smiling. The photo was featured on *Hockey Night in Canada* as Toews talked about winning the Stanley Cup and the Conn Smythe Trophy as playoff MVP on the night Chicago broke a 49-year championship drought. There was no mention of why Toews was wearing a Chicago sweater in the photo, but it seemed to set the scene for a perfect update. The Blackhawks captain gathered around with his teammates as photographers snapped new shots of Toews in his Chicago uniform on the night of June 9, 2010 — this time with the Cup in the middle of the frame.

It was not the first time Toews had worn the 'C' on a winner. When he was just nine years old, he captained a team to the city championship in Winnipeg, Manitoba, where he was born. Not many nine-year-olds are named captain of a hockey team but Toews and leadership just seem to go together. The team Toews was playing for at the time were decided underdogs, but that did not deter the youngster in any way. The other boys, inspired by their captain, worked very hard to overcome the odds and took the title in 1997. The coach of the team, Bob Saelens, recalled that Toews had more desire and dedication than the average nine-year-old. Andree remembers a son who talked about making it to the NHL and how he dreamed about winning the Stanley Cup. By the age of 22, Toews had done just that and added an Olympic gold medal in 2010 to cover another one of his boyhood goals.

Even though his greatest success came in the 2009–10 season, Toews was winning important awards well before then. In 2005, he captained the Canada West team (and was named the MVP of the tournament) at the World Under-17 Hockey Challenge, defeating a team representing another Canadian region to win the gold medal. In 2006 and 2007, he won back-to-back World Junior Championships as a member of Team Canada. He then played for Canada at the 2007 World Championship, notching seven points in nine games and taking home another gold medal. His gold medals made Toews the first player to win at both the senior and junior levels in the same season. Toews' international experience was certainly noticed by Canadian management when they selected the best NHL stars for the 2010 Winter Games. Toews' only goal of the tournament came in the gold medal game versus Team U.S.A. and he finished with eight points in seven games to be named top forward of the event.

In Chicago, the 6-foot-2, 209-pounder is known as 'Captain Serious' for his very strict approach to the game. If things are not going well, Toews will sit and analyze what went wrong and vow to do better. He gets teased by his Chicago teammates, who see their leader as someone who is 22 going on 40. Toews is very mature and extremely focused on what he wants to accomplish. He spoke about how he could not sleep the night before the last game of the 2010 Stanley Cup final because he kept imagining how it would feel if the Blackhawks won the championship. He then went out and set up Chicago's first goal by Dustin Byfuglien, a very important tally in the Blackhawks' 4–3 overtime victory to seal the title.

Toews did not play his best hockey in the final against Philadelphia, battling some nagging pains and the stifling checking of hulking Flyers defenseman Chris Pronger. However, when it was all said and done, Toews had tied a Chicago playoff record with 29 points (including seven goals) in 22 games. If Toews had not been so outstanding against Nashville, Vancouver and San Jose, there was no chance of the Blackhawks winning their first Cup since 1961. Chicago is relatively young and could dominate for a few years if team management makes the right choices about who to keep and who to let go because of salary cap constraints.

It is a certainty Toews is staying in the 'Windy City' and will add to his impressive total of 191 career points in 222 games. He's inked to a five-year contract extension that pays roughly $6.3 million annually. Having such a great leader around almost assures Hawks fans they won't have to wait another half-century for an encore championship.

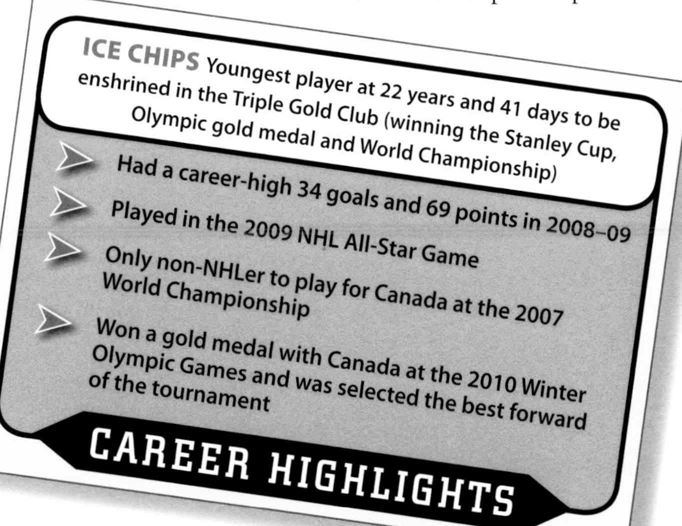
ICE CHIPS Youngest player at 22 years and 41 days to be enshrined in the Triple Gold Club (winning the Stanley Cup, Olympic gold medal and World Championship)

- Had a career-high 34 goals and 69 points in 2008–09
- Played in the 2009 NHL All-Star Game
- Only non-NHLer to play for Canada at the 2007 World Championship
- Won a gold medal with Canada at the 2010 Winter Olympic Games and was selected the best forward of the tournament

CAREER HIGHLIGHTS

The Colorado Avalanche were a very poor team in 2008–09, winning just 32 games, losing 45 and accumulating only 69 points, finishing last in the Western Conference and third last overall. Changes came rapidly once the season was over. GM François Giguère was fired and coach Tony Granato was soon let go as well. Players such as veterans Ryan Smyth, Ian Laperriere and Tyler Arnason were moved out or allowed to leave, while longtime star Joe Sakic retired. However, there was a plan implemented that allowed the Avalanche to inject a strong group of young players into their lineup for the 2009–10 season. Matt Duchene, drafted third overall in 2009, and Ryan O'Reilly, 33rd overall in '09, were inserted after a great training camp. Other youngsters included Chris Stewart, T.J. Galiardi, Brandon Yip, Kyle Quincey, Kyle Cumisky and later, Peter Mueller, who was acquired in a deal with Phoenix for Wojtek Wolski. But the best of the bunch is 24-year-old center Paul Stastny.

Stastny became a hockey player just like his Hall of Fame father, Peter Stastny, and two uncles and former NHL stars Anton and Marian. He was born in the province of Quebec, while his father was starring for the Nordiques. He was constantly around the game while his family lived in Canada. Never pushed by his father to excel at hockey, it was still only natural that young Paul would be drawn to the game. He played on a pond near the family home in Quebec, but left for the United States at age five when his father was traded to the New Jersey Devils. Another move was made when Peter played his final two NHL seasons in St. Louis. Paul started to play on indoor rinks once he moved south of the border. He and his brother, Yan, may not have had the quality of competition in the U.S. they would have seen had they stayed in Canada, yet both made it to the NHL.

By the time he was 18 years old, Paul was playing for the River City Lancers of the United States Hockey League. He had 30 goals and 77 points in 56 games, including a league-leading 47 assists, before heading to the University of Denver, where he recorded 17 goals and 45 points in 42 games as a freshman during the 2004–05 season. The Avalanche drafted the 6-foot, 205-pound center with the 44th overall selection of the 2005 NHL draft. He returned to play one more season with Denver, scoring 53 points in 39 games, and played for Team U.S.A. at the 2007 World Hockey Championship despite his Canadian birth certificate. It was not the first time Stastny had worn the red, white and blue. He was able to do so because of his dual citizenship. He had lived in the U.S. for a number of years and felt a strong attachment to his American roots and it helped that most of his hockey friends were American. He was named to the U.S. Olympic team for the 2010

Winter Games, where he contributed three points in six games and picked up a silver medal.

In 2006–07, Stastny made the Avalanche and the rookie notched 28 goals and 78 points in 82 games. He lost out on the Calder Trophy to Evgeni Malkin of the Pittsburgh Penguins, but did make the NHL's All-Rookie Team. Since his rookie year, Stastny has led the Avalanche in points twice, including the 2009–10 season when he had 79 in 81 games. It was a good bounce-back season for the skilled pivot, who had only played 45 games the previous season due to injuries, but still managed to record 36 points. The Avs got off to a great start in 2009–10 and although they faltered somewhat as the season moved along, they did manage to hang on to the West's eighth and final playoff spot. A first round loss to the No. 1-seeded San Jose Sharks was not unexpected, but Stastny acquitted himself very well with a goal and five points in six games.

Stastny has a very good imagination on the attack and is a pinpoint passer. He is not overly aggressive, but knows how to use his size to create space while playing a solid two-way game. His 264 points in 274 NHL games indicate Stastny is a No. 1 center who should be able to score more goals (83 career markers thus far) in the future. Having youth on their side will help Stastny and the entire Colorado team get better soon.

ICE CHIPS As a rookie, he set an NHL record for first-year players by posting a point in 20 consecutive games

- Had a career-high 79 points in 2009–10
- Named to the NHL All-Rookie Team in 2006–07
- Has at least 70 points in three of his four NHL seasons
- Won a silver medal with Team U.S.A. at the 2010 Olympics

CAREER HIGHLIGHTS

Since the Columbus Blue Jackets entered the NHL in 2000, they have made the playoffs just once and were swept by the Detroit Red Wings in four games during the opening round of the 2009 post-season. The team has not only struggled to make the playoffs, it has had precious few star players to build around, despite a number of high first round draft choices. One player the Blue Jackets have had who has been able to raise his level of play to great heights is Brampton, Ontario, native Rick Nash. Columbus selected the now 6-foot-4, 218-pound left winger first overall at the 2002 NHL draft. Blue Jackets management traded its third overall pick (Jay Bouwmeester) plus a conditional first-rounder in 2003 to Florida for the chance to pick Nash. It was obviously one of the best moves in franchise history — possibly the only good move.

Since the Blue Jackets were an underachieving expansion team, Nash was able to make the club on his first try and registered 17 goals as a rookie in 2002–03; good but not great. However, the next season saw a remarkable performance by the then 19-year-old Nash — 41 goals, good for a share of the NHL's goal-scoring lead (tied with Jarome Iginla and Ilya Kovalchuk) and the Rocket Richard Trophy. Nash had only 16 assists that season, an indicator that he was a pure goal-scorer and that the Blue Jackets had little else on the roster. Nash spent the lockout season playing in Europe, but when NHL action resumed, he added to his goal-scoring prowess with 31 tallies in 2005–06. Selected to play for Team Canada at the 2006 Winter Olympics, Nash came away without a medal and just one assist in six games. He slumped slightly to 27 goals the next season, but then added seasons of 38 and 40 goals to his impressive career statistics. His 79 points were a career high in 2008–09, but Nash's performance in the playoffs was much like his team's — nothing to get excited about, even though he did have three points in the four post-season games.

Appearing in the playoffs was supposed to be the start of something big for Columbus, but the 2009–10 season was one filled with great disappointment. A return to the post-season was expected, but the Blue Jackets were well back in the Western Conference, second-last with just 79 points. Nash had a good season again with a team-high 33 goals and 67 points, but it seemed he was not at the top of his game for most of the year. He was once again selected to the Canadian Olympic team and was a major contributor to the gold medal-winning side, recording two goals and five points in seven games after a sluggish start to the tournament, easily the highlight of his season. But questions were raised about Nash's ability to play under pressure since he has experienced virtually none when playing with the Blue Jackets. To his credit,

Nash never lashes out at the critics and in his own quiet way goes about the business of simply scoring goals.

A very intense competitor, Nash has always shown a knack for scoring, ironic considering he started out as a lacrosse player thinking he might be a goalie. But when his father suggested he make a choice between net or forward, the 10-year-old decided to leave the goalie equipment behind. He scored 61 goals and 115 points in 31 games playing midget triple-A for the Toronto Marlboros of the Greater Toronto Hockey League before joining the Ontario Hockey League's London Knights. Seasons of 31 and 32 goals with the Knights were not outlandish by junior standards, but the Blue Jackets saw great potential in the young winger — and they were correct. Nash goes to the net at full speed with great determination and his soft hands allow him to finish plays in close. During one game against Detroit in 2008–09, Nash became the first NHL player in 61 years to score an unassisted hat trick, an amazing feat, although another example of a lack of playing partners.

Clearly Columbus' best player, the Jackets made the young star their captain after veteran defenseman Adam Foote left the team in 2008. Nash is not a loud leader by any means and is still learning how to embrace the role. When he had a chance to leave Columbus via free agency, his childhood favorite team the Toronto Maple Leafs would have been a sure bidder, but Nash declined the opportunity to leave his adopted home. His $7.8 million-a-year contract through 2018 is more than fair, but unless the Blue Jackets turn their fortunes around, it might be a choice Nash regrets one day.

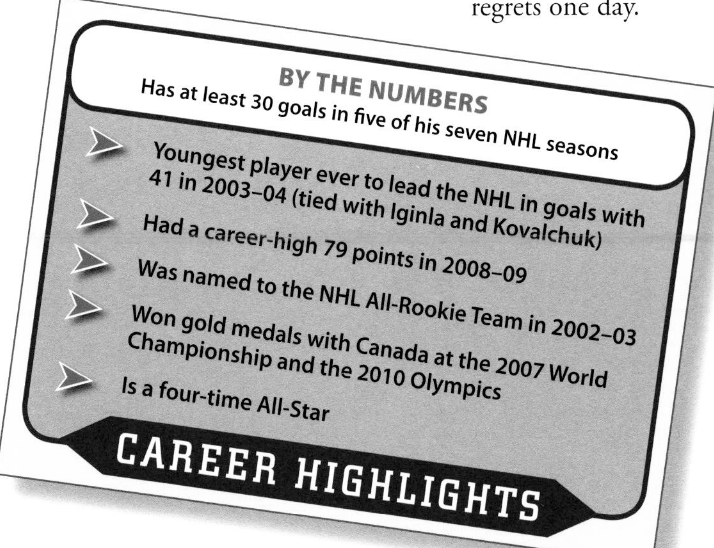
BY THE NUMBERS

Has at least 30 goals in five of his seven NHL seasons

- Youngest player ever to lead the NHL in goals with 41 in 2003–04 (tied with Iginla and Kovalchuk)
- Had a career-high 79 points in 2008–09
- Was named to the NHL All-Rookie Team in 2002–03
- Won gold medals with Canada at the 2007 World Championship and the 2010 Olympics
- Is a four-time All-Star

CAREER HIGHLIGHTS

Many hockey fans wondered exactly why Dallas Stars left winger Brenden Morrow was selected to the Canadian Olympic team for the 2010 Winter Games held in Vancouver. It was his style of play that led to his inclusion. He competes physically each and every shift and is unafraid to run into anybody, anytime. Morrow readily admits there is nothing exceptional about his rugged approach to playing hockey, but he is hard to play against and ultimately Team Canada executive director Steve Yzerman decided he needed such a player on the roster. Selecting the Dallas team captain was obviously a good strategy as Canada won gold in a very competitive tournament with an overtime victory against the United States. In seven games, Morrow scored twice and added one assist and was a very effective player throughout the Olympic tournament.

The management group of Team Canada must have really liked Morrow because he had missed most of the previous season with a severe knee injury. The injury occurred November 20, 2008, during a game against the Chicago Blackhawks and at first Morrow did not think he was badly hurt, but it turned out he had torn his anterior cruciate ligament. His season was over just 18 games into the campaign and the Stars, missing his drive and enthusiasm, finished out of the playoffs for the first time in seven years. Despite missing so much time, Morrow was invited to the Olympic orientation camp in August 2009 and then added to the final roster December 30, 2009 — quite a comeback from such a potentially serious injury. Morrow patterned his game after that of former Boston Bruins great and Hockey Hall of Fame member Cam Neely — the prototypical Canadian power forward.

Morrow is especially good on the forecheck, where he can zone in on and rattle defensemen with heavy bodychecks and create loose puck opportunities. He will battle along the boards and is excellent in front of the net, where he scores the majority of his goals. Morrow has never scored more than 74 points in a season, but he will do whatever it takes to win a game — block shots, kill penalties, fight. His grit, character and determination are recognized by both teammates and opponents, but at times he needs to understand that he cannot take too many penalties (he has recorded over 100 minutes in penalties six times). The 2009–10 season saw Morrow spend just 69 minutes in the sin bin while managing to score 20 goals, including nine on the power play, and 46 points in 76 games, although that was again not enough to get the Stars into the post-season. Dallas is a team going through something of a transition stage, but with a contract that pays him $4.1 million per season through 2013, it appears Morrow is there to stay.

Morrow was raised in Carlyle, Saskatchewan, and was used to walking to a nearby arena where he could skate anytime he wanted. In 1994, at the age of 15, he left home to play bantam for the Estevan Bruins of the Saskatchewan Minor Hockey Association; he scored 117 goals and 189 points in 60 games. He then played major junior with the Portland Winter Hawks in the Western Hockey League, winning the Memorial Cup in 1998 by contributing 18 points in 16 playoff games. The Dallas Stars made Morrow a first round draft choice in 1997 with the 25th overall selection. He played another year of junior, scoring 41 goals and 85 points in 61 games while racking up 248 penalty minutes. The next season — 1999–2000 — Morrow was in the NHL, scoring 14 goals and 33 points as a rookie. He has been a big part of the Dallas club ever since, both as a leader and a scorer, posting six seasons of 20 or more goals.

In addition to the gold medal Morrow won in Vancouver, he has represented Canada many times both as a junior and as a professional — a World Junior tournament, four World Championships, a World Cup and the 2010 Olympics. But no matter the circumstances, Morrow will always give the kind of performance that *Hockey Night in Canada* commentator Don Cherry would give thumbs up to.

BY THE NUMBERS

Had 32 goals and 74 points, both career highs, in 2007–08

- Was second in the NHL with a 20.0 shooting percentage in 2002–03
- Won an Olympic gold medal with Canada in 2010
- Was a career-high plus-30 in 2005–06
- Has scored at least 20 goals six times in his career
- Led the Stars with 12 power play goals in 2007–08

CAREER HIGHLIGHTS

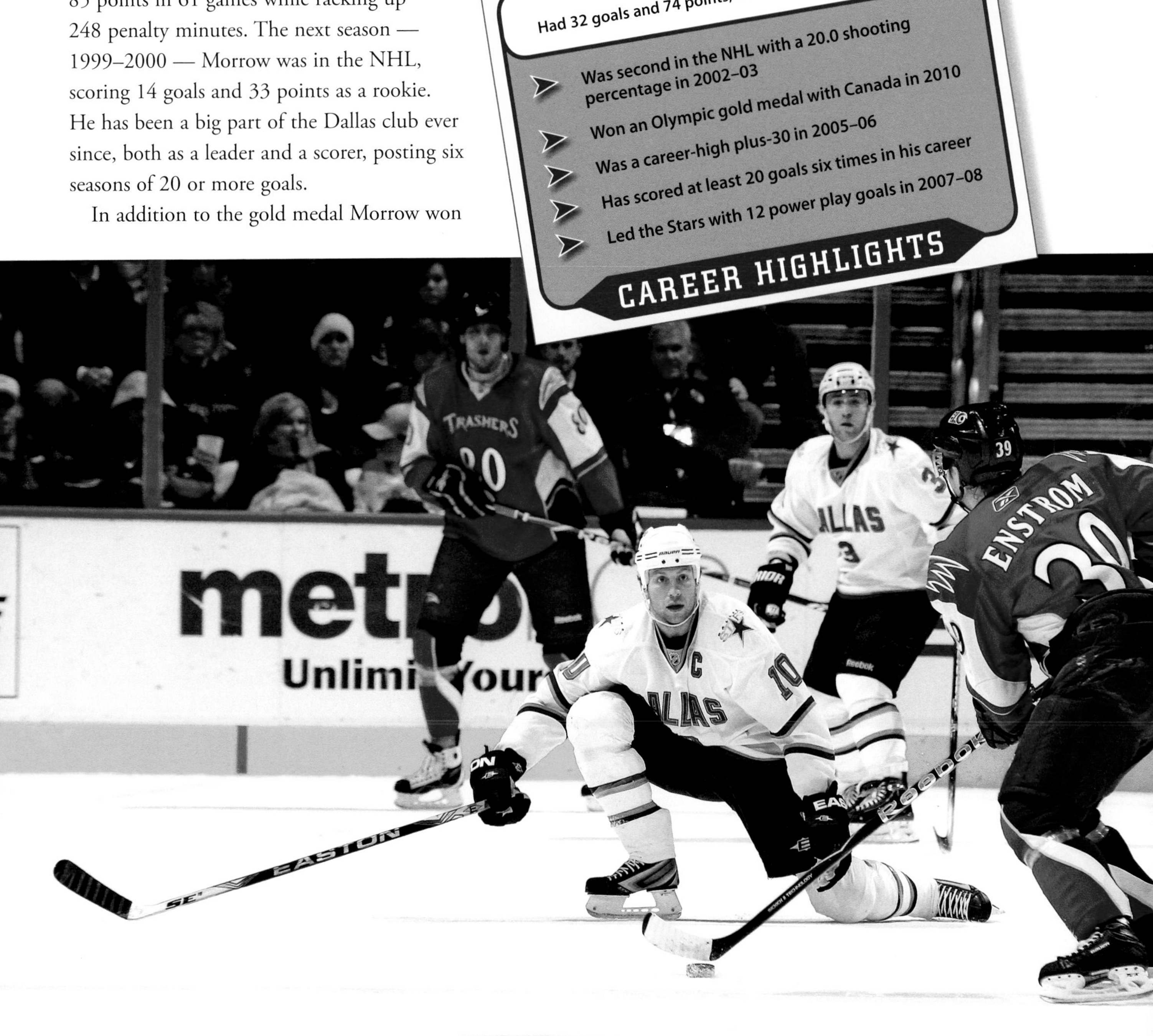

The sigh of relief coming out of the Detroit Red Wings' front office in June of 2010 could be heard all over the hockey world when 40-year-old defenseman Nicklas Lidstrom decided to return for at least one more year. Lidstrom's decision was the source of much speculation as soon as the 2009–10 season ended, but the star defender moved quickly to end any doubt, giving his team more flexibility to make off-season moves. Detroit GM Ken Holland has often joked that he will leave his post as soon as Lidstrom announces his retirement. Luckily for Detroit fans, that day is not at hand yet and may not be for some time to come.

Part of the reason Lidstrom decided to return is that the Swedish blueliner thinks his team can win another Stanley Cup. Already a four-time winner of the NHL championship, the Detroit captain would like to add another ring to his collection before he hangs up the skates for good. There is really little else for Lidstrom to accomplish since he has won the Norris Trophy as the league's best defenseman six times and been a First Team All-Star nine times. He's also been a major trailblazer for European players, holding the distinction of being the first Euro to win the Conn Smythe Trophy as playoff MVP in 2002 and the first to captain his team to a Cup win in 2008. He is also the only European defenseman in league history to record 1,000 career points. All this means Lidstrom is a sure bet to enter the Hall of Fame when his career finally ends.

Lidstrom's game is built around his superb finesse skills, which have still not left him despite his advanced hockey age. On offense, Lidstrom controls the point like a conductor leads an orchestra. His shot will never blow anyone away, but he is very accurate and is able to set up teammates for tip-ins or deflections. Lidstrom is able to assess his best option from his perch on the blueline and if all else fails, he will shoot wide in the hopes of creating a rebound to one of the Red Wing forwards. He is one of the best tape-to-tape passers in the history of the game and can make the long stretch pass from his own end with great ease. His offensive instincts have allowed him to score 237 goals and add 809 assists in 1,412 games to date — all Detroit club records for defensemen.

As good as Lidstrom is on the attack, he is just as deft playing in his own end of the ice. He will not smash anyone into the boards or dish out devastating bodychecks, but through proper positioning and the use of his quick stick, Lidstrom is one of the best shutdown defenders in the NHL. He is rarely beaten in a 1-on-1 situation and uses the poke check effectively to break up many opposition rushes. Lidstrom will battle in front of his net without taking a penalty (he has only 466 career penalty minutes) and once he gets the puck on his stick, he makes a great first pass to get his team out of trouble. Although he has good size at 6-foot-1 and 190 pounds, Lidstrom is actually much stronger physically than most people might realize. He works out steadily in the gym and knows his way around the weight room.

The 2009–10 season saw Lidstrom average just over 25 minutes a game, which was down only slightly from the days when he was on the ice for nearly 29 minutes per contest. He managed to play in all 82 games, but his numbers were down to nine goals and 49 points, one of the lower totals in his illustrious career. He was not nominated for the Norris Trophy, but he is very respected by his peers and of course by his teammates, many of whom he now mentors. Numerous Detroit players past and present have benefited from working alongside Lidstrom over his nearly 20 years in the Motor City.

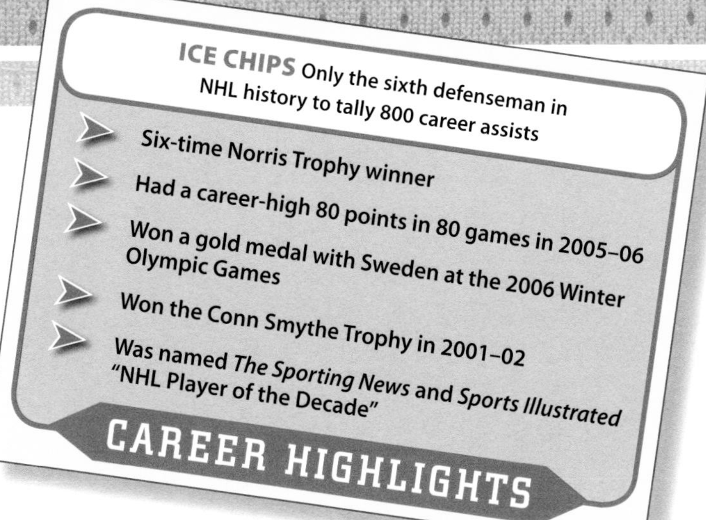

ICE CHIPS Only the sixth defenseman in NHL history to tally 800 career assists

- Six-time Norris Trophy winner
- Had a career-high 80 points in 80 games in 2005–06
- Won a gold medal with Sweden at the 2006 Winter Olympic Games
- Won the Conn Smythe Trophy in 2001–02
- Was named *The Sporting News* and *Sports Illustrated* "NHL Player of the Decade"

CAREER HIGHLIGHTS

Lidstrom agreed to take a pay cut of over $1 million to play another season in Detroit and it is quite likely he will continue to sign one-year contracts until the time he decides he's had enough of hockey. Holland thinks the superstar defender could play until he is 45 and, judging by his most recent performances, who could argue?

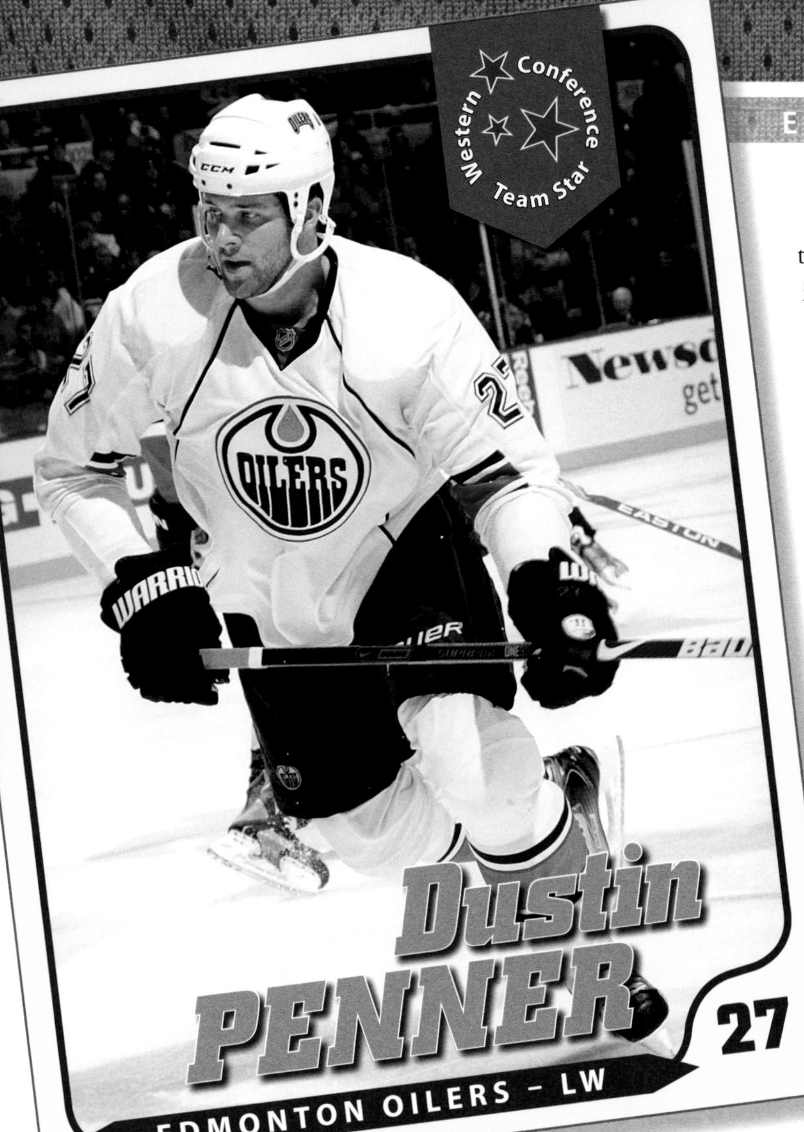

More than one eyebrow was raised when the Edmonton Oilers signed restricted free agent Dustin Penner to a massive offer sheet in the summer of 2007. The deal called for the 6-foot-4, 245-pound left winger to average $4.25 million dollars a year for the next five seasons — quite an impressive package for a player who had not recorded more than 45 points in any single campaign. The Anaheim Ducks were less than pleased — to put it mildly — with Edmonton for attempting to poach Penner, but decided to take compensation rather than match the offer because the Ducks believed the deal was far too lucrative for a player of his caliber. For two straight seasons it appeared the Ducks had done the right thing as the hulking winger struggled to find his niche in Edmonton. He did score 23 times in his first year as an Oiler, but that dropped to 17 in the 2008–09 season and Edmonton's critics were howling over his performance. Just when it appeared the situation was only going to get worse for Penner, he redeemed himself somewhat in 2009–10 and may yet prove to be quite a valuable asset for the Oilers.

Penner's problems in Edmonton were directly related to former coach Craig MacTavish, who implied his player was lazy and unwilling to pay the price for success. He was even a healthy scratch on occasion and an obvious source of frustration for a team that has missed the playoffs each of Penner's three seasons with the Oilers. The lack of a playoff appearance cost MacTavish his job and the coaching duties were given to Pat Quinn, a longtime NHL bench boss who was assisted closely by Tom Renney, also an experienced coach. The change did a world of good for a revitalized Penner, who came out of the gate scoring goals. Through his first 20 games, Penner had 12 goals and 23 points and earned some early consideration for the 2010 Canadian Olympic team. He was unable to sustain that performance the entire year, but did finish with career-high marks of 32 goals and 63 points despite playing for the worst team in the NHL. Penner became just the third Oiler to score 30 or more goals in the past 10 seasons (Mike Comrie and Ryan Smyth were the others) and the questions about his performance were at least pushed to the background for one year.

A native of Winkler, Manitoba, Penner's hockey abilities have always been underestimated. He could not make the Manitoba Junior Hockey League's Winkler Flyers and went to play at Minot State University, a U.S. junior college in West Minot, North Dakota, scoring 20 goals in 23 games in 2001–02. He then went to the University of Maine and did not post overwhelming numbers, but managed to catch the eye of David McNabb, a scout with the Anaheim organization. Never drafted by an NHL team, Penner was available as a free agent and the Ducks inked him to a deal and assigned him to the American Hockey League for most of the next two seasons. He started to play very well while with the Portland Pirates in 2005–06, scoring 39 goals and 84 points in 57 games. Those numbers got Penner promoted to the Ducks for 19 games, where he recorded seven points and he played in 13 post-season games, recording six more points. He was rewarded with full-time employment in Anaheim the following year. His 29 goals during the 2006–07 season readied him for the playoffs and he scored three goals and eight points in 21 post-season games as the Ducks won their first Stanley Cup. It was that 2006–07 performance that landed Penner his big deal in Edmonton.

Penner is something of a gentle giant with just 216 career penalty minutes and that fact alone might keep him from getting more open ice to do what he does best. In close to the net is where Penner excels with his soft hands and a deft touch when everything is going well. His large body makes him difficult to handle, but when he plays a soft game, it is very noticeable because he is so big. If Penner keeps his conditioning level high, he will be better able to keep up from a skating point of view and get to the places where he can score goals.

It is ironic that Penner would have his best year when his team finished so low in the standings. He might be trade bait for the Oilers who look to add many new players to an organization in desperate need of rebuilding.

BY THE NUMBERS

Scored 29 goals in his first full season in 2006–07

- Had career highs of 32 goals and 63 points in 2009–10
- Won the Stanley Cup as a rookie with Anaheim in 2007
- Has played 82 games in three of the last four seasons
- Produced 84 points in 57 games for Portland (AHL) in 2005–06

CAREER HIGHLIGHTS

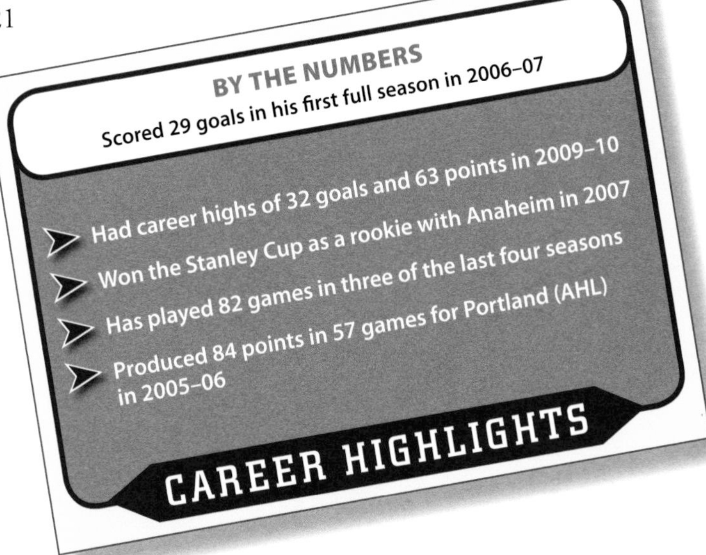

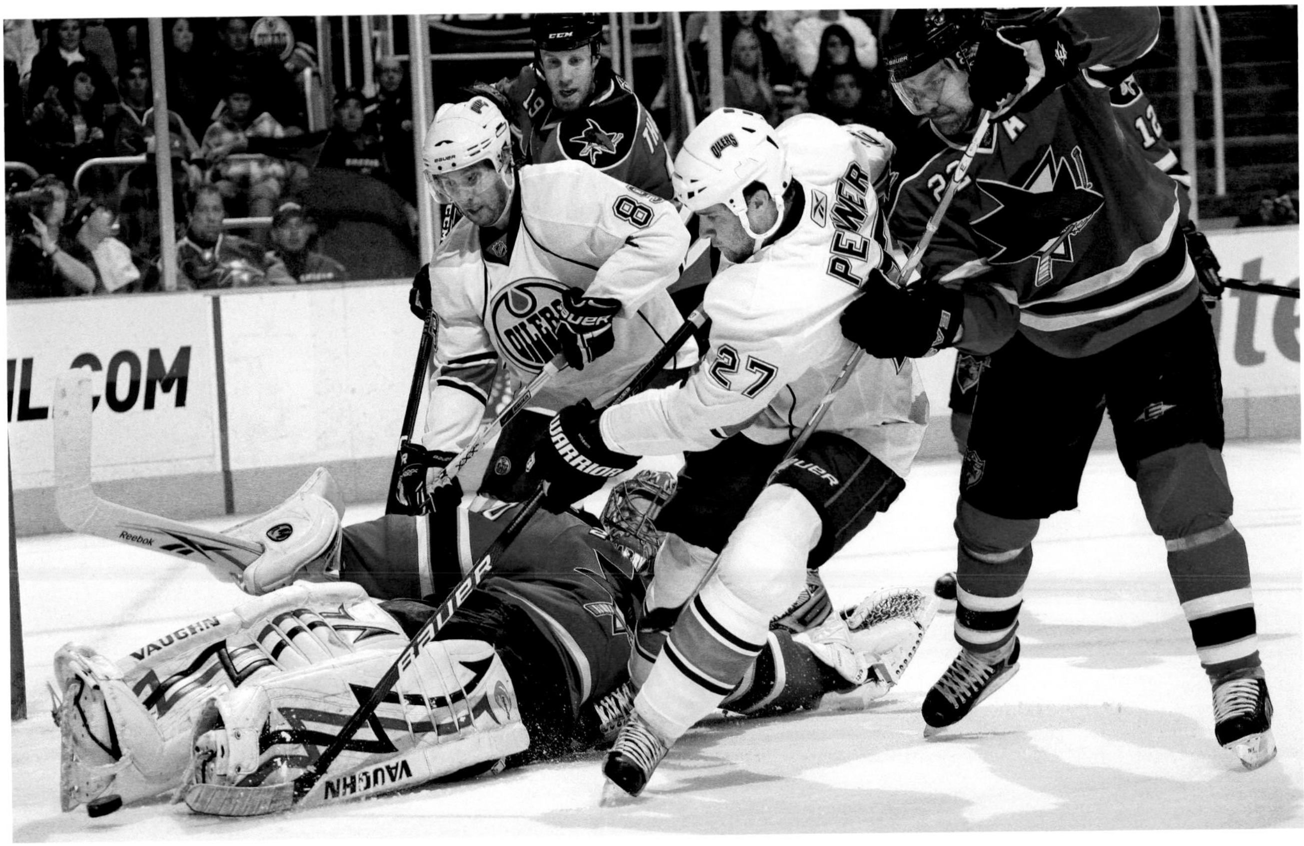

In addition to his great hockey skills, Anze Kopitar holds one other very noteworthy distinction — he is the first and thus far only NHL player born in Slovenia. Mind you, when Kopitar was born on August 24, 1987, the nation of his birth was still known as Yugoslavia. It wasn't until 1991 that Slovenia became an independent state with the collapse of the former federation. In a nation of two million people, young Anze was one of the few who wanted to be a hockey player. Most kids he grew up with wanted to play soccer or basketball, but Kopitar's father, Matjaz, was a former hockey player who had his son skating before he turned four. A small outdoor rink was built for Kopitar in the backyard of his home and his father gave him his first hockey stick. Kopitar first played hockey in his hometown of Jesenice, a small industrial area, and he dominated with 196 points in 91 games at various levels of play. In order to play against better competition, Kopitar moved to Sweden when he was 17 years old. He lived on his own and often felt lonely, but it paid off when the Los Angeles Kings took him 11th overall during the 2005 NHL draft.

Every NHL team was aware of Kopitar's exploits despite his relatively obscure beginnings, though many felt they couldn't get an accurate read on his potential because he hadn't played against enough high-level competition. The Kings were a team that saw Kopitar early on and ranked him the third-best prospect behind only Sidney Crosby and Jack Johnson by the time the '05 draft rolled around. Kopitar produced 49 points in 30 Swedish junior league games during the 2004–05 season, but certain teams were still leery about his background. The youngster felt his home country was being devalued as a hockey nation and he fully believed he could play with the best in the world. Kopitar has been proving the Kings made an accurate assessment since his first game in the NHL.

Kopitar made his debut in Los Angeles at the age of 19 and produced 20 goals and 61 points in 72 games for a rather weak team in 2006–07. He had 32 goals and 77 points the next season when he played 82 games, but slipped back a little in 2008–09, when he recorded 66. The Kings were undergoing a major reconstruction and missed the playoffs in each of Kopitar's first three seasons in the league. But that didn't stop the club from rewarding their young star with a seven-year contract extension worth $47.5 million in October 2008. The battlefields of war-torn Yugoslavia seemed a long way off as Kopitar moved his family to southern California. In the summer of 2009, Kopitar dedicated himself to getting into better condition and it showed with a strong effort that saw him score a career-high 34 goals and 81 points during the 2009–10 season. He also decided to pay more attention to his defensive game and for the first time ever was a plus player with a plus-6 rating.

At 6-foot-3 and 222 pounds, Kopitar is an impressive package of size and skill. He has great hands in close and will use his big body to go to the net most of the time. Kopitar is also a terrific passer and shows an excellent eye for creativity when he wants to make a play. His shot is above average and he needs to use it more often because he has shown he can score goals. Although he has committed to playing a two-way game, his defensive work still needs to improve and that will come with experience playing away from the puck. Kopitar spent much of 2009–10 on a line with veterans Ryan Smyth and Justin Williams, but the two wingers suffered injuries that hurt the pivot's production as the season wore on. The Kings finally made the playoffs in 2010 and took a 2–1 series lead on the Vancouver Canucks in Round 1 before ultimately losing in six games. Kopitar's first playoff exposure saw him record five points and he will no doubt benefit from that experience.

Los Angeles has taken the slow and steady approach to building its team and has given young talent like Kopitar every chance to prove their worth. This method is finally paying off and a few key additions could elevate the Kings to elite status.

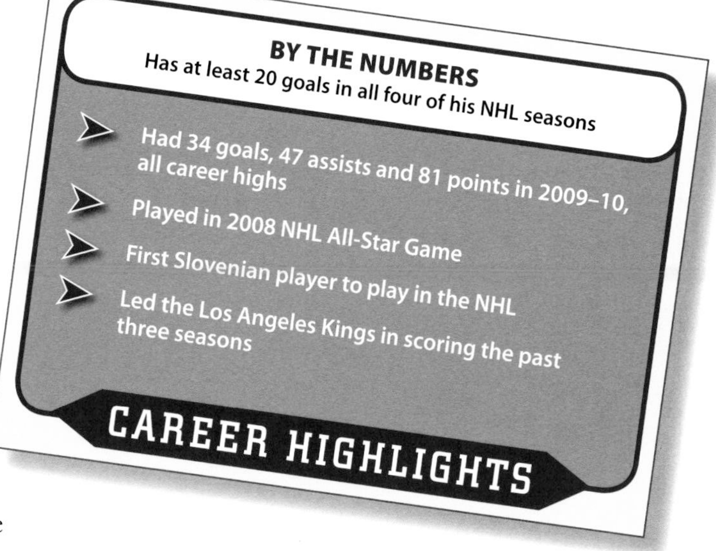

BY THE NUMBERS

Has at least 20 goals in all four of his NHL seasons

- Had 34 goals, 47 assists and 81 points in 2009–10, all career highs
- Played in 2008 NHL All-Star Game
- First Slovenian player to play in the NHL
- Led the Los Angeles Kings in scoring the past three seasons

CAREER HIGHLIGHTS

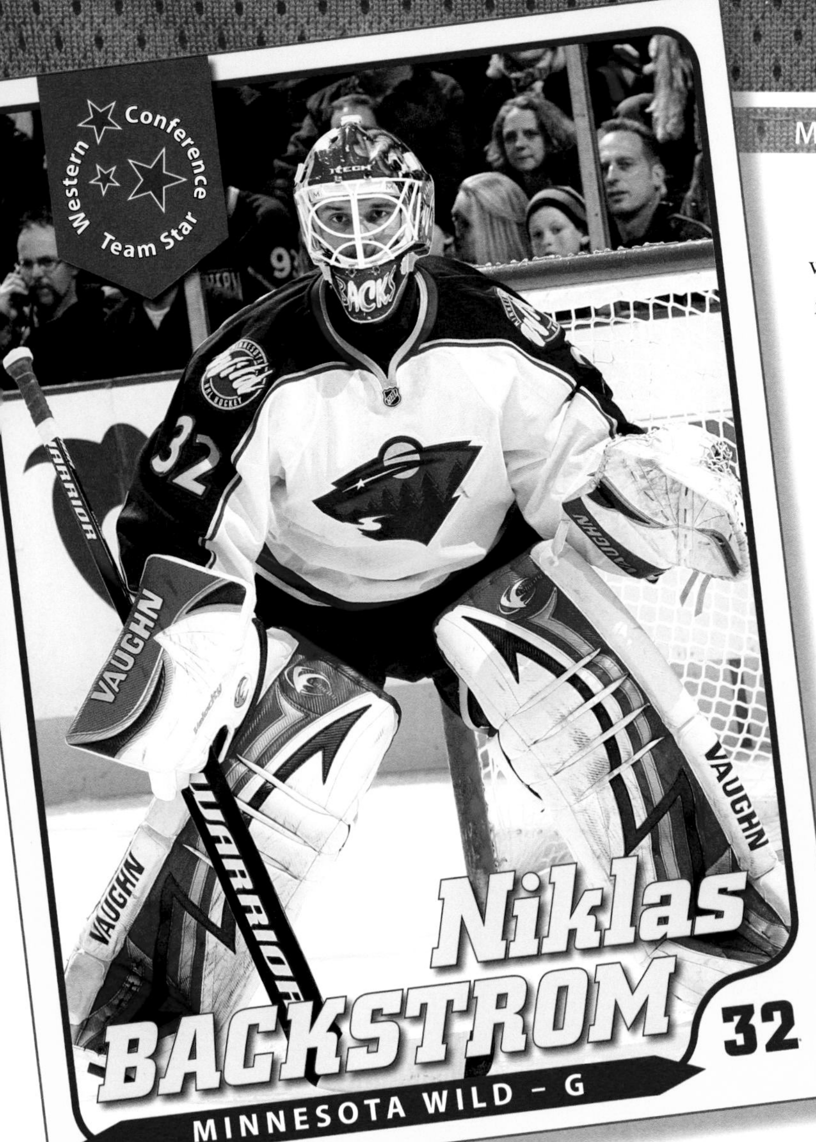

The Minnesota Wild have been in the National Hockey League for a decade now, but haven't had a great deal of success. They did make it to the Western Conference final in 2003 and made the post-season on two other occasions, but have missed the playoffs in six other seasons. When the club fell short of the big dance in 2009, management and coaching changes were the order of the day, with Chuck Fletcher and Todd Richards named GM and coach, respectively. There was plenty of room for improvement in all areas of the team, but one position was essentially trouble free because Niklas Backstrom was the No. 1 netminder and one of the hardest-working players on the squad.

Backstrom first came to the attention of the Wild based on his good play in Europe, posting an impressive winning record over his last four years. He played primarily in his home country of Finland before former Minnesota GM Doug Risebrough brought him over to North America. Seen as a depth netminder at the time, Backstrom signed a one-year deal with the Wild in June of 2006. He was likely headed to play in the minors, but backup Josh Harding suffered an injury and starting netminder Manny Fernandez got off to a poor start. By the time the 2006–07 season ended, Backstrom played in 41 games, posting a 23–8–6 mark. His .929 save percentage and 1.97 goals-against average were both league-leading marks and he pitched five shutouts to boot. Although the Wild made the playoffs, their post-season lasted just five games. Still, it was quite a start for a 28-year-old who was essentially unknown on this side of the Atlantic.

As a boy, Backstrom always sought to be a netminder with his friends in the schoolyard and the idea of being a goaltender may have been passed on to him through his father and grandfather, both of whom played the position. However, he may have learned the most about the position from Boston Bruins puckstopper Tim Thomas, who played with and against Backstrom when he was in Europe. It is interesting to note both goalies have gone on to success in the NHL. Thomas arrived in the big show first in 2005–06, but Backstrom had never given up on the dream of playing in North America, even if he was quite happy in Finland. Luckily for the Wild, Backstrom could not pass up the opportunity. One of the reasons Backstrom did so well as an NHL rookie is that he was quite comfortable playing in Minnesota, a place that reminded him of his home country. The fishing Backstrom loves to do is great in both places and all four weather seasons are prominent in each location as well. There are many people in Minnesota who have a Scandinavian background and it has large, wide-open areas similar to Finland. He also had to like that the Wild were an organization known for attention to defensive detail, especially under former coach Jacques Lemaire.

Backstrom continued his strong play in his second NHL season, earning 33 victories in 58 appearances with a .920 save percentage and also winning two playoff games. If that was not convincing enough, the 6-foot-1, 195-pounder won 37 games in 2008–09 and earned a Vezina Trophy nomination. He was in the top five among all the important goalie statistical categories, but a lack of offense kept the Wild from making the post-season. Fletcher tried to rebuild other parts of the team, but was unable to hold onto star forward Marian Gaborik. Martin Havlat was signed as a free agent to help fill the void, but it was the Wild's best player and Backstrom's fellow Finn, Mikko Koivu, who led the team in points with 71. Injuries held Backstrom to 60 games, but he did manage to win 26 times and record a .903 save percentage — a stat that has never been below .900 for the goalie since he arrived in Minnesota.

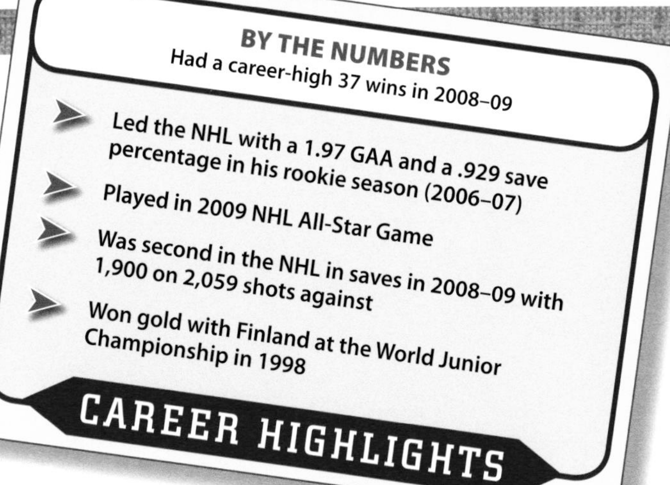

BY THE NUMBERS
Had a career-high 37 wins in 2008–09

- Led the NHL with a 1.97 GAA and a .929 save percentage in his rookie season (2006–07)
- Played in 2009 NHL All-Star Game
- Was second in the NHL in saves in 2008–09 with 1,900 on 2,059 shots against
- Won gold with Finland at the World Junior Championship in 1998

CAREER HIGHLIGHTS

Backstrom's strong performance earned him a $24 million dollar deal with the Wild that will keep him in Minnesota until 2013. Although he is, by his own admission, very emotional at times, the team likes his steadying influence and the fact Backstrom can get over a bad goal quickly. His strong positional play will be counted on by the Wild if they are to return to the playoffs and make their second decade much more memorable than the first.

A big part of today's NHL game is blocking shots. Coaches talk about it all the time and the league keeps statistics on what has become a very desirable skill. However, if you watch the Nashville Predators play, it's obvious players tend to scatter when Shea Weber unleashes his howitzer from the point. Clocked as fast as 103.4 miles per hour, no opponent or teammate wants to get in the way when Weber delivers his blistering shot. Words used to describe Weber's shot range from 'heavy and vicious' to 'rocket and cannon' by players on other teams. But players on the Predators are just as concerned about broken bones if they get in the way — especially on the power play, where Weber gets a little more space to pound the puck. To keep the injury list as short as possible, the best-case scenario for Nashville is to have the puck go straight in from the point when the Preds have the man advantage. Weber had seven power play goals in 2009–10 and led Nashville with 10 the previous year.

When the 2010–11 season begins, Weber will be just 25 years old, but he is already considered one of the best defensemen in the NHL. After just four full NHL campaigns, Weber boasts an impressive package of power, physical play, mobility and pure skill, which he uses to dominate. He uses his 6-foot-3, 220-pound frame to deliver clean, bone-jarring hits (his career high in penalty minutes was 80 in 2008–09) and his foot speed to take on attackers 1-on-1 and get the puck back. Once the disc is on his stick, Weber starts a breakout with the first pass as well as anyone in the world. What makes Weber a special defender is his willingness to join the attack, with 57 total assists the past two seasons. When the time is right, he unleashes his extraordinary shot, exemplified by his 64 career goals in 320 NHL games.

Weber, selected 49th overall in the 2003 NHL draft, developed his great shot while growing up in Sicamous, B.C., where he found lots of time to practice with his brother and their friends. The Weber boys used plywood as launching pads and hung soda cans from the net to develop accuracy. By 13, Weber's shot was already registering 78 mph on the radar gun! Weber eventually made his way to the Western Hockey League's Kelowna Rockets, where he won the Memorial Cup in 2004, contributing 17 points in 17 playoff games. He was also a key member of the gold medal-winning Canadian team at the 2005 World Junior Championship. Dion Phaneuf was a fellow blueliner on that junior squad and the two defensemen have often been compared, despite the fact Phaneuf went ninth overall at the 2003 NHL draft, while Weber was selected 40 picks later.

The star defender played just 46 minor league games for the American Hockey League's Milwaukee Admirals in 2005–06 (he did play in the AHL playoffs for the

Admirals when NHL season ended) before being promoted to the NHL, where he recorded 10 points in 28 Nashville games. He has been in the NHL ever since and impressed enough that he was selected to Team Canada for the 2010 Winter Olympics. The Games were held in Vancouver, which was a homecoming of sorts for the British Columbian. He had an exceptional tournament with six points, including two goals, in seven games while demonstrating why he's one of Canada's top blueliners, showing the entire hockey world how much his game has developed.

Nashville qualified for the 2010 NHL playoffs, but lost in five games to Chicago. The Predators lost the fifth game of the series despite being up by a goal with a minute to play while on the power play. Weber was on the ice when Chicago tied the game, indicating he, his teammates and coaches have a lot to learn about post-season play.

BY THE NUMBERS Had 222 shots on net in 2009–10, which ranked him third for NHL defensemen

- Had career highs of 23 goals and 53 points in 2008–09
- Won a gold medal with Canada at the 2010 Winter Olympic Games and was named to the tournament All-Star Team
- Played in 2009 NHL All-Star Game
- Named team captain in July 2010

CAREER HIGHLIGHTS

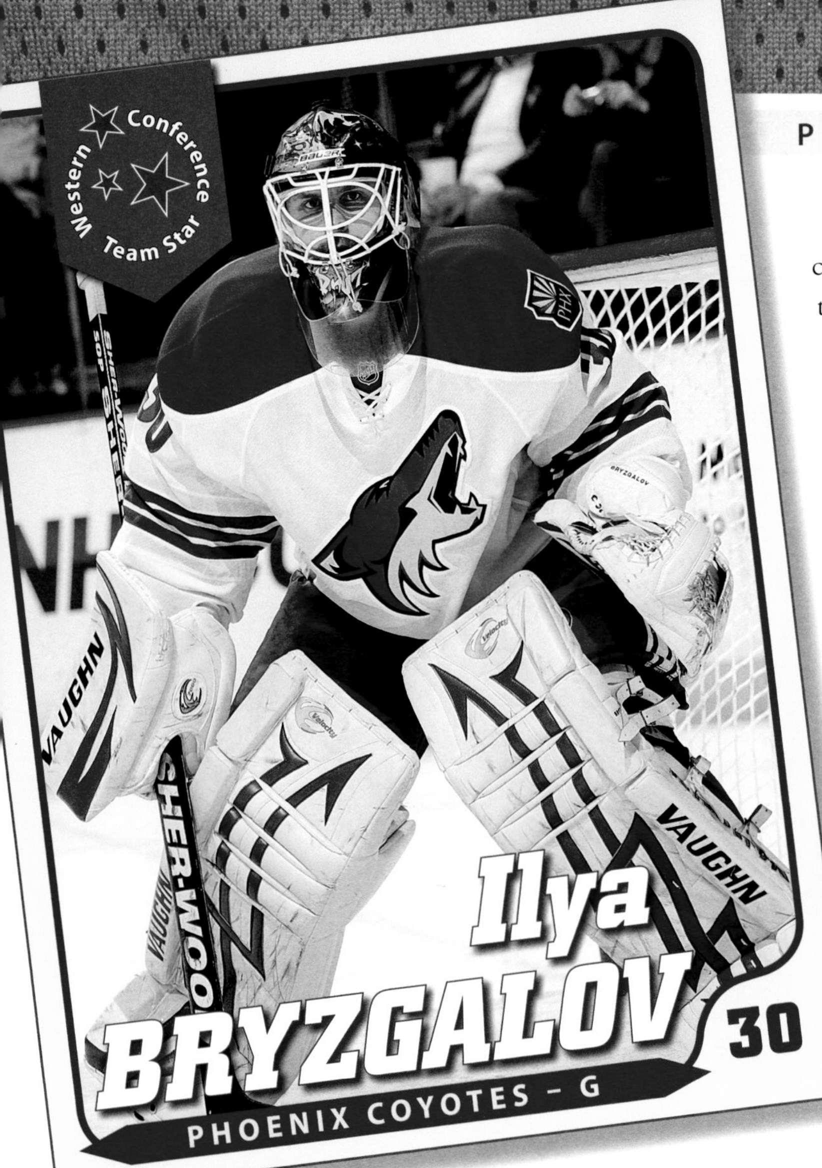

In today's world, it is becoming a very rare thing to see the man who is happy to do his job quietly and blend into the background. When it does happen, it is very appreciated as was certainly the case with goaltender Ilya Bryzgalov. He was allowed to leave the Anaheim Ducks and join the Phoenix Coyotes without any compensation for his original team. Former Anaheim GM Brian Burke was thankful for what Bryzgalov had given to the organization, most notably leading Anaheim to a first round victory over the Minnesota Wild in 2007 while filling in for No. 1 goalie Jean-Sebastien Giguère. The latter eventually returned to the crease and the Ducks went on to win the Cup that year. Bryzgalov never complained about being a backup, even though he had the talent to be a starter. When Burke found he couldn't get fair market value in return when trying to deal Bryzgalov, he simply put him on waivers and Phoenix stepped up to take the 6-foot-3, 200-pounder. It turned out to be a stroke of genius on the Coyotes' part.

Bryzgalov went to Phoenix and was an instant success during the 2007–08 season. He had played in nine games for the Ducks (posting a 3–2–1 mark) to start the year before the Coyotes claimed his rights in the middle of November. He played 55 games for Phoenix through that season and won 26. The big netminder got off to another good start in 2008–09 and although he won 26 times again, his rather ordinary second half ran his loss total to 31, taking the Coyotes right out of the playoff picture. Bryzgalov's save percentage was still a very good .906, but he was playing behind one of the youngest teams in the NHL and the young defense was prone to making major errors. Coach Wayne Gretzky made the decision that youth would be served and, for a while, it looked like he might be right. However, a long NHL season can take its toll on a green club and the Coyotes started counting on their goalie to be their savior every night.

The 2009–10 season started out very differently for Phoenix, which was not even sure it would be playing in Arizona due to a long and very messy court battle for ownership. Eventually it was decided the Coyotes would stay, but that Gretzky would no longer be the coach. In came an experienced bench boss in former Dallas Stars coach Dave Tippett and he went with a more veteran lineup while implementing a defensive system to help out in the Coyotes' end of the ice. The plan was executed to near perfection and Bryzgalov had his best season to date. He played 69 games, winning 42 times and recording eight shutouts during the regular season. His save percentage was a stellar .920 and he took the club back to the playoffs for the first time since 2002. The crowds picked up in Phoenix as the season wore on and the Coyotes entered the playoffs as the West's No. 4 seed

BY THE NUMBERS

Recorded a career-best 2.29 GAA in 2009–10

- Had a career-high 42 wins in 2009–10, which ranked him third in the NHL
- Was 7–0 for the gold medal-winning Russian team at the 2009 World Championship
- Originally drafted 44th overall by the Mighty Ducks in 2000
- Was second in the NHL with eight shutouts in 2009–10

CAREER HIGHLIGHTS

after recording the first 100-point campaign in franchise history. A first round matchup with Detroit proved to be an exciting series and Phoenix had a chance to win the seventh game at home, but the Red Wings were too strong, winning the decisive contest 6–1. Still, the Coyotes are a team on the rise and will continue counting on their goalie for great things in the future.

Although he was born in Russia, Bryzgalov does not reinforce many of the stereotypes associated with players from that country. He enjoys joking and being light-hearted and will tease the media with all sorts of answers that nobody can really decipher. He is very well read and will quote from what he has seen on television or from a book he might be enjoying. Bryzgalov likes to promote hockey and doing so gets him into the limelight as well. His teammates react well to the quirky netminder and like the fact he will accept the blame for a bad goal and move on.

The athletic goalie with a terrific glove hand also uses his great size to cover much of the net. He tends to be down quite a bit and excels at taking away the bottom of the net. Like many goalies, he has some difficulty with traffic in front of his crease, but he should get better at dealing with that issue as he plays more as a No. 1 NHL goalie.

Since being traded to the San Jose Sharks on November 30, 2005, center Joe Thornton has played in 383 regular season games for the team and produced 116 goals and 477 points. The Sharks have been in the playoffs every year since Thornton's arrival in California and their regular season win totals are 44, 51, 49, 53 and 51 over that time span. They have also won a Presidents' Trophy for having the best record in the league in 2008–09. The 6-foot-4, 235-pound Thornton has taken home the Hart and Art Ross Trophies and gained two All-Star Team nominations — one First, one Second — since he first put on the Sharks' teal blue sweater. So why are so many hockey experts unhappy with Thornton's performance? The answer is rather easy — no Stanley Cups, no appearances in the final and only 47 points in 56 post-season games for the man known as 'Jumbo Joe.'

Thornton has never really changed much since his days growing up in St. Thomas, Ontario, just a little south of the city of London. He is still the same polite kid who was bigger than most of his opponents, even when he was a young boy. A rather shy individual, Thornton has always been very easy to coach and manage. He would play on defense when asked and never complained because he loved to play the game. Thornton also hated to lose and each loss would affect him, but he was always able to bounce back. His skills were always exceptional, evidenced by his 40 goals and 104 points in 50 Jr. B games for the St. Thomas Stars in 1994–95. He then played for the Sault Ste. Marie Greyhounds of the Ontario Hockey League for two seasons, before the Boston Bruins selected him first overall in 1997.

It took him awhile to get going in Boston, but by the time he was 20, Thornton was a steady 60- to 70-point center. He had a breakout season in 2002–03, when he produced 101 points, including 65 assists. However, just two short years later, the Bruins decided they weren't getting everything they wanted from the big pivot and dealt him to San Jose. The Sharks gave up three players in return, but there was no doubt Thornton was the best player in the deal. He quickly asserted himself in San Jose with 20 goals and 92 points in just 58 games to give him 125 total points on the year to top all NHL scorers. Both Thornton and his team have enjoyed great regular season success since the big trade, but the playoffs have proven to be a very different story.

The 2010 post-season was actually a bit of a breakthrough for Thornton and the San Jose club. A first round win over Colorado and then a Round 2 romp over the Detroit Red Wings got the Sharks to the Western Conference final for the first time since 2004. The Chicago Blackhawks quickly ended any hope of an appearance in the final with a four-game sweep, but at least the Sharks had advanced much further than their first round ouster at the hands of the Anaheim Ducks in 2009. Thornton had 12 points in 15 2010 playoff games, but once again disappeared for portions of the post-season. More questions were raised about Thornton's ability to perform in the clutch, including whether or not he could keep up to the pace of a high-speed game. His totals during the 2009–10 regular season were down to 20 goals and 89 points — great numbers for many players, but not quite up to the level expected of a $7.2 million dollar player. However, it should be noted Thornton and linemates Dany Heatley and Patrick Marleau combined for 103 goals during the season and played together for the gold medal-winning Canadian team at the Winter Olympics.

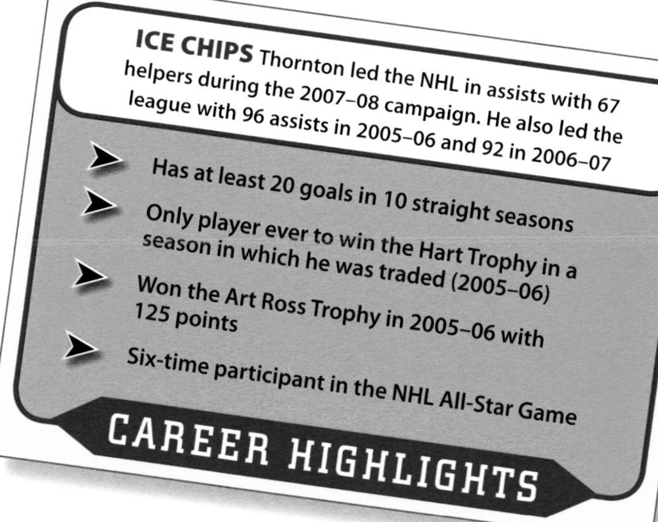

ICE CHIPS Thornton led the NHL in assists with 67 helpers during the 2007–08 campaign. He also led the league with 96 assists in 2005–06 and 92 in 2006–07

- Has at least 20 goals in 10 straight seasons
- Only player ever to win the Hart Trophy in a season in which he was traded (2005–06)
- Won the Art Ross Trophy in 2005–06 with 125 points
- Six-time participant in the NHL All-Star Game

CAREER HIGHLIGHTS

Thornton can be a very aggressive player at times, but he does not seem to have as much intensity in the playoffs when he is the obvious target of every team the Sharks face. A truly gifted passer who seems to see the game in slow motion at times, Thornton has never been a big goal-scorer despite owning a very good shot. Perhaps a high goal total in the season would provide the incentive to shoot more in the playoffs.

Thornton now has 931 career points thanks largely to 646 assists and will likely hit the 1,000-point milestone during the 2010–11 campaign. He still has the firm belief that he will one day hoist the Stanley Cup and silence his critics.

When the Vancouver Canucks tendered a free agent contract to St. Louis Blues center David Backes in the summer of 2008, it left one team very hopeful and the other very upset. The Canucks had visions of snagging a player who was a little under the radar, since the 6-foot-3, 225-pound Backes had only scored 13 goals in 2007–08 and had played just 121 career games to that point. The Blues were a very angry group because they felt Vancouver was trying to poach one of their young prospects by giving him a contract he had not yet earned (a three-year deal which totaled $7.5 million dollars). The Blues were not about to let Backes, a player they had selected 62nd overall in 2003, walk away, so they matched the offer and the youngster remained in St. Louis, which is where he wanted to be all along. It turned out to be a wise decision for the Blues since Backes turned in a great season in 2008–09 by scoring 31 goals and adding 23 assists in 82 games. The 2009–10 campaign wasn't nearly as productive for Backes as he found the net just 17 times, but he did make the U.S. Olympic Team and played very well as the American squad won the silver medal in Vancouver.

A native of Blaine, Minnesota, Backes attended Spring Lake Park High School, where he scored 46 goals and recorded 112 points in 48 career games between 1999 and 2001 for a team known as the Panthers. The 17-year-old then joined the United States Hockey League and played briefly in Chicago before moving on to play in Lincoln, Nebraska. His prolific goal-scoring in the USHL (70 goals in 112 games) got him into Minnesota State-Mankato, where he developed for three seasons. Backes had been a straight 'A' student for most of his academic career and majored in mechanical engineering at the university. He turned professional in 2005–06 and played for the Blues' American Hockey League farm team in Peoria, scoring a total of 15 goals in 43 games over two years for the Rivermen. His 10 goals to start the 2006–07 season got him promoted to St. Louis and he has never been back to the minors. As a rookie, Backes scored 10 goals in 49 games and showed he could play in the NHL. He became a more effective player when the Blues switched him to a new position.

When center Yan Stastny got injured, St. Louis coach Andy Murray decided to give Backes a try at the position. Murray wanted a bigger body in the middle, preferably someone who was tough to play against both offensively and defensively. The former Blues bench boss got more than he expected because it turned out Backes was also a good playmaker and not afraid to set up in front of the opposition net or go into the corners. At his best when he is physical, Backes got more space by using his body to deliver hard hits. The opposition was leery about getting Backes riled up as word got around of how he broke the neck of a Swiss player with a devastating bodycheck during the World Championship in 2009. During the 2009–10 season, he got into fights with Rick Nash of Columbus, Corey Perry of Anaheim and Jonathan Toews of Chicago, and he more than held his own, admitting a loss only to the bigger Nash.

Backes' all-around play got him a spot on Team U.S.A. for the Olympics and he quickly showed it was a good choice by scoring the winning goal in the first game of the tournament. Backes grabbed the puck in front of his own net and took it all the way down the ice, showed his speed down the boards, swept past Swiss defender Yannick Weber before putting a shot behind netminder Jonas Hiller. It was a highlight goal and the Swiss defense could not handle the very aggressive Backes all game long. He finished the Olympics with three points in six games and when he returned to St. Louis he was given an 'A' on his sweater, a sign the team saw his leadership skills coming forth.

Backes has modeled his NHL style after retired power forward Keith Tkachuk, whom he spent the past four seasons playing alongside in St. Louis. If all goes to plan, Backes will soon have the same impact Tkachuk — a two-time 50-goal scorer — did in his prime. At the age of 26, the time is now for Backes to show his true mettle.

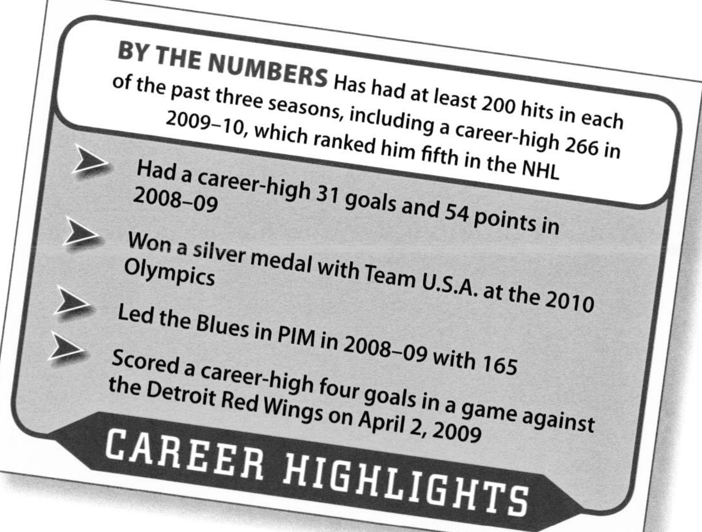

BY THE NUMBERS Has had at least 200 hits in each of the past three seasons, including a career-high 266 in 2009–10, which ranked him fifth in the NHL

- Had a career-high 31 goals and 54 points in 2008–09
- Won a silver medal with Team U.S.A. at the 2010 Olympics
- Led the Blues in PIM in 2008–09 with 165
- Scored a career-high four goals in a game against the Detroit Red Wings on April 2, 2009

CAREER HIGHLIGHTS

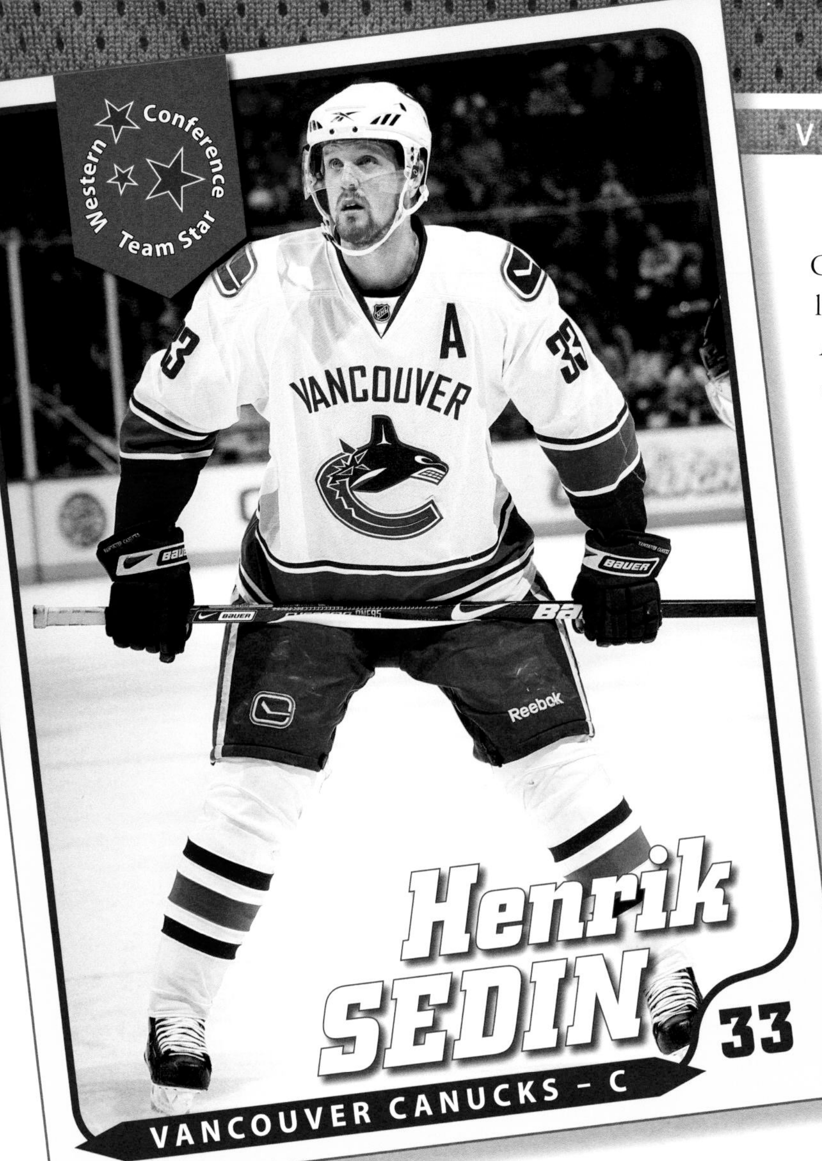

Entering the 2009–10 season, the Vancouver Canucks never had a player claim the Art Ross Trophy as the league's top scorer since their inception in 1970–71. They had a couple close calls with former captain Markus Naslund finishing second on two occasions, and former stars Pavel Bure, Alex Mogilny and Todd Bertuzzi all finished as top-ten scorers at various points, but no Canuck had ever finished ahead of everyone else in the league. That all changed when Henrik Sedin won both the Art Ross with 112 points and the Hart Trophy as league MVP, finishing ahead of megastars Alex Ovechkin and Sidney Crosby for that coveted piece of hardware. Sedin's point total established a new team record surpassing the mark of 110 held by Bure, and his 83 assists broke his own Canucks standard of 71. Playing on an electrifying line with his twin brother Daniel and feisty forward Alex Burrows, Sedin produced the best regular season a Canuck has ever enjoyed.

While his brother missed 19 games with a broken foot, Sedin seemed to understand he now had to produce without a winger he was so used to having by his side. Whereas he might have been behind the opposition net trying to set up his brother with a pass, Sedin was now in the high slot trying to score a goal. He wanted to show everyone he could play good hockey even if Daniel was out of the lineup, so he changed his game a little from the pass-first mentality that has been ingrained in him since his days as a youngster in Sweden. While it is difficult to prove, Sedin's time away from his brother may have made him more comfortable with his other teammates and it might also be true that the 'A' sewn on his sweater also gave him a renewed sense of purpose. He made other players, particularly Burrows, better and was the Canucks' best player throughout the entire season. The bottom line was that Sedin surpassed his career-best point total by 30 — a remarkable amount given that he was already 29 years of age.

The 6-foot-2, 190-pound Sedin has missed a grand total of eight games over his career. He has played an 82-game schedule seven times since he joined the team in 2000–01 and has recorded 57 or more assists for five consecutive years, totaling 434 in 728 career games. His lack of goal-scoring was evident early in his career when he had just nine markers in his first season as a Canuck and only his last two years have been respectable from a goal production point of view, as he set a career high with 29 in 2009–10. Perhaps he will now shoot the puck more often, but it will be hard for Sedin to change his style of play completely. Another noticeable trend from his statistics is Sedin's lack of penalty minutes, never recording more than 66 in a season. He has the size to be more physical, but it is not in his nature to seek out any trouble. At times his timid nature holds him back and the lack of aggressive play may keep him from being considered an elite NHL player despite his impressive performance as the league's leading point-getter.

Vancouver fans certainly appreciated Sedin's performance during the regular season and he won just about every team award imaginable including Most Valuable Player, most three star selection points and leading scorer. As much as Sedin had been able to improve his numbers, he has not been able to turn in a superb playoff performance yet. More disturbingly for Vancouver fans is the fact Sedin has virtually disappeared in two second round losses to the Chicago Blackhawks in 2009 and 2010. The challenge for Sedin is clear: improve to the point where he can lift the Canucks deep into the playoffs.

BY THE NUMBERS

Won the Art Ross Trophy in 2009–10 with 112 points

- Hasn't missed a game in the past five seasons
- Has led the Canucks in scoring the past three seasons
- Played in 2008 NHL All-Star Game
- Won a gold medal with Sweden at the 2006 Winter Olympic Games

CAREER HIGHLIGHTS

74 Craig Anderson – Colorado Avalanche
76 Patrice Bergeron – Boston Bruins
78 Dan Boyle – San Jose Sharks
80 Mike Fisher – Ottawa Senators
82 Marc-Andre Fleury – Pittsburgh Penguins
84 J-S Giguère – Toronto Maple Leafs
86 Mike Green – Washington Capitals
88 Jaroslav Halak – St. Louis Blues
90 Jonas Hiller – Anaheim Ducks
92 Duncan Keith – Chicago Blackhawks
94 Ilya Kovalchuk – New Jersey Devils
96 Henrik Lundqvist – New York Rangers
98 Joe Pavelski – San Jose Sharks
100 Dion Phaneuf – Toronto Maple Leafs
102 Chris Pronger – Philadelphia Flyers
104 Tuukka Rask – Boston Bruins
106 Brad Richards – Dallas Stars
108 Daniel Sedin – Vancouver Canucks
110 Jordan Staal – Pittsburgh Penguins
112 Martin St-Louis – Tampa Bay Lightning

IMPACT PLAYERS

Players who elevate their game with everything on the line.

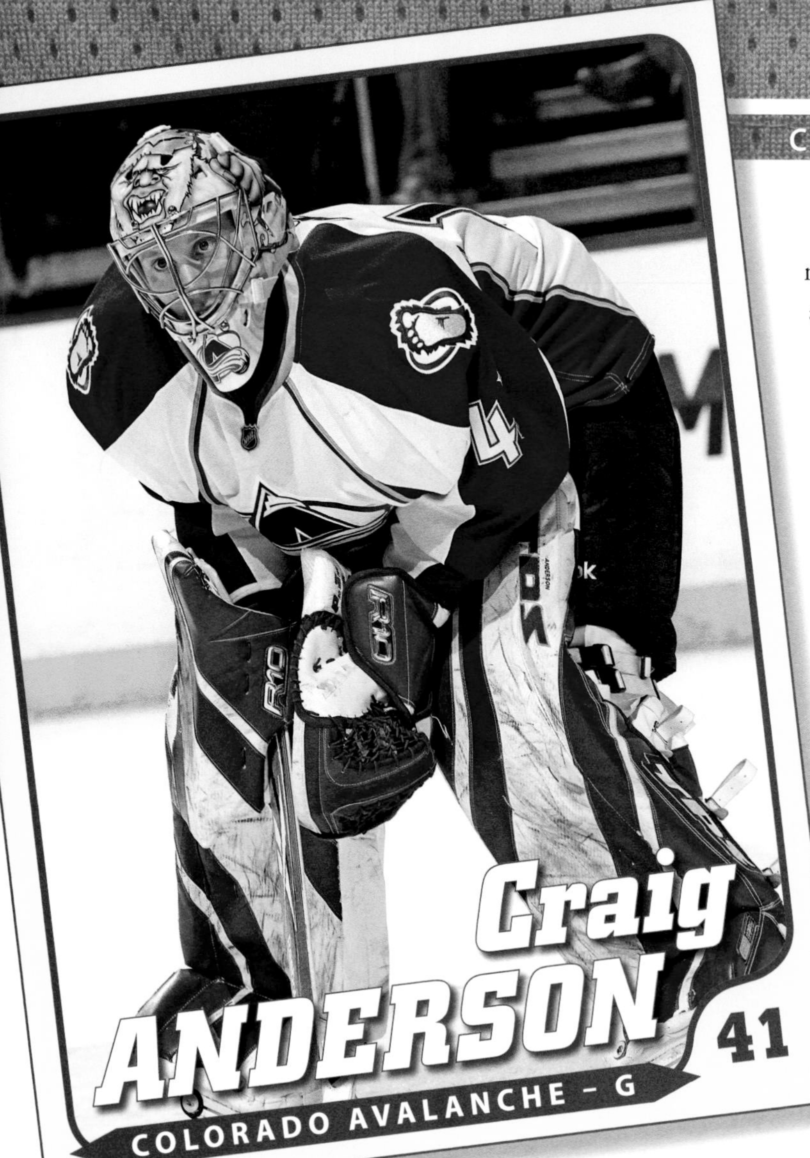

In the summer of 2009, at age 28, netminder Craig Anderson figured it was time for him to become a No. 1 goalie. The trouble was he did not have a job lined up after the 2008–09 season and the prospects of getting the opportunity to be a starting goaltender seemed rather bleak. But the Colorado Avalanche came along at just the right time and offered the 6-foot-2, 180-pound Anderson the chance he was looking for. The Avs' goaltending was in a state of flux as the club was only too happy to let Andrew Raycroft leave as a free agent, while the goalie still on its roster, Peter Budaj, was viewed as a backup, at best. Colorado liked Anderson's athleticism, size and the fact he had at least some NHL experience. Anderson was offered a two-year deal worth roughly $1.8 million annually and was in no position to turn it down. With Greg Sherman in as Colorado's new GM and Joe Sacco taking over as a rookie head coach in the NHL, the Avalanche were looking to start a different chapter in their history and Anderson turned out to be the perfect free agent signing for a team in transition.

A native of Park Ridge, Illinois, Anderson's road to the NHL was, to say the least, very rocky. He played his minor hockey in the Chicago area, but then went to play for the Guelph Storm of the Ontario Hockey League. He did not play in a lot of games during his first two seasons with the Storm, but he did get drafted 77th overall by the Calgary Flames in 1999. However, Anderson never signed a contract with Calgary and re-entered the draft two years later. In 2000–01, he played in 59 games with the Storm, winning 30 and posting a .918 save percentage and that got him selected once again in the third round (73rd overall) — this time by the Chicago Blackhawks. He played in a grand total of 56 games for Chicago, but spent most of his time with the Norfolk Admirals of the American Hockey League. He also bounced around the NHL on waivers, but ended up back with the Blackhawks and appreciated the opportunity he was given to develop his skills, even if it was at the minor league level.

In June 2006, Chicago decided to give Anderson a chance with another organization and dealt him away for the cheap price of a 2008 sixth round draft choice from the Florida Panthers. However, Anderson was the third goalie on Florida's depth chart in 2006–07, behind veteran Ed Belfour and Alex Auld. Once again he saw little playing time and another stint in the minors, this time with the Rochester Americans, where he posted a quality 23–10–1 record. His good play earned him more NHL games over the next two seasons, including 31 appearances in 2008–09, which saw him go 15–7–5. Strong as Anderson's play was, unseating Tomas Vokoun as the Panthers' starter was not going to happen, so he decided

BY THE NUMBERS

Led the NHL with 2,047 saves in 2009–10

- Had a career-high 38 wins in 2009–10
- Ranked third in the NHL with seven shutouts in 2009–10
- Was originally drafted 77th overall by the Flames in the 1999 NHL draft
- Has a career .913 save percentage

CAREER HIGHLIGHTS

to look for another team, as he became an unrestricted free agent. The Avalanche liked that Anderson had played behind such netminders as Belfour and Nikolai Khabibulin, both Stanley Cup winners. Colorado opted to take a chance on Anderson, who had yet to prove he was capable of being a No. 1 puckstopper.

Any doubts were soon erased as Anderson took over in goal for a team not expected to compete for a playoff position. In 71 games, Anderson faced a league-high 2,233 shots and stopped 2,047 of them (also a league high) for a .917 save percentage. He also won 38 games and allowed only 186 goals against. The young Avs squad responded to the confidence their new stopper gave them and put up a surprising 95 points, good for the eighth and final playoff spot in the Western Conference. A late-season slump put Colorado in danger of losing its playoff spot, but the Avalanche rallied to capture the last post-season position ahead of favored teams like Calgary, St. Louis and Anaheim.

Anderson was outstanding during the first NHL playoff action of his career and was the sole reason the Avalanche were able to win two contests against the San Jose Sharks, who dropped Colorado in six first-round games. His determination to succeed made Anderson one of the best stories in the NHL during the 2009–10 season and it was good to see that two parties had made the right choice during free agency — something that does not always happen. If the Avalanche and Anderson continue on the same path, Colorado may be able to reach its former lofty heights.

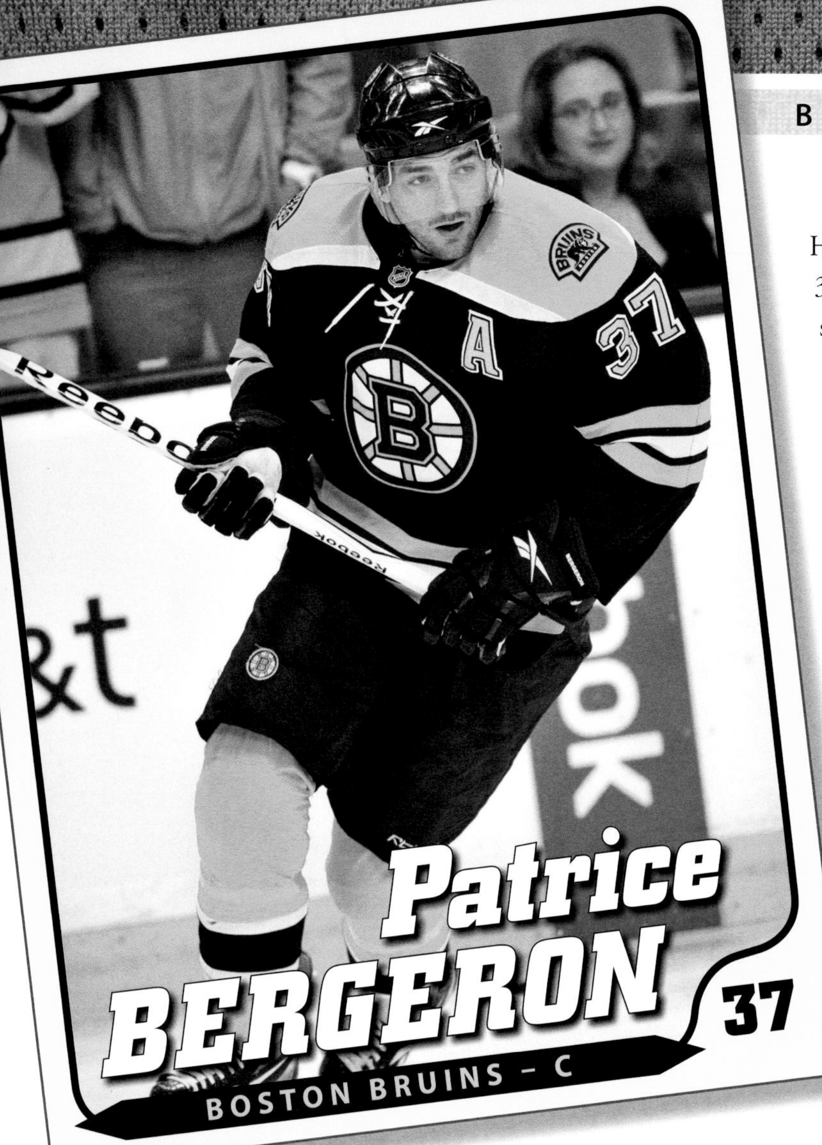

When the Canadian hockey team that would represent the country for the 2010 Winter Olympics was named December 30, 2009, the roster selection garnered a great deal of discussion, mostly for those players who were not picked. The one player whose inclusion also sparked strong debate was Patrice Bergeron. It's not that people didn't believe the Boston Bruins center was a good player, but with so much high-end talent in the mix to make Team Canada, Bergeron seemed like a bit of a long shot to skate in Vancouver. The decline in his offensive numbers had been driven by a severe concussion sustained 10 games into the 2007–08 season that caused him to miss the rest of that campaign. There were days when Bergeron thought his career was over, fighting nausea and headaches for many months.

He came back to play 64 games in 2008–09, recording 39 points, but scoring just eight times. He was much stronger in 2009–10 when he had 12 goals and 37 points in the first 54 games of the year and that got him a nod for the most scrutinized team of the year. Although he played in a limited role and registered just one assist in seven games, Bergeron was useful as an extra forward and for defensive-zone faceoffs, embracing his limited role enthusiastically.

Bergeron had played well for Canada before, which likely had a big influence on his selection for the Olympic team. In fact, he is the first Canadian player to participate in the World Championship before the World Junior Championship. After winning gold at the 2004 Worlds, Bergeron, playing alongside Sidney Crosby, led the 2005 World Juniors in scoring with 13 points in six games and took home another gold medal for his trouble. He also scored a goal in the gold medal game during a 6–1 whipping of Russia. Bergeron was on Team Canada at the 2006 World Championship and had 14 points in nine games while once again being teamed with Crosby. Posting such good numbers while wearing the Team Canada sweater, coupled with his play beside Crosby, should have made Bergeron's selection in 2010 much more understandable.

Selected 45th overall by Boston in the 2003 NHL draft, Bergeron surprised everyone by making the Bruins as an 18-year-old rookie. He acquitted himself rather well by scoring 16 goals in 71 games in 2003–04, but was forced down to the Providence Bruins of the American Hockey League the following year during the NHL lockout, scoring 21 goals and 61 points in 68 games. The experience made him a better player for his second NHL season, when he had 31 goals and totaled 73 points in 81 games in 2005–06. He followed that up with a career-high 48 assists the next year and had 71 points in 77 games. But then the concussion ruined the majority of 2007–08 and cast a pall over his entire career. He is only now getting back to the point where he is producing quality offensive numbers, while still trying to fully restore his game to its previous level.

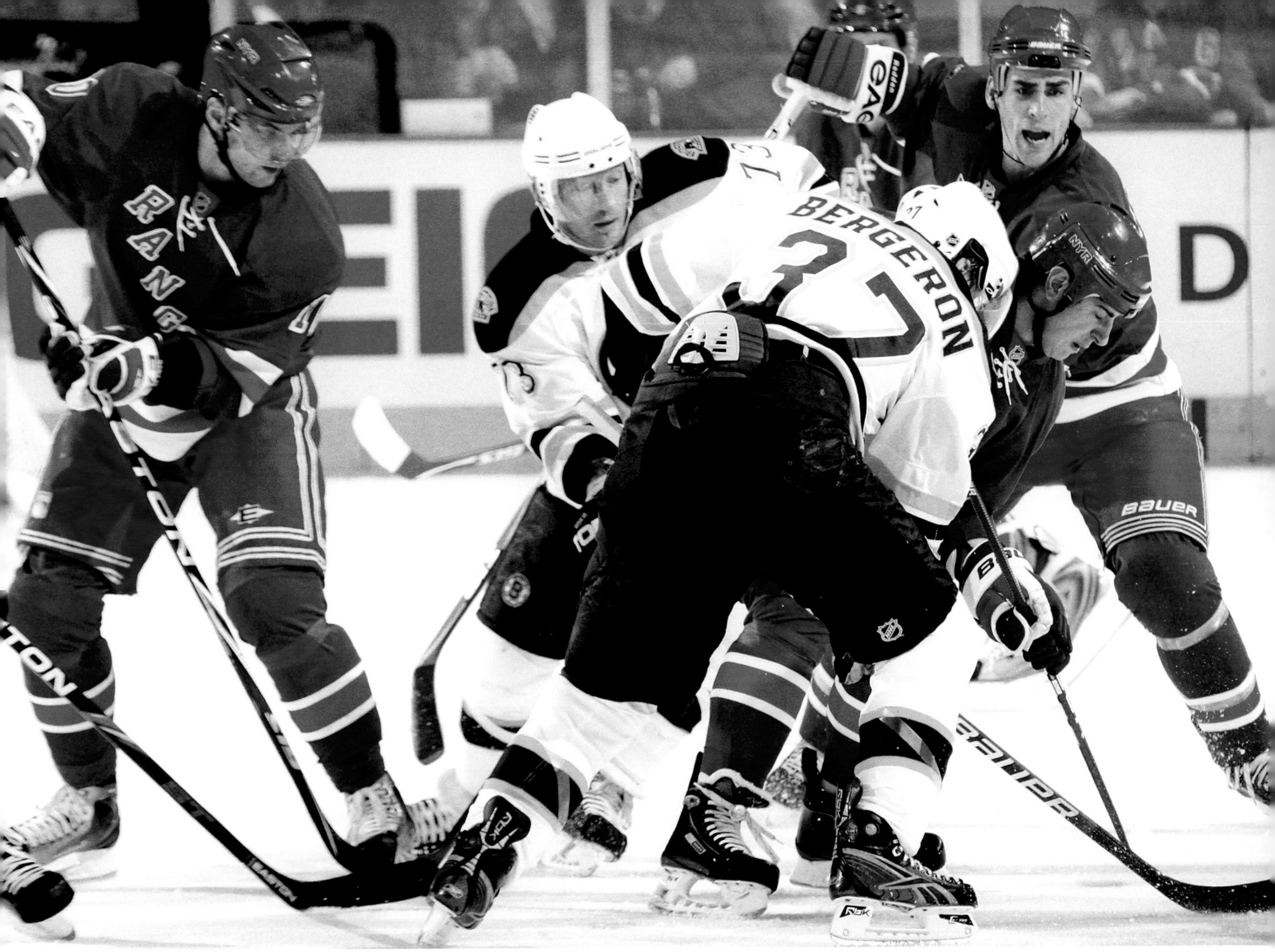

Bergeron got his weight back up to 194 pounds and worked on his strength to survive the rigors of the NHL regular season. He also started to focus more on the defensive side of the game, going from minus-28 in 2006–07 to plus-6 in 2009–10, and continuing to grow in the role of being an effective two-way player. The Bruins managed to make the playoffs with a late-season surge to end 2009–10 and knocked out the favored Buffalo Sabres in the first round. The year ended in very bitter fashion as Boston coughed up a 3–0 series lead against the Philadelphia Flyers in Round 2, but with 11 points in 13 playoff games, Bergeron showed he can be an impact player.

When Bergeron is at his best, he is a very smart playmaker who can easily spot an open teammate. Bergeron can use his 6-foot-2 frame to great effectiveness at times, but his penalty minute total has not hit the 30 mark in any one season thus far. He can backcheck very well and can take the puck away with a very quick stick. Though his concussion history would indicate he might be susceptible to further head injuries, his on-ice vision should be able to keep him out of trouble and allow him to keep improving as a player.

BY THE NUMBERS

Had career highs of 31 goals and 73 points in 2005–06

- Was just 18 years old when he cracked the Bruins lineup
- Won a gold medal with Canada at the 2010 Winter Olympic Games
- Drafted 45th overall by Boston in 2003
- Posted back-to-back 70-point seasons with Boston from 2005–07

CAREER HIGHLIGHTS

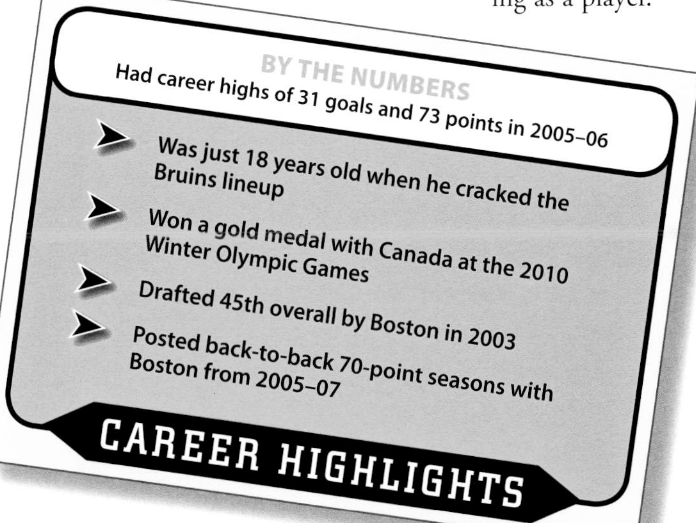

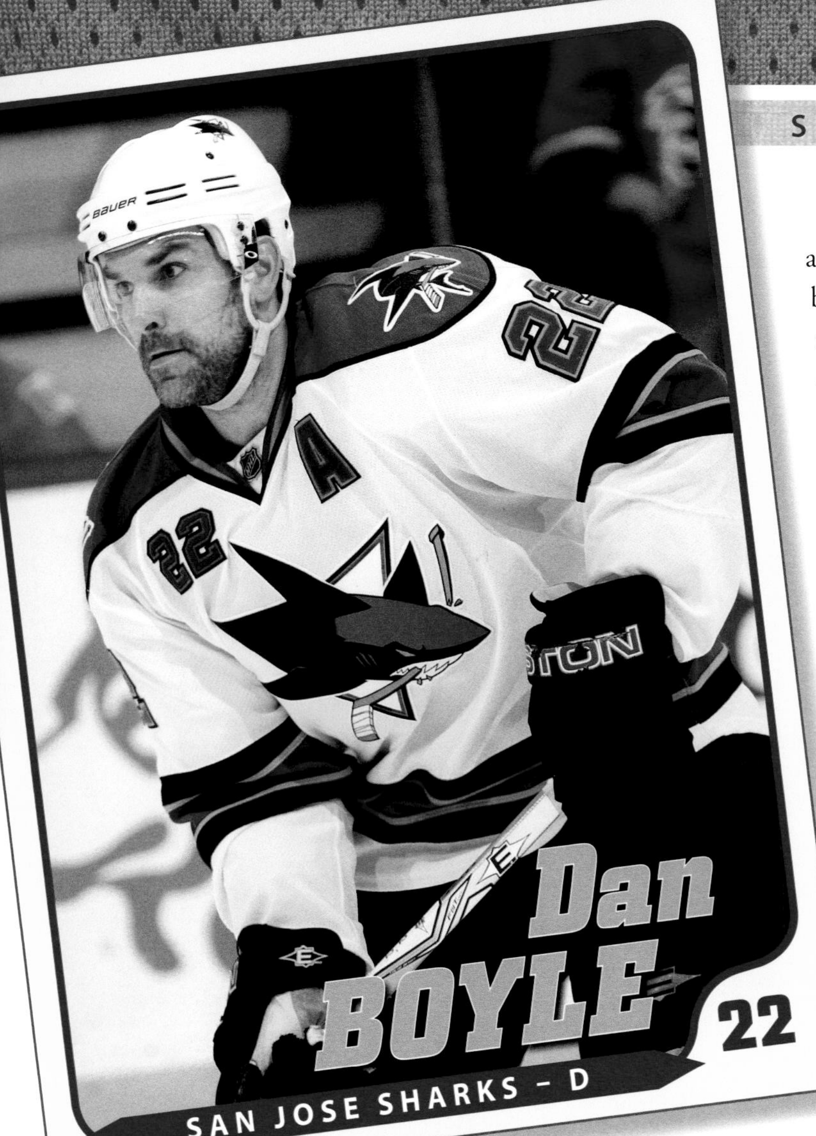

Defenseman Dan Boyle knows all about heartache and triumph in the Stanley Cup playoffs. The 2010 post-season brought back many memories for the talented blueliner, especially after the third game of the first round playoff series between Boyle's San Jose Sharks and the Colorado Avalanche. The teams had split the first two contests and Game 3 went into extra time tied 0–0. Just 51 seconds into the overtime session, Boyle was trying to clear a puck in his own end from the corner when his pass just ticked off the stick of Avalanche forward Ryan O'Reilly, squeezing past Sharks netminder Evgeni Nabakov on the short side to give Colorado a stunning 1–0 win and a 2–1 series lead. It was a nightmare scenario for the top-seeded Sharks and for Boyle; he could not wait to get back out there and make amends. As Boyle replayed the horrible bounce in his mind, the Sharks were getting ready to rally around their star defenseman. They never lost another game to Colorado and then beat Detroit in the next round. Many believed Boyle's gaffe was the galvanizing force behind San Jose's recovery in the post-season.

Overcoming hurdles is nothing new for Boyle, who was never drafted and only made the NHL after being signed as a free agent in 1998 by the Florida Panthers, who later dealt him to Tampa Bay for a fifth round pick. His goal-scoring mistake in 2010 was not the first time Boyle faced adversity in the playoffs. In 2004, while he was with the Lightning, his house suffered extensive damage because of a fire as he and his teammates lost the opening game of the Stanley Cup final to the Calgary Flames. Boyle lost many of his possessions and the value of the damage was believed to be around $300,000. Luckily, much of his hockey memorabilia was saved, but it was quite a distracting turn of events.

Boyle and the Lightning recovered to win the Cup in seven games and if anything bothered the defenseman, he certainly did not show it, recording 10 points in 23 post-season games. A bad goal against in 2010 must have seemed trivial by Boyle's standards.

Boyle became a Shark after a deal in the summer of 2008 was completed between San Jose and Tampa Bay. The Lightning had just signed Boyle to a new deal earlier that year, but new owners Len Barrie and Oren Koules decided his $6.7 million annual stipend was too rich for their taste. Even though he had a no-trade clause in his deal, Boyle was more or less forced to accept a new home by Barrie and Koules, who believed his best years were behind him after he posted a horrible minus-29 rating during a rough 2007–08 season in Tampa for himself and the team. Perhaps the pair — who no longer own the team — were too quick to disregard Boyle's earlier work, which included a spot on the NHL's Second All-Star Team in 2006–07. On the other hand, the Sharks were pleased to land a high-quality defender and gave up a first round draft choice in 2009, a fourth-rounder in 2010, plus the rights to Matt Carle and Ty Wishart to complete the deal.

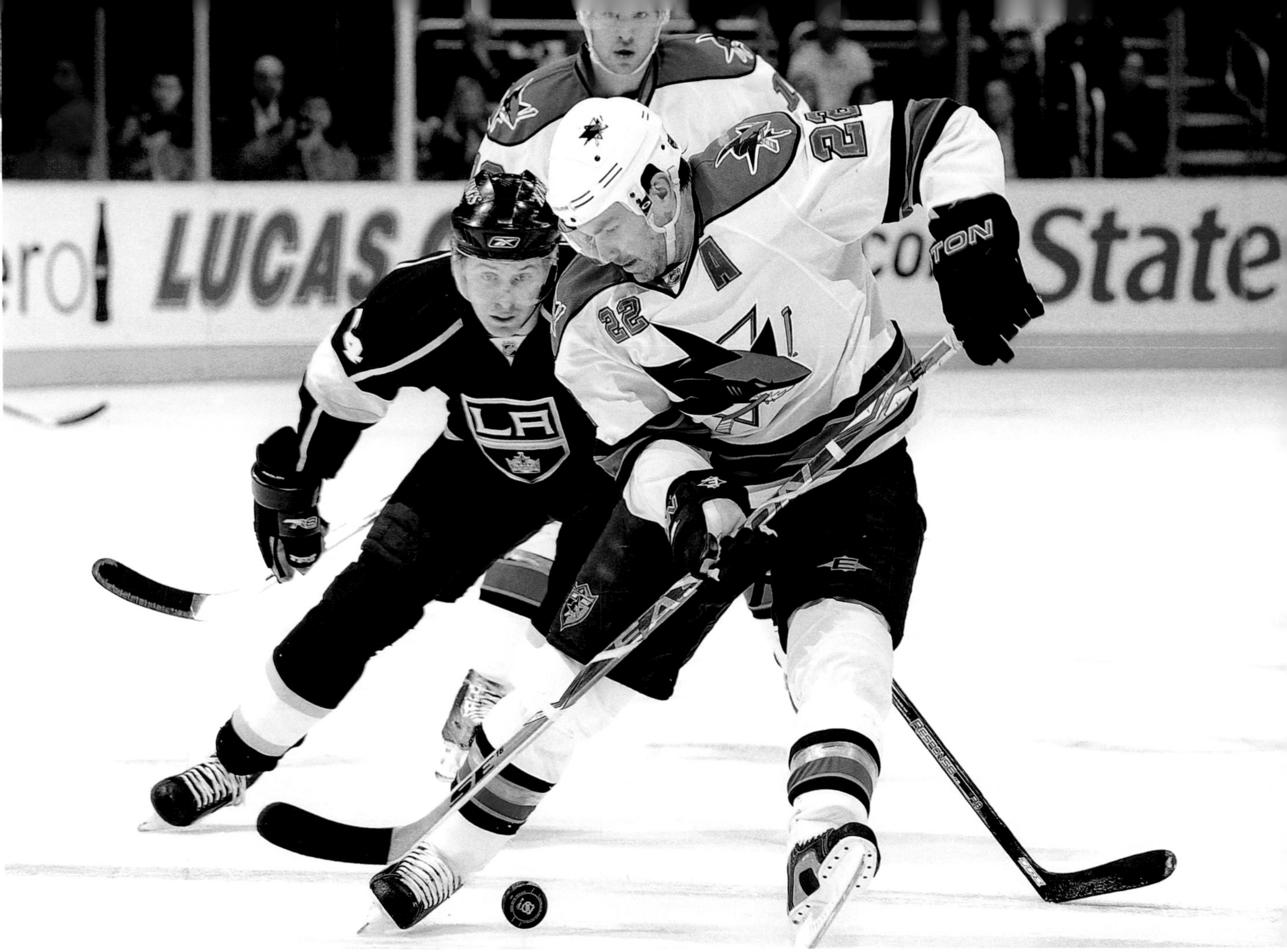

The 2008–09 season saw Boyle return to his previous form with another Second All-Star Team selection based on his 16-goal, 57-point performance. The 5-foot-11, 195-pounder showed he still had not lost his superb puck-moving skills and his ability to quarterback the power play. Boyle's skill set was ideally suited for San Jose, a team loaded with high-scoring forwards. He is very poised with the puck and can spot an open teammate for a pass or let go a rising shot that can often hit the back of the net. His cool, calming nature is a big asset and he also exhibits many leadership qualities.

Boyle's 2009–10 season was highlighted by his selection to Team Canada for the Winter Olympics. He played his usual efficient game and lugged the puck out on many occasions. He scored once and added five assists in the seven-game tournament and proved he was still one of the best defensemen in the world with his steady performance. He finished the regular season with 15 goals and 58 points for the Sharks, adding 14 more in 15 playoff contests. Unfortunately, the Sharks were not able to continue their momentum in the third round and were ousted by Chicago. At 34, Boyle should still be a productive 50- to 60-point blueliner for at least a few more seasons and perhaps be a part of another Cup-winning team.

BY THE NUMBERS Has led the San Jose Sharks in average ice time the past two seasons

- Had a career-high 20 goals and 63 points in 2006–07 while playing for Tampa Bay
- Originally signed by Florida as an undrafted free agent in 1998
- Has been named a Second Team All-Star twice: 2007, 2009
- Won a gold medal with Canada at the 2010 Winter Olympic Games

CAREER HIGHLIGHTS

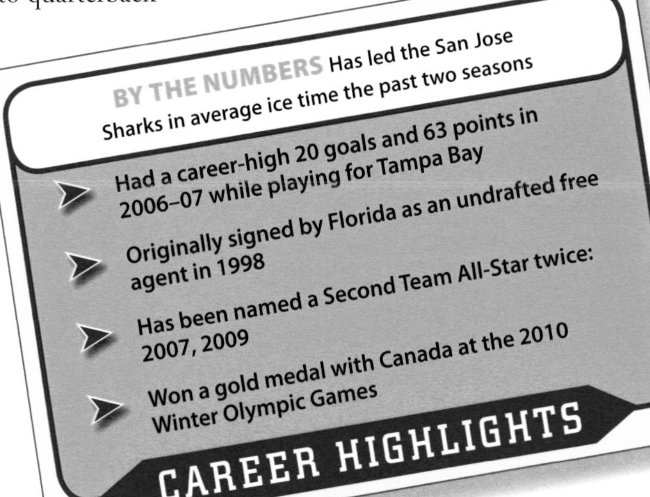

Mike Fisher had a very good year in 2009–10, both on and off the ice. The Ottawa Senators center made his best move off the ice when he announced his engagement to the beautiful Carrie Underwood in December of 2009. The couple had always been rather coy about their relationship with the media, but when word got out that Fisher had proposed, there was no denying it from either side. In fact, Fisher confirmed the story at a team practice the next day, saying he was thrilled his lovely girlfriend had accepted his offer. Fisher first met Underwood in November of 2008, when the former *American Idol* winner performed a concert in Ottawa. The country singer/songwriter and actress was seen at many Senator games both in Ottawa and on the road, although the blonde beauty was often camera shy when her face showed up on the big screen. The Oklahoma-born 26-year-old Underwood is a devout Christian, as is the 29-year-old Fisher and both believe in old-fashioned values. Fisher's relationship has made him very happy away from hockey and he said it helped with his game on the ice, too.

The 6-foot-1, 205-pound Fisher had a difficult season in 2008–09, when he scored only 13 goals and totaled just 32 points in 78 games. Normally, the rock-solid pivot is good for more than 20 goals and around 50 points a year. The Senators needed Fisher to regain his form in 2009–10 and he did not disappoint with 25 goals and 28 assists for 53 points. He was easily Ottawa's most consistent performer and when lengthy injuries struck Senators stars like Daniel Alfredsson and Jason Spezza, the team turned to their alternate captain for leadership. Fisher started the season on fire with 28 points in 31 games, earning himself some consideration for the Canadian Olympic team, though he was ultimately not given a spot. His confidence level eroded somewhat as the season progressed, but he was being asked to fulfill a No. 1 center role that does not really suit him.

The most notable thing about Fisher is how hard he works every time he is on the ice. He can create offense and score goals, dish out a hit or he can come back to his own end and make a strong defensive play. Ottawa coach Cory Clouston loves the fact Fisher is hard to play against and does not hesitate to give his best two-way middle man the assignment of going against the opposition's best line. He will go into every corner of the rink to battle for a loose puck and Fisher's hard, clean hits — the only kind he delivers — can cause real damage. He can defend all his actions with a scrap if he has to and has spent 521 minutes in the penalty box in 620 career games. His good shot has resulted in 153 goals so far and if Fisher was not so defensively conscious, he would most likely have a higher total. Fisher is also one of the best special teams players in the

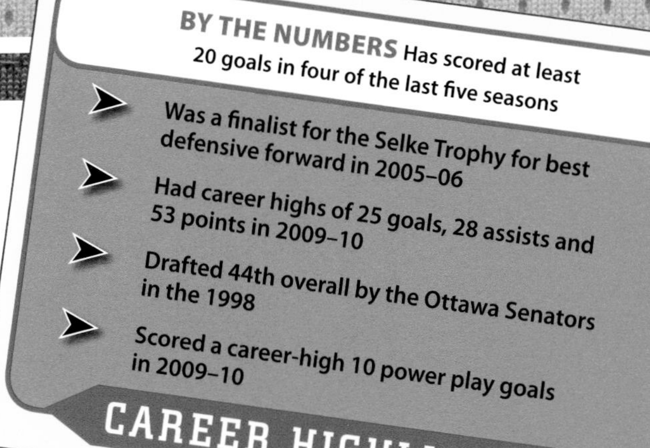

league, scoring a career-high 10 power play goals in 2009–10.

Fisher came to the Senators in the 1998 NHL draft when he was selected 44th overall. The native of Peterborough, Ontario, played for his hometown Jr. Petes of the Ontario Jr. A circuit as a 16-year-old, netting 56 points in 51 games in 1996–97. He then went on to play two years for the Ontario Hockey League's Sudbury Wolves and had his best year in 1998–99 when he recorded 41 goals and 106 points in 68 games. He never played a game in the minors and was something of a slow starter with only 11 goals over his first two NHL seasons. He was plagued with injuries for four of five seasons, but the 2005–06 campaign saw Fisher score 22 times. He followed that with years of 22 and 23 goals before he faltered in 2008–09, when the puck simply would not go in for him. Fisher's good bounce back in 2009–10 was also indicative of how his team played despite numerous injuries. Ottawa made the playoffs with 44 wins and 94 points, good for fifth in the Eastern Conference. The Senators could not compete with the Pittsburgh Penguins in the first round of the playoffs and were ousted in six games, although Fisher did contribute five points. The Sens would have had trouble even making the post-season without Fisher's consistent efforts.

There's been a tendency by some to overrate the talent level in Ottawa, but with Fisher, what you see is what you get — and that is a very fine hockey player.

BY THE NUMBERS Has scored at least 20 goals in four of the last five seasons

- Was a finalist for the Selke Trophy for best defensive forward in 2005–06
- Had career highs of 25 goals, 28 assists and 53 points in 2009–10
- Drafted 44th overall by the Ottawa Senators in the 1998
- Scored a career-high 10 power play goals in 2009–10

CAREER HIGHLIGHTS

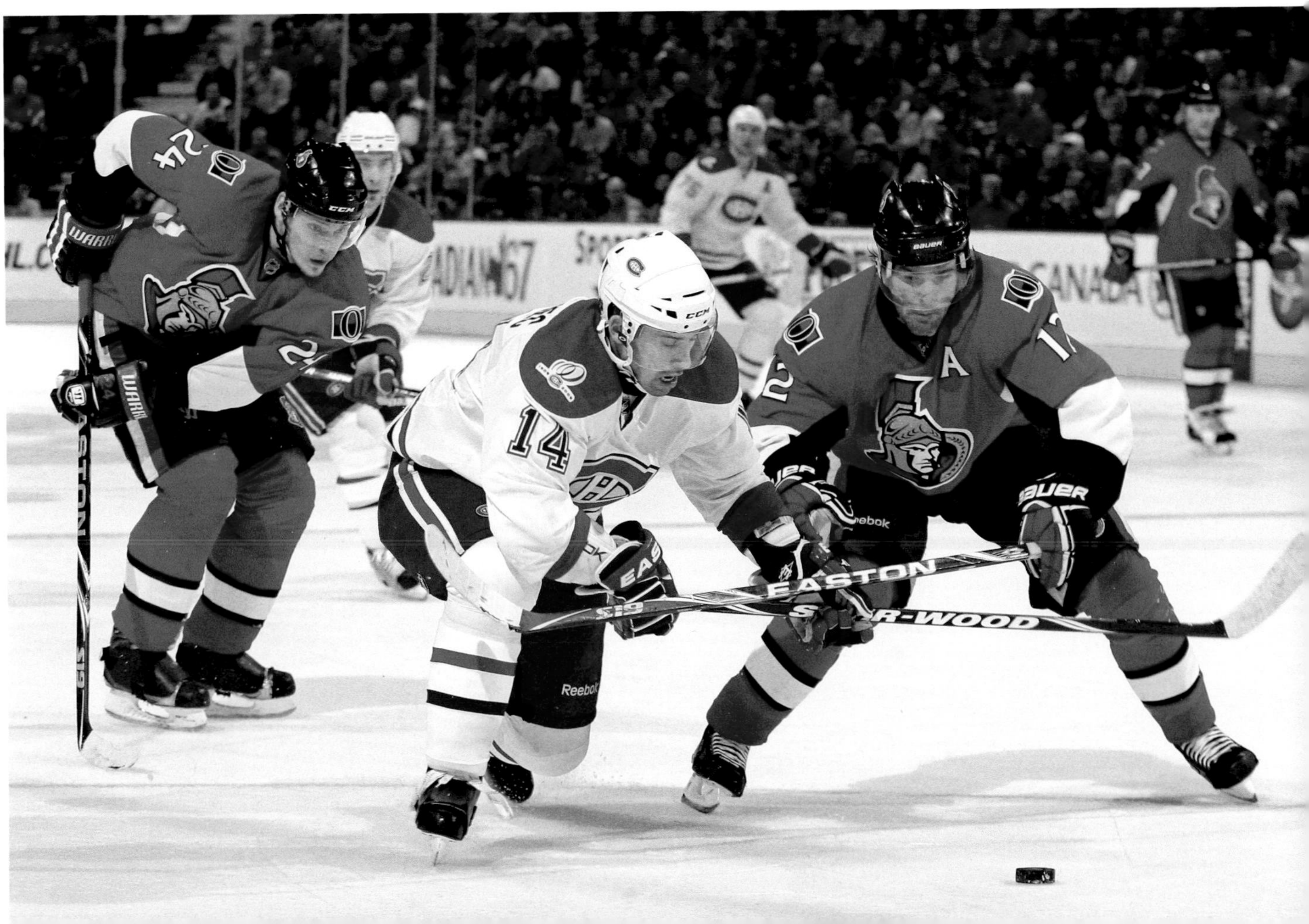

Trailing 2–1 in Game 7 of the 2009 Stanley Cup final, the Detroit Red Wings managed to get a faceoff in the Pittsburgh Penguins zone with 6.5 seconds left in regulation time. Henrik Zetterberg got the puck back to Brian Rafalski, whose attempted shot never made it to the Pens goal. The puck came out to Zetterberg and he let go a quick shot that Penguins netminder Marc-Andre Fleury denied with a quick pad save. Wings defenseman Nicklas Lidstrom jumped up to whack the rebound on net, but Fleury dove across the crease and just managed to get there in time to block Lidstrom's well aimed drive with a shoulder save. The game was finally over and the Penguins swarmed their goalie in celebration of their first Stanley Cup win since 1992, when Hall of Fame legend Mario Lemieux captained the team to the title. For Fleury, it was the save of a lifetime and erased many bad memories for a goalie who was supposed to be a winner, but until that magic moment, had failed to deliver on his great promise.

Fleury was supposed to lead the Penguins to success from the time they drafted him first overall in 2003, one of many very high picks that helped turn the team around. He played 21 games for the Pens in 2003–04, posting a 4–14–2 mark on a very bad team. Fleury was ultimately sent back to major junior, but not before he committed a big blunder on the international scene. Suiting up for Canada at the 2004 World Junior Championship, Fleury accidentally bounced a clearing attempt off a teammate and into his own net for the decisive goal in the gold medal game versus Team U.S.A. He spent the next season with the Penguins' American Hockey League farm team in Wilkes-Barre/Scranton and showed he was a capable netminder with a 26–19–4 record in 2004–05 when the NHL was shutdown for the season.

Fleury had one more up-and-down year with a young Penguins team in 2005–06 before breaking out with 40 wins in 2006–07 as the club started to really hit its stride. In 2008, Pittsburgh made it all the way to the Cup final, but lost out in six games against the veteran-laden Wings. Fleury had some rough patches, but was also brilliant at times, especially in a triple-overtime win in Game 5 to keep the series alive. But he gave up an especially bad goal to Zetterberg that cost the Penguins severely in a 3–2 Game 6 loss, which clinched the series for Detroit. The Penguins vowed things would be different in 2009 when the same two teams met for the Cup, though Pittsburgh once again lost the first two games in Detroit. After the Pens bounced back for two home victories, Fleury was pulled in a 5–0 Game 5 loss. However, he shut the door on Detroit after that as Pittsburgh won consecutive 2–1 games to claim the Cup. No goalie had won the Stanley Cup by taking Game 7 on the road since Ken Dryden had done it for Montreal in 1971 when the Canadiens beat the Blackhawks in Chicago. Fleury had now repeated that rare feat.

Fleury plays a classic butterfly style and his trademarks are his incredible quickness and athleticism. He has learned over the last few years to economize his movement and get into better position instead of just relying on his great reflexes. His save percentage has been over .900 in each of his past four seasons and Fleury's goals-against average has been below 3.00 over those same years, a notable accomplishment since the Penguins are not always interested in playing defense. To be more effective in the future, Fleury will have to work on his consistency and get better defensive help in his own end.

Just when Fleury might have thought the ghosts of the past were buried, his 2010 playoff performance indicated otherwise. He got the Penguins past an injury-weakened Ottawa Senators club in the first round, but was very ineffective at times during the second round series against Montreal. He was awful in a 5–2 Game 7 loss and was pulled from the contest in front of the Penguins home crowd. At 25, he is still young enough to redeem himself once more and Pittsburgh figures to be a contender for at least a few more years.

ICE CHIPS Marc-Andre Fleury was honored by his junior team, the Cape Breton Screaming Eagles, when they retired his No. 29 jersey prior to a game between Cape Breton and Lewiston

- Drafted first overall by Pittsburgh in 2003
- Won the Mike Bossy Trophy in 2003 as the QMJHL's top prospect
- Has recorded 148 wins and 16 shutouts in 302 career games
- Has 38 wins in 62 career playoff games

CAREER HIGHLIGHTS

Considering Jean-Sebastien Giguère was easily the greatest goaltender in the history of the Anaheim Ducks, he did not get treated with the greatest level of respect. A Conn Smythe Trophy winner in 2003 and a Stanley Cup champion in 2007, Giguère couldn't prevent Jonas Hiller from taking his net away. There were good reasons why Hiller was given the opportunity to take Giguère's job, but it seems there was no room for loyalty. Giguère was not as good as he had been in the past during the 2008–09 season, when he won only 19 games after winning 30-plus games four times during his stay in Anaheim. His father's death and the continuing health concerns with his son no doubt played a part in Giguère's faltering performance, but he was not ready to see Hiller take over. As Hiller's stock rose, Giguère's name was soon in most trade rumors involving the Ducks since they were not going to keep paying a backup $6 million annually. As the 2009–10 season unfolded, it was obvious Giguère was not going to regain his No. 1 status. He did not perform well when given a shot to play (a 4–8–5 record) and became more willing to consider waiving his no-trade clause. The Toronto Maple Leafs were looking for an accomplished veteran to solidify a very troubling netminding situation. The Leafs managed to swing a deal to take Giguère and his large contract in exchange for forward Jason Blake and netminder Vesa Toskala. Leaf fans could not believe their good fortune.

Giguère is listed at 6-foot-1 and 200 pounds, but when he puts on all the goalie equipment, he seems much bigger. He thrives at covering most of the net with his butterfly style and when he is on his game, Giguère is great at anticipating the play. The hard-working netminder prepares himself as well as any goalie in the NHL and is virtually impossible to beat with low shots. His focus may wander at times, but more often than not pucks hit him square on the logo because he is usually very well positioned. If there is one noticeable flaw in his game it would have to be his puckhandling skills outside of the net. It's not unusual for Giguère to struggle with the puck on the end of his stick, but that can be managed if he can coordinate his efforts with the defensemen.

It was ironic the Maple Leafs came to Giguère's rescue since they had drafted his older brother, Stephane, 111th overall in 1986. Giguère welcomed the move to Toronto because he needed a change and said he was re-energized in the new environment. He made a quick impression by recording shutouts in his first two appearances as a Leaf and the fact both games were played on home ice only upped the excitement. It was easier on Giguère knowing he was going to play and his competitive juices were flowing once again. The Leafs added many new and young players to close out the 2009–10 season and it was easy to see the veteran netminder had a steadying influence on his teammates. In 15 games as a Leaf he posted a 6–7–2 record — not overwhelming by any means — but he did register a .916 save percentage and a 2.49 goals-against average, both better numbers than he had in Anaheim earlier in the year. It is interesting to note he won only once on the road all season long, that coming in the form of a 4–3 overtime victory versus Montreal in the last contest of the year.

The Leafs signed free agent netminder Jonas Gustavsson prior to the 2009–10 campaign and many believed the man they call 'The Monster' was going to be Toronto's No. 1 goalie. Heath issues and inexperience proved to be major obstacles for Gustavsson, but he was also playing better to close the year out, finishing with a 16–15–11 record. Getting guidance from Giguère and goaltending consultant François Allaire made the Swedish rookie a calmer and more effective puckstopper. Many seem to think Giguère was brought in strictly to mentor Gustavsson, but the veteran made it clear he was out to prove he could still be a starter. He reminded everyone that he was only 32 years old and that Allaire was his coach in Anaheim when he had his greatest success. The 2010–11 campaign promises to be an interesting one for Giguère since he is in the last year of his contract and will be out to show the entire league he can regain his former status as one of the game's best goalies.

ICE CHIPS Was the fifth player in history to receive the Conn Smythe Trophy as part of a losing team

- Originally drafted 13th overall by the Hartford Whalers in 1995
- Broke his own Anaheim record with a 2.12 GAA in 2007–08
- Boasts a career goals-against average of 2.52
- Recorded shutouts in his first two games with the Maple Leafs

CAREER HIGHLIGHTS

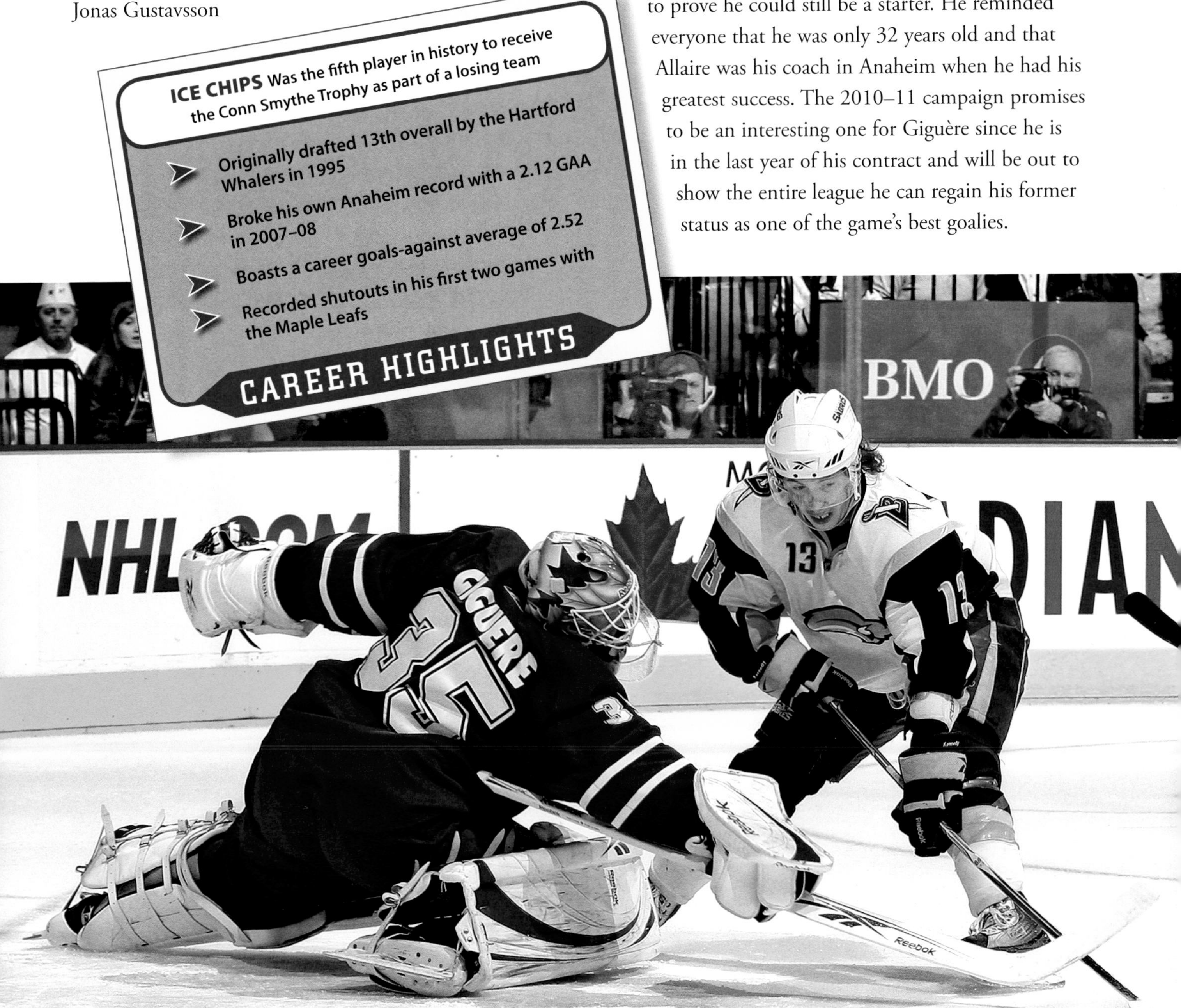

When Bruce Boudreau took over as coach of the Washington Capitals in November of 2007, he told defenseman Mike Green, a virtual unknown at the time, to go out and try to score some goals. The two had been together in Hershey of the American Hockey League and the new bench boss certainly knew what the young blueliner could do. It took Green just two minutes to notch his first goal under Boudreau's direction when the Capitals met the Philadelphia Flyers in the first game of the new regime. Before Boudreau arrived on the scene, Green had played close to 115 games under previous coach Glen Hanlon and had managed just six goals. Green went on to finish the 2007–08 season with 18 goals and then added another 31 markers the following year to lead all defensemen. Under Boudreau's guidance Green became a player who could bring any fan to the edge of their seat and a defenseman everyone was talking about.

A big part of Green's transformation was his willingness to employ a gambler's mentality on the ice. He was actually a bit of a rambunctious kid growing up in a working class district of Calgary and always enjoyed trying new things. He liked riding dirt bikes, racing go-karts and wakeboarding. Green also had another adventure as a youngster and that involved riding sheep on a family farm located an hour from his home. He and other kids in his family would ride the sheep by grabbing onto the sides of the animal, but after he got tossed on one ride, such adventures were banned. Growing up as he did also taught Green the value of hard work. His father, Paul, was an outdoor labor worker for the city, while his mother, Kate, worked two jobs; she was an insurance agent by day and re-stocked greeting cards at local pharmacies by night. His mother would usually take the three kids to games in between her jobs, but the pace got to her eventually and she suffered a heart attack. Green was very upset by what happened to his mother and did his best to care for her whenever possible. When the Capitals signed him to a new four-year contract at just over $5 million per year, it took a lot of pressure off the family.

Green was not much of a point-producer or goal-scorer until his draft year of 2003–04, when he had 14 goals and 39 points in 59 games for the Saskatoon Blades of the Western Hockey League. The Capitals had three first round picks in the '04 NHL draft, taking Alex Ovechkin first overall, defenseman Jeff Schultz with the 27th pick and then nabbing Green with the 29th selection. All three have made it to the NHL, but the two with the most impact are Ovechkin and Green. The young defenseman returned to junior for one more season before going to Hershey, where he put up 43 points in 46 games in 2005–06. The floundering

Capitals had Green on the roster for two seasons, but he was accomplishing little until Boudreau came on board.

Green is very successful because he is so unpredictable on the ice. He's just as likely to be found behind the opposition's net as his own. Green will read the play on his own side of center with the idea of intercepting a pass and starting the attack. At 6-foot-1 and 208 pounds, Green has decent size, but does not make it a point to use his body — though opponents have learned that when he decides to dish out a hit, they better be aware. His greatest attribute is a devastating shot, which he likes to put high on goal. He has come to realize most netminders excel at blocking the lower part of the net, leaving no choice but to put his hard drives up and over the shoulders. Green loves to creep in from the blueline and let a howitzer go from the faceoff circle. He plays on a fine edge that gives both his team and the opposition an equal chance to score, but the Capitals are content to live with his risky style.

The 2009–10 season saw Green lead all defensemen in goals (19), assists (57) and points (76), but he had just three assists in a stunning seven-game loss to the Montreal Canadiens in Round 1 of the playoffs. He must elevate his game further in the post-season if the Capitals are to have any shot at the Stanley Cup.

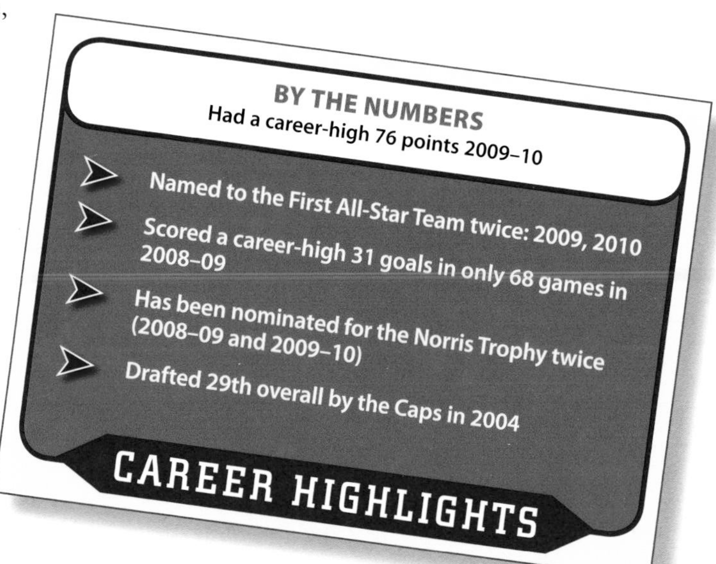
BY THE NUMBERS

Had a career-high 76 points 2009–10

- Named to the First All-Star Team twice: 2009, 2010
- Scored a career-high 31 goals in only 68 games in 2008–09
- Has been nominated for the Norris Trophy twice (2008–09 and 2009–10)
- Drafted 29th overall by the Caps in 2004

CAREER HIGHLIGHTS

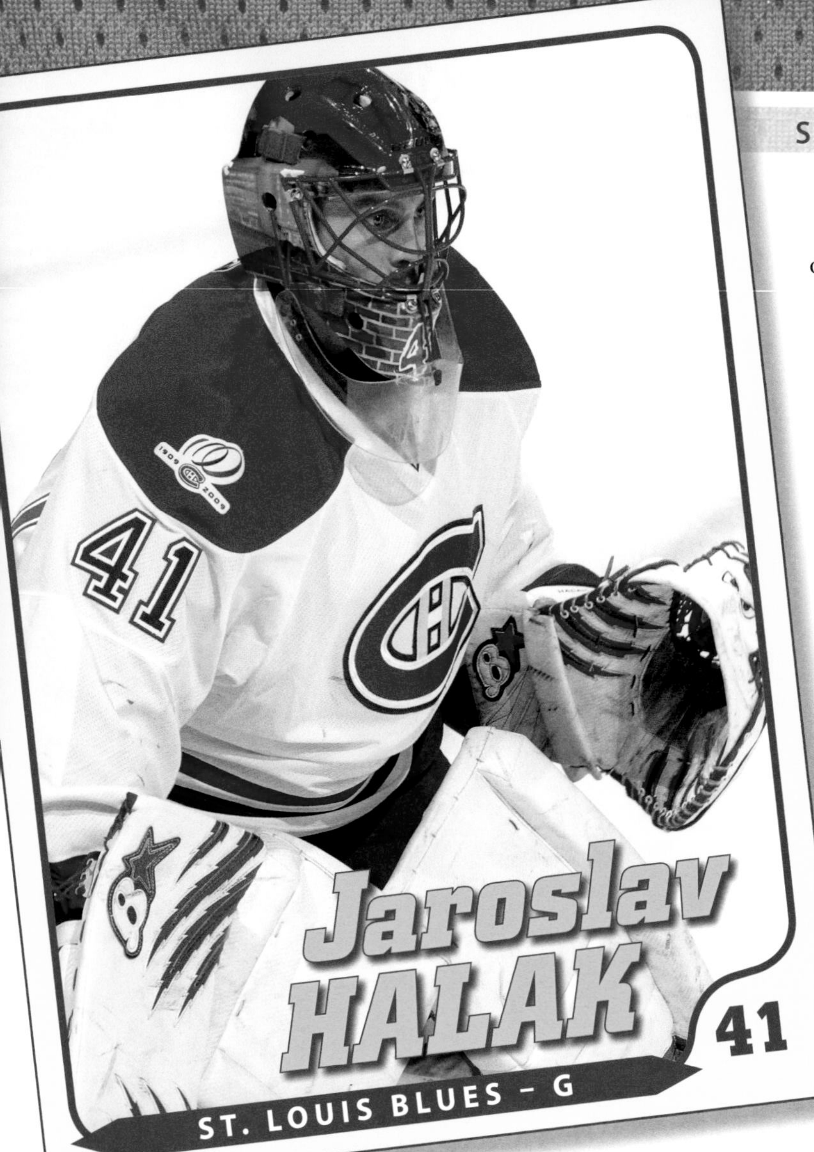

The Montreal Canadiens surprised the entire hockey world by scoring two major upsets in the 2010 playoffs, bouncing the Washington Capitals and Pittsburgh Penguins in a pair of seven-game series. But the most shocking Montreal move came after the season, when the club sent playoff hero Jaroslav Halak to the St. Louis Blues for a pair of prospects.

The Canadiens have 24 Stanley Cup titles to their credit, a number of which have been won thanks to all-world goaltending by past greats like Ken Dryden and Patrick Roy. In the 2010 post-season, it was relatively unknown Halak who led the charge for a 25th championship. A ninth-round selection in the 2003 NHL draft, 271st overall, the 5-foot-11, 182-pound Halak was the 26th of 28 goalies taken that year. The native of Bratislava, Slovakia, played a season in the Quebec Major Junior Hockey League and then played his first season as a professional in the ECHL. He was promoted to the Hamilton Bulldogs of the American Hockey League for part of the 2005–06 campaign and split 2006–07 between Montreal and Hamilton, posting a winning record in each city. He played most of 2007–08 in Hamilton and acquitted himself rather well with a 15–10–2 record. The 2008–09 campaign saw him play 34 contests for the Canadiens and he won 18 games, establishing that he was going to be at least a backup goalie, if not more. The problem facing Halak was that Montreal management seemed to favor Carey Price, a bigger goalie drafted fifth overall in 2005 who had led Canada to a World Junior Championship and the Bulldogs to a Calder Cup title.

Halak did not get much action early in 2009–10, but when Price started to falter, he stepped in and won seven of nine starts and recorded two shutouts. Halak's good play got him onto the Slovakian team for the 2010 Winter Olympic Games and the highlight of the tournament for the young netminder was defeating the Russians 2–1 in a shootout. Gaining valuable confidence from his Olympic performance, Halak kept the No. 1 role with Montreal and got the club into the playoffs with a 26–13–6 record. However, gaining a playoff berth got the Habs a matchup with Washington, which racked up more points than any other team in the NHL. Few, if any, gave the Habs a chance to win the series, but then again, not many anticipated where Halak was about to take his game.

After falling behind 3–1 in the series, the Canadiens refused to quit and ended up winning the set in seven games, taking the last contest in Washington. There is no way the Habs would have had any chance if not for the great play of their netminder and soon crazed Montreal fans were thinking they might have another Dryden or Roy on their hands who could pull out a surprise Stanley

Cup like those goalies had in 1971 and '86. Soon T-shirts with stop signs were made up, except the word 'stop' was removed and replaced with 'Halak.' One cartoonist from Quebec suggested Halak could stop the oil leak off the Gulf of Mexico! Things got even wilder when the Canadiens were able to repeat the magic and oust the Penguins in another seven-game series. Halak tried to take it all in stride and told anyone who listened he was just an ordinary person and a regular goalie. In total, Halak had to face 562 shots in the post-season and he somehow managed to stop 519 of them for a save percentage of .923. The Philadelphia Flyers burst Montreal's balloon in the Eastern Conference final, taking out the Cinderella team in five games, despite the fact Philly had finished just one slot higher than the eighth-seeded Habs.

Montreal GM Pierre Gauthier had a very tough decision to make after the season, with both Halak, 25, and Price, just 23, due for new contracts. Despite Halak's heroics, Gauthier opted to send him to the Blues for two young prospects in Lars Eller and Ian Schultz, banking on the belief Price can still realize his full potential. If he doesn't and Halak reprises his incredible play in St. Louis, where he is now signed for the next four years, the deal could come back to haunt the Habs for a long time.

BY THE NUMBERS Ranked fourth in the NHL with a .924 save percentage in 2009–10

- Recorded a career-high 26 wins in 2009–10
- Was the starting goalie for the Slovakian team at the 2010 Winter Olympic Games
- Was selected 271st overall in the 2003 NHL draft
- Had five shutouts in 2009–10, which placed him tied for seventh in the NHL

CAREER HIGHLIGHTS

Jonas Hiller is a finicky type of guy, which actually makes him a pretty standard member of the notoriously odd goalie fraternity. Before a game he will be adjusting one of the following items: mask, pads, stick or skates. Hiller loves to tweak all these pieces of goalie paraphernalia and his teammates often marvel at how he loves to make changes on his own, including skate sharpening, usually the domain of the equipment manager. Hiller needs to feel confident with all the goalie tools so he can do what he wants on the ice. He also sees the need to make improvements if he is going to get better at his craft.

Hiller must be doing something right because he has been improving his performance each season in the NHL. Signed as a 25-year-old free agent by the Anaheim Ducks in 2007, Hiller was looking for a chance to establish himself as a backup netminder first. The Ducks had some success with another Swiss-born goalie when they drafted Martin Gerber 232nd overall in 2001. Gerber did not stay long in Anaheim, but had some success during stops in Carolina and Ottawa. Hiller wanted to work with goaltending consultant François Allaire, someone he had met while working at hockey schools over a number of summers. The goalie put up good numbers playing in the Swiss League and won two championships with Davos. Hiller knew he needed guidance if he was going to make it in the NHL and Allaire was always looking to develop two goaltenders for the Ducks. Hiller played in just six minor league games in 2007–08 before getting the call to Anaheim.

The biggest hurdle for Hiller to overcome was that the Ducks were very strong in net with proven performers Jean-Sebastien Giguère and Ilya Bryzgalov, who had combined to win the Stanley Cup in 2007. However, the Ducks were impressed enough by Hiller that they decided to break up the winning tandem by placing Bryzgalov on waivers. In doing so, the team was also able to keep its word that it would attempt to find Bryzgalov a place where he could compete for the starter's job and he was claimed by Phoenix. Hiller played 23 games in 2007–08 and posted a 10–7–1 mark, very respectable for a rookie. His save percentage was a sparkling .927 and suddenly the Ducks thought they just might have a No. 1 goalie in the making, not just a backup. Giguère's play was never as good after he won the Cup and soon Hiller was pushing the veteran for the lead goaltender role. Even though they were in competition, Giguère was good to Hiller, acting as a mentor and demonstrating great respect for the youngster's athleticism and hard work.

As the 2008–09 season progressed, it was clear Hiller was taking over as Anaheim's top goalie. He appeared in 46 games and won 23 times, reducing Giguère's playing

time by a significant amount. Hiller also won a playoff round for the Ducks and that pretty much sealed Giguère's fate with the team. When Toronto was finally able to swing a deal in January of 2010, Giguère became a Maple Leaf and Hiller officially became the everyday goalie in Anaheim. The 2009–10 season saw Hiller win 30 games for the first time and he signed a four-year, $18 million dollar contract with the Ducks. He had come a long way in just a short time.

The highlight of the season for Hiller came at the 2010 Winter Olympics as he backstopped the Swiss team to the quarterfinals before losing to the United States. Hiller was brilliant, holding his team in games they should have lost by a large margin. If people knew little about the 6-foot-2, 195-pounder, they certainly knew what he was all about after he posted a .918 save percentage thanks to great games against elite competition.

Hiller has fast reflexes and covers the net very well. He seems to play the entire game on his knees, but he has strong, fast legs that get him across the crease. He is a very composed netminder who does not get rattled easily. Hiller's attitude before he got the No. 1 job with the Ducks was that he would improve every day and his only interest was in giving his team a chance to win — a fact that endeared him to coach Randy Carlyle. If he keeps improving, Hiller will make everyone in Anaheim very happy.

BY THE NUMBERS Had a 2.23 GAA and a .943 save percentage in 13 games in the 2009 NHL playoffs

- Was the starting goalie for the Swiss team at the 2010 Winter Olympic Games
- Has a career .920 save percentage
- Recorded a career-high 30 wins in 2009–10
- Has a career 2.49 goals-against average

CAREER HIGHLIGHTS

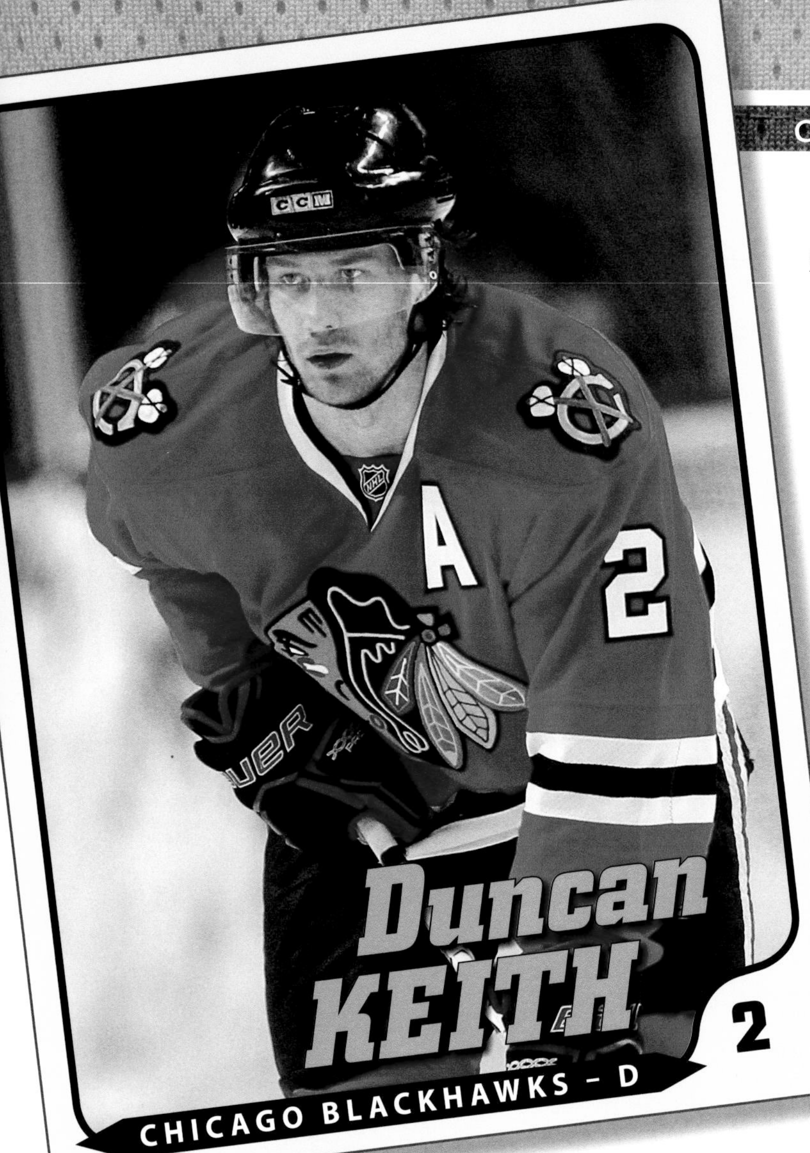

At the end of the 2010 Stanley Cup playoffs, the writers who vote for the prestigious Conn Smythe Trophy, given annually to the MVP of the playoffs, decided to give the award to Chicago Blackhawks captain Jonathan Toews. While Toews was a worthy winner, many in the hockey world believed Chicago defenseman Duncan Keith deserved the honor. A tireless defender, Keith played close to 30 minutes a game each and every night and bailed the Blackhawks out in their own end time after time. Without his strong efforts, which included 17 points in 22 playoff games, the Blackhawks might have learned that you cannot expect to win a Stanley Cup without great goaltending. Sure, Antti Niemi was good most nights at guarding the Chicago net, but if Keith had not been in front of him, it might have been the Philadelphia Flyers celebrating a championship.

The 2009–10 season saw Keith fully blossom as an NHL defenseman — some say the best in the league. His 14 goals, 55 assists and 69 points were all career highs for the native of Winnipeg, Manitoba. When Chicago drafted the youngster 54th overall in 2002, they were hopeful he might become an NHL player, but were not totally sure. He was rather small at the time and looked like he could be overwhelmed by larger, tougher players. The budding blueliner originally attended Michigan State of the NCAA, but made the jump to the Western Hockey League's Kelowna Rockets because he felt it would better prepare him for life in the NHL.

Keith had always impressed his coaches with his desire to improve all aspects of his game. When he was told to be better defensively, he worked hard at it despite his inherent offensive instincts. Keith had scored 68 goals and totaled 226 points in just 163 games when he played Jr. A hockey for the Penticton Panthers of the British Columbia Hockey League, so defending wasn't necessarily what came naturally to him. The Blackhawks did the smart thing and sent the young defenseman to Norfolk of the American Hockey League for some much-needed seasoning. In two years with the Admirals, Keith did not produce great offensive numbers, but did learn to play the pro game. He was up with Chicago at the age of 22 and muddled through a rookie year that saw him go minus-11 and score nine times and record just 21 points in 2005–06. His point totals rose over the next three years and he scored 12 goals in 2007–08, the first indication he was starting to figure out how to lead the attack from the blueline.

By the start of the 2009–10 campaign, Keith was seen as one of the rising stars in the NHL. He was selected to play for Team Canada at the 2010 Winter Olympics and got his first taste of winning with a gold medal. He performed very capably for the Canadian side and was

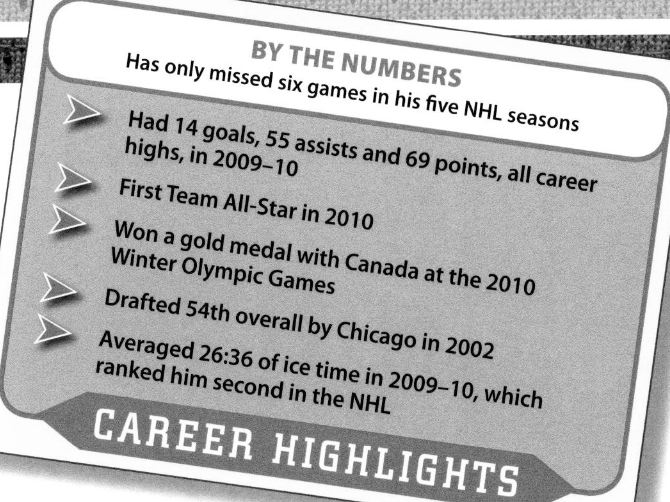

considered one of the top four defenders on the elite squad. He did not score, but helped to set up six goals in seven games. By this point everyone knew the 26-year-old defenseman deserved to be mentioned among the very best players in the world. That notion was further cemented when Keith claimed the 2010 Norris Trophy as the league's best defenseman.

Keith's game is really all about his superb skating abilities. He has exceptional speed and even though many teams throw the puck into his corner, few are able to get in on him for a bone-rattling check. Keith knows how to protect his body and bounce off any attempt to hit him. He now stands at 6-foot-1 and 205 pounds and although he is not overly aggressive, no opponent will ever take advantage of him physically. It also helps Keith greatly that he is often paired with fellow blueliner Brent Seabrook, a stay-at-home type who will back up his teammate at all times.

Keith also showed just how tough he is when he blocked a shot in the playoffs that resulted in him losing seven teeth. Although he looked like an old-time hockey player, Keith did not miss any games as a result of the mishap and his lovely girlfriend told the TV audience after the Blackhawks won the Cup that she was still going to marry him — a wise choice considering he is signed for the next 13 years and will pocket some $72 million over the life of the deal.

BY THE NUMBERS

Has only missed six games in his five NHL seasons

- Had 14 goals, 55 assists and 69 points, all career highs, in 2009–10
- First Team All-Star in 2010
- Won a gold medal with Canada at the 2010 Winter Olympic Games
- Drafted 54th overall by Chicago in 2002
- Averaged 26:36 of ice time in 2009–10, which ranked him second in the NHL

CAREER HIGHLIGHTS

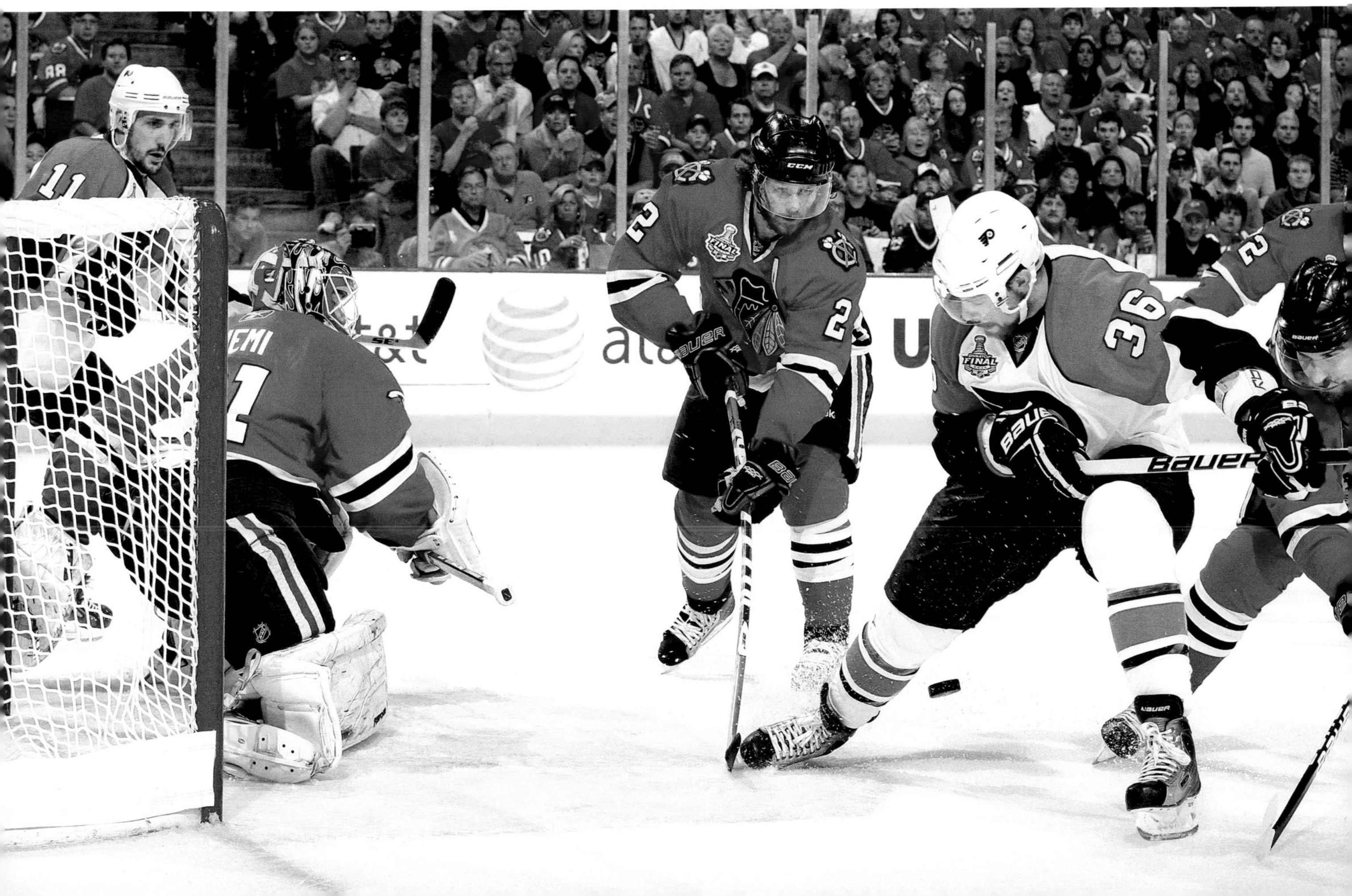

How many hockey players can turn down $100 million? The answer is few, if any, but that didn't stop Ilya Kovalchuk from doing just that. The Atlanta Thrashers made Kovalchuk the first player taken in the 2001 NHL draft and he played seven full seasons there. However, with his contract due to expire at the end of the 2009–10 season, Kovalchuk's future in Georgia became cloudy. Atlanta GM Don Waddell did everything he could to keep the superstar with the Thrashers, but his long-term offer that would have given the player $100 million over the life of the deal was turned down. It was obvious the talented Russian was not interested in continuing his career in Atlanta, despite some public posturing.

Knowing he had no other alternative, Waddell put Kovalchuk on the trade market partway through the 2009–10 campaign.

The New Jersey Devils were enjoying a very good regular season, but felt they could strengthen their club further with a legitimate 40-goal forward. With no assurance Kovalchuk would sign a contract with them when he became an unrestricted free agent, the Devils sent forward Niclas Bergfors, defenseman Johnny Oduya, prospect Patrice Cormier and a swap of draft picks to Atlanta for the mercurial Kovalchuk. The Thrashers were not able to make the playoffs even with the influx of Bergfors and Oduya, but were not far off the mark, missing the post-season by five points. Kovalchuk, on the other hand, indicated he was happy to be joining a perennial contender.

New Jersey hoped Kovalchuk would adjust quickly to his new environment and while he posted just 10 goals in 27 games with the Devils, he was able to register 27 points. Despite his stats, anyone who watched Kovalchuk with the Devils did not see the same player who had always been the Thrashers' most dynamic force. He struggled to find the open ice he had in Atlanta and his shots did not hit the back of the net very often. Part of the explanation for this performance was that his wife was expecting a child, plus all the turmoil that goes with changing teams mid-season. A couple of goals in the playoffs did nothing for the second-seeded Devils, who were out in a shocking five-game loss to the seventh-seeded Philadelphia Flyers. Questions about Kovalchuk's future with the team began almost immediately.

Kovalchuk has been a very consistent performer since he entered the league, scoring 29 goals as a rookie in 2001–02. Blessed with speed and a blazing shot, Kovalchuk is a top-notch talent who has twice eclipsed the 50-goal barrier in his career, earning a share of the Rocket Richard Trophy with Rick Nash and Jarome Iginla in 2004, when he was also named a Second Team All-Star. He has ranked in the top ten in goals scored in every year but his first and has been in the top three on three separate occasions. He has a variety of moves and is especially adept at putting a shot over the goalie's shoulder, making him especially dangerous in shootouts. Kovalchuk never backs away from physical play and has on occasion dropped the gloves to fight. He was essentially allowed to keep his focus solely on offense during his time in Atlanta, but that changed when he landed in Jersey. Adjusting to a new system proved to be a choppy experience for Kovalchuk, who was suddenly playing under one of the most stringent defensive coaches of all-time, Jacques Lemaire. Perhaps Lemaire's decision to hang up his coach's whistle will have some impact on where Kovalchuk decides to play in 2010–11. With new bench boss John MacLean in place and sniper Zach Parise continuing to climb the ranks of stardom, the Devils look more offense-minded than ever. That was enough to convince Kovalchuk — who is sometimes frustrating, but always electric — to re-sign with New Jersey.

BY THE NUMBERS Has scored at least 40 goals in each of the past six seasons

- Had a career-high 52 goals in 2005–06 and 2007–08
- Second Team All-Star in 2004
- Won the Rocket Richard Trophy in 2004 along with Jarome Iginla and Rick Nash
- Drafted first overall by Atlanta in 2001
- Named to the 2002 NHL All-Rookie Team
- Led the NHL with 27 power play goals in 2005–06

CAREER HIGHLIGHTS

It's been tough sledding for the New York Rangers the last few seasons. Only a couple of first round playoff series victories — one versus New Jersey in 2008 and another against Atlanta in 2007 — have given Blueshirts fans anything to cheer about since 1997. Many players have come and gone, a variety of free agents have been tried and more than one big trade has been completed — all to little or no avail. However, since 2005 there has been one player keeping the Rangers at least competitive — goaltender Henrik Lundqvist. Luckily for the Rangers — or they would be in even worse shape — they selected the splendid Swede 205th overall in the 2000 NHL draft.

Every Rangers skater recognizes that Lundqvist is the team's most valuable player. In fact, the 6-foot-1, 198-pound stopper has been named team MVP each of the past four seasons, including the 2009–10 campaign. Only Hall of Fame defenseman Brian Leetch (a six-time recipient) has won the award more often than Lundqvist, who bested the record of three consecutive team MVPs by Hall of Famer Andy Bathgate in the 1950s. The Rangers netminder has been a consistent performer, winning at least 30 games each of his five years in the NHL. Twice he's recorded 10 shutouts in a season and twice he's finished seasons with save percentages of .920 or better. The past four seasons have seen Lundqvist appear in 70 or more games, including a career-high 73 in 2009–10, proving he is a reliable workhorse who can be counted on night in and night out.

Having Lundqvist behind them has given his teammates the confidence to take chances. Mentally tough, Lundqvist is a goalie who battles as hard as he can and his competitive nature endears him greatly to his teammates and coaches. A good example of how well Lundqvist can play came on the final day of the 2009–10 season when he faced 47 shots in Philadelphia and kept the score tied 1–1 at the end of regulation with some great saves. It was Lundqvist's 17th straight start to end the year. A win would have given the Rangers an Eastern Conference playoff spot, but they lost in the shootout. At the end of the game the Rangers players lamented the fact they had let their goalie down.

Lundqvist anticipates the play very well and moves across his crease quickly without losing his spot in relation to the net. If he gives up a rebound, Lundqvist is quick to recover and makes some of his most dazzling saves in such a way. He is very good at challenging shooters and his competitive nature means he's happy to play so many games. The Rangers have not been able to find a backup netminder to complement their star and until they do, Lundqvist can expect to start the vast majority of the Blueshirts' games. It is interesting to note that Lundqvist played 45 games and allowed two goals or fewer during the 2009–10 season, indicating that if he was fatigued in any way it did not show up in the statistics.

Lundqvist had a distinguished career in Sweden with the Frolunda Indians prior to heading to the NHL. He won the Swedish Elite League championship, three consecutive goalie of the year awards and was named the league MVP his final season. He has also represented his country at World Hockey Championships and has twice been an Olympian, leading Sweden to the gold medal at the 2006 Winter Games held in Turin, Italy. Sweden beat long-time rival Finland in the '06 gold medal game, setting off a great celebration in Sweden. Lundqvist's performance at the Olympics solidified his position as the best goalie Sweden has produced since the late Pelle Lindbergh, who played in the NHL with Philadelphia during the early 1980s.

Lundqvist is quite capable of leading a team to the Stanley Cup, but the Rangers must improve their team overall to see that dream come to fruition.

BY THE NUMBERS

Has had at least 30 wins in all five of his NHL seasons

- Led the NHL with 10 shutouts in 2007–08
- Played in 2009 NHL All-Star Game
- Boasts a career goals-against average of 2.33
- Won Olympic gold with Sweden in 2006
- Named to the NHL's All-Rookie Team in 2006

CAREER HIGHLIGHTS

Considering Joe Pavelski has become a fairly consistent 20-goal man in the NHL, it is interesting to learn he was selected 205th overall by the San Jose Sharks in the 2003 NHL draft. That fact is even more surprising when you consider Pavelski's rather decorated hockey career as he rose through the ranks. The native of Plover, Wisconsin, first came to prominence in high school, with his team winning the state championship in 2002. He went on to play Jr. A hockey for Waterloo of the United States Hockey League for a couple of years, making the All-Rookie and All-Star Team in his first season, which saw him score 36 times in 60 games. His solid performance got him drafted by the Sharks, but there was little else to go on, making his late-round selection a little more understandable. The 5-foot-11, 195-pounder was also a little undersized, but he did manage to score 21 goals his second year in the USHL and then helped his team win the league championship with 12 points in 12 playoff contests. He later attended the University of Wisconsin for two seasons, where he gained All-Star status once again, scoring 39 goals and 101 points in 84 career games. He split the 2006–07 season between the NHL and the Sharks' American Hockey League farm club in Worcester and has remained on the San Jose roster since then.

Pavelski's first full NHL season saw him score 19 times and total 40 points in 82 games, but he was even better in 2008–09 when he scored 25 times and upped his point total to 59. The 2009–10 season saw Pavelski net 25 once again, this time in only 67 games, but it was in the post-season where he really excelled and began earning a reputation for being a clutch performer. In a six-game series against the Colorado Avalanche, Pavelski led his team with five goals and eight points. His most important goal came late in Game 2 of the series with Sharks goalie Evgeni Nabokov on the bench and San Jose already trailing 1–0 in the set. Pavelski's goal tied the game and the Sharks won the contest in overtime, thus avoiding losing the first two meetings at home. The plucky center wasn't done though, as he scored the overtime winner in Game 4 and then finished off Colorado with the series-clinching goal in the sixth contest. Pavelski seemed to thrive on the excitement of the home crowd in San Jose and he relished the playoff pressure — something that could not be said of some of his more highly paid and higher-profile teammates. Pavelski continued his hot streak into the next series against Detroit with two goals, including the game-winner, and one assist in a 4–3 Sharks triumph in the first game. He followed that up with two power play tallies and one assist to secure another 4–3 San Jose victory in the second contest. The Sharks made mincemeat of the Red Wings by winning in five games, but Pavelski and the rest of the team was no match for

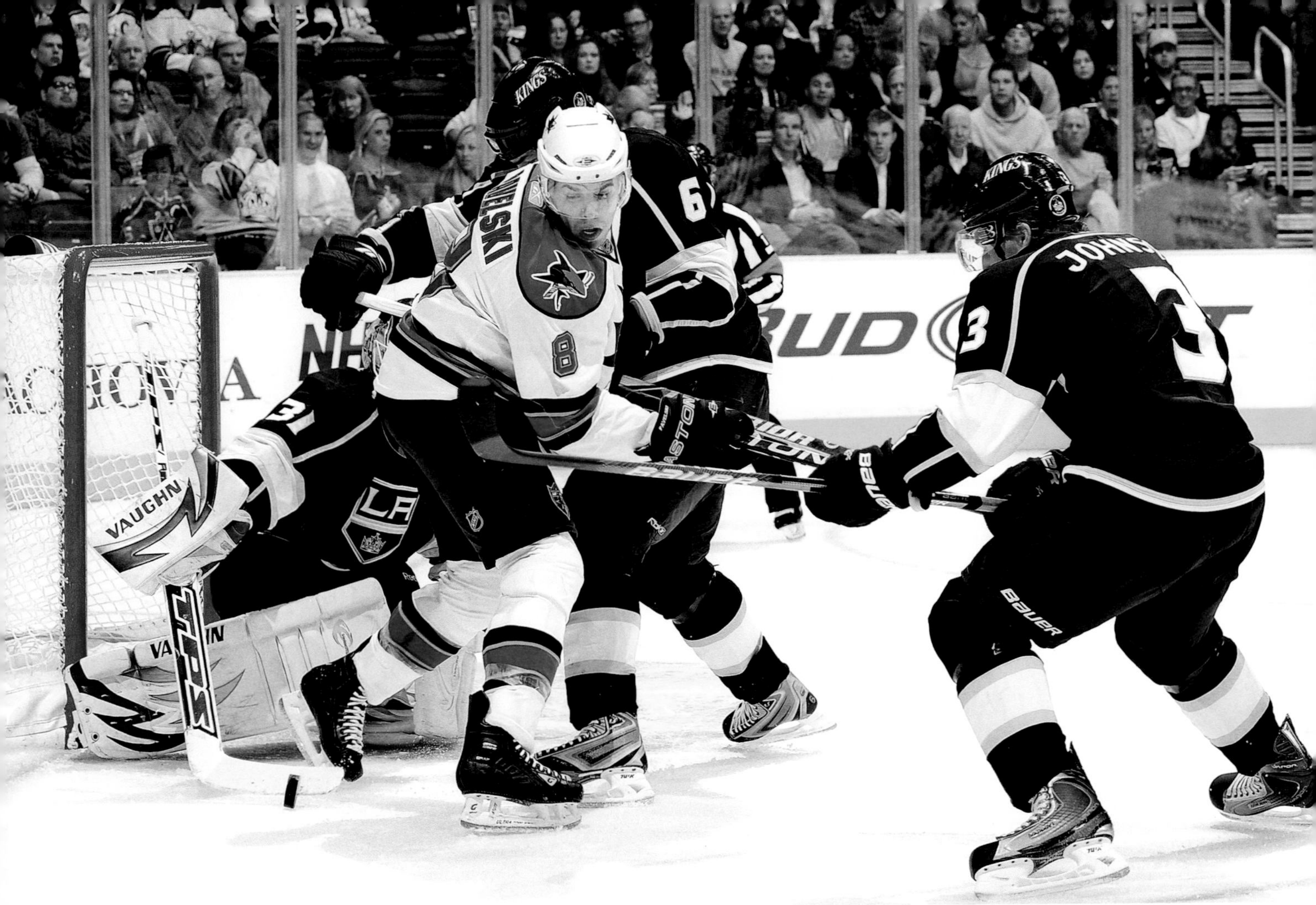

the Chicago Blackhawks in the Western Conference final, losing in four straight contests.

The 2010 playoffs brought out the best of Pavelski's game on an almost nightly basis. His creativity with the puck was very noticeable and his ability to pass made him very dangerous on the attack. Pavelski showed he had a strong, accurate shot that he would not hesitate to use when the moment was right. He was not afraid to go hard to the net and that got him many of his post-season goals. Pavelski is especially good on the power play (five of his nine playoff goals were with the extra man) where he seems to find holes in the opposing defensive system and make a pretty cross-ice pass or let one of his own bullet shots go. He worked well with linemates Devin Setoguchi and Ryane Clowe and they were a dynamic force throughout San Jose's playoff run. The trio forced opponents to worry about more than just the Sharks' big line of Joe Thornton, Patrick Marleau and Dany Heatley.

Depending on what GM Doug Wilson does with the rest of the team, the Sharks may have found a second line that can one day help lead them to the Stanley Cup final. It has become very clear the Sharks' so-called best players need the secondary help if they are to go all the way. However, it may be that Pavelski and a few other youngsters on the Sharks become the team's top guns very shortly.

BY THE NUMBERS Has recorded back-to-back 25-goal seasons from 2008–10

- Had a career-high 59 points in 2008–09
- Drafted 205th overall by the Sharks in the 2003 NHL draft
- Has at least 200 shots on net in each of the past three seasons
- Won silver medal with Team U.S.A. at the 2010 Winter Olympic Games

CAREER HIGHLIGHTS

The events of January 31, 2010 were shocking to fans of defenseman Dion Phaneuf. He had been a member of the Calgary Flames since they selected him ninth overall in the 2003 NHL draft. The tough blueliner had enjoyed some great years as a Flame, including a 20-goal rookie season in 2005–06. Phaneuf's play earned him a robust contract averaging $6.5 million a year, but when defender Jay Bouwmeester was acquired via trade and signed to an even larger contract by the Flames, it was obvious that the team had too many big-money players on the back end. Phaneuf's game tailed-off somewhat in his final two seasons in Calgary and reports that he had disagreements with the coach and some teammates made the once unthinkable thought of dealing him quite possible.

The Toronto Maple Leafs were floundering at the same time and GM Brian Burke knew he had to do something drastic. The Leafs brass had made earlier inquires about Phaneuf's availability and were initially rebuffed, but when the low-scoring Flames' season was about to take a terrible turn, they moved the aggressive defender and two others to Toronto in exchange for help at forward in Matt Stajan, Niklas Hagman and Jamal Mayers, and a replacement on defense in Ian White. The trouble for the Flames was that Phaneuf was clearly the best player in the deal and their fans were left wondering if they had seen a repeat of the 1992 deal between the same two teams that saw Calgary give up Doug Gilmour to Toronto. The final results of the trade are not yet in, but the Maple Leafs could not be happier.

As soon as Phaneuf arrived in Toronto he seemed to put whatever happened in Calgary behind him. He made the Leafs' dressing room a louder, more boisterous place and took command of a rudderless team in a very positive way. In his first game as a Leaf against New Jersey, he played 24-plus minutes, rocked star winger Zach Parise and fought tough Devils defenseman Colin White. He acquitted himself well and Toronto's home crowd was pleased with a 3–0 win, but more so with a more spirited on-ice product. While it was just one game, the Leafs' coaches and management liked what they saw from the belligerent Phaneuf, who has never been afraid to inject his personality into any contest his team plays. The Leafs seemed to rally around their new approach from the time Phaneuf arrived on the scene and posted a 13–10–3 mark, a much better showing than they had recorded all season long. Too far behind to make up playoff ground, the Leafs finished 29th overall in 2009–10, but for the first time in a number of years there was light at the end of the tunnel.

Phaneuf first started to play hockey in his hometown of Edmonton, Alberta, and developed his hard shot by breaking windows and light bulbs in the basement of his

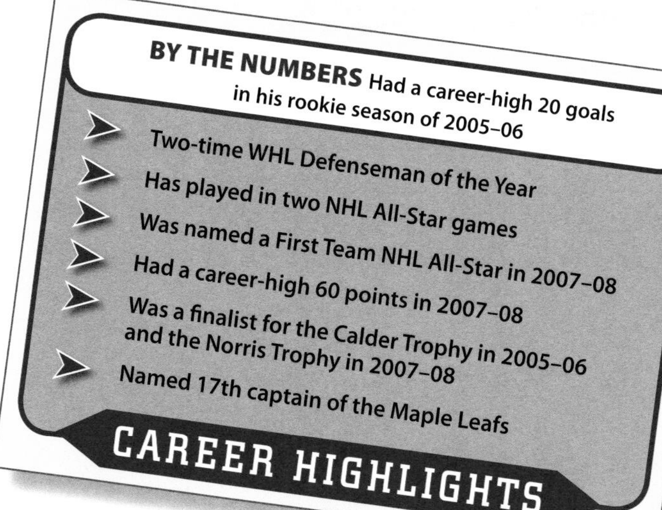

BY THE NUMBERS Had a career-high 20 goals in his rookie season of 2005–06

- Two-time WHL Defenseman of the Year
- Has played in two NHL All-Star games
- Was named a First Team NHL All-Star in 2007–08
- Had a career-high 60 points in 2007–08
- Was a finalist for the Calder Trophy in 2005–06 and the Norris Trophy in 2007–08
- Named 17th captain of the Maple Leafs

CAREER HIGHLIGHTS

parents' house. His mother, Amber, was a former figure skater; his father, Paul, worked in the construction business. Paul also dared to put on goalie pads to face his son's wicked drives. He had bruises and welts to show for his efforts, but all the work paid off for young Dion, who soon joined the Western Hockey League's Red Deer Rebels. He played for former NHLer Brent Sutter in Red Deer (ironically, the Flames' coach on the day Phaneuf was traded) and also starred for Team Canada at the World Junior Championship in 2005 when the Canadian team went unbeaten en route to capturing the gold medal. Phaneuf modeled his game after the legendary Scott Stevens (a tough-as-nails, Hall of Fame defenseman) and he was NHL ready at the age of 20. He was a finalist for the Calder Trophy as the league's best rookie in 2006 and was named to the NHL's First All-Star Team in 2008 as well as being nominated for the Norris Trophy after scoring 17 goals and 60 points in 82 games, but finished second to Detroit's Nick Lidstrom.

The Leafs are obviously hoping Phaneuf returns to his All-Star form — they named him team captain during the summer of 2010 after just 26 games with the team. He was the obvious choice to help firmly establish a new leadership group in Toronto to replace those who floundered since the end of the NHL lockout. On the last night of the 2009–10 season, Phaneuf scored the overtime-winning goal in Montreal to give the revitalized Leafs a 4–3 victory. It was only the second goal he scored with Toronto, but it was hopefully a sign of big things to come for the 25-year-old and his new team, which had been transformed into one of the youngest in the league by season's end.

The Philadelphia Flyers generally like to employ big, physical and nasty players on their hockey team. When they had the chance to acquire the largest and meanest defenseman in the entire National Hockey League, they did not hesitate to complete a deal for Chris Pronger. The 6-foot-6, 222-pound blueliner came to the Flyers with eight career suspensions on his resume and a reputation for bending the rulebook and smirking at opponents who did not like it — in other words, the prototype of the perfect Philadelphia Flyer. When he arrived in the 'City of Brotherly Love,' Pronger said he was meant to wear the orange and black uniform and who exactly was going to argue with him?

The other noticeable item about Pronger's career is that he is a proven winner. He was drafted second overall in 1993 by the Hartford Whalers, but lacked the focus early in his career to be an impact player. That all changed when the Whalers traded Pronger to St. Louis in 1995. His rise with the Blues culminated with him being named the Norris Trophy winner as the league's best defenseman and Hart Trophy winner as MVP of the NHL in 2000. Following a 2005 trade to Edmonton, Pronger helped lead the eighth-seeded Oilers to within one win of the Stanley Cup in 2006. Not finding Edmonton to his liking, he demanded a trade and was with Anaheim when it won the Cup in 2007. When the Ducks realized they could not afford Pronger's contract, they traded the four-time league All-Star to Philadelphia in exchange for a package of players and high draft choices. The Flyers wanted the 35-year-old to go up against the likes of Alex Ovechkin and Sidney Crosby, the two greatest stars in the Eastern Conference, and make the front of the Philly net an uncomfortable place to be. It all nearly backfired as the team was initially rife with rumors about how Pronger did not fit in well with some of the younger players. The Flyers needed a shootout win on the season's final day just to eke into the playoffs, but it was during the post-season that Pronger showed his true value.

Pronger has become a much wiser defenseman as he has aged and gained more experience. He measures each step so that no energy is wasted. Pronger does not chase the puck, preferring to let the game come to him. By playing in such an efficient manner, he can play a great number of minutes and still be very effective. His passes are very precise and he knows when to put some juice behind his feed to a teammate or if he needs a feather touch to advance the puck. The rangy blueliner can find an open teammate with his great vision and his shots from the point are laid in perfectly for a deflection. He has never scored 20 goals in a season, but has recorded 30 or more assists a total of nine times and has a career total of 509 helpers.

CAREER HIGHLIGHTS

BY THE NUMBERS
Was a career-high plus-52 in 1999–00

- Four-time league All-Star
- Won the Hart and Norris Trophies in 2000
- Originally drafted second overall by Hartford in 1993
- Won Olympic gold with Canada in 2002 and 2010
- Has tallied 120 points in 170 career playoff games

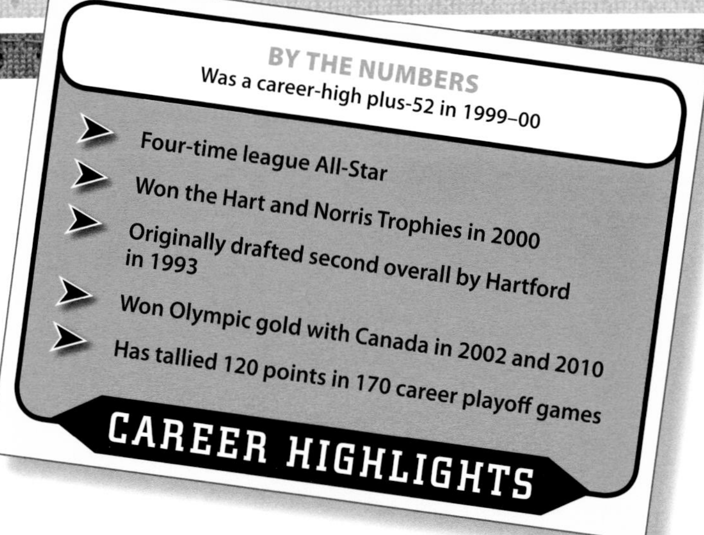

Pronger does not take any backward steps when it comes to physical play. He is heartless in letting opposing forwards know he does not want them near the Flyers goalie. High sticks, slashes and elbows are all part of his repertoire and he really doesn't worry about other people's opinion of him. He could be called for a penalty on virtually every shift, but has learned to be just subtle enough — most of the time, anyway — to avoid the referee's wrath.

After a 10-goal, 55-point season, Pronger was simply outstanding in the 2010 playoffs as the Flyers made it all the way to the final. An easy win over New Jersey was followed by an amazing comeback from a 3–0 series hole versus the Boston Bruins. Pronger and the Flyers then easily dismissed the Montreal Canadiens before dropping the final in six games to Chicago. Pronger was all over the ice for his team, often playing nearly half the game. He had 18 points in 23 playoff contests and almost certainly would have taken the Conn Smythe Trophy if the Flyers had prevailed in the final.

Was the playoff performance of 2010 the final great moment in Pronger's career or does he still have another Cup in his future?

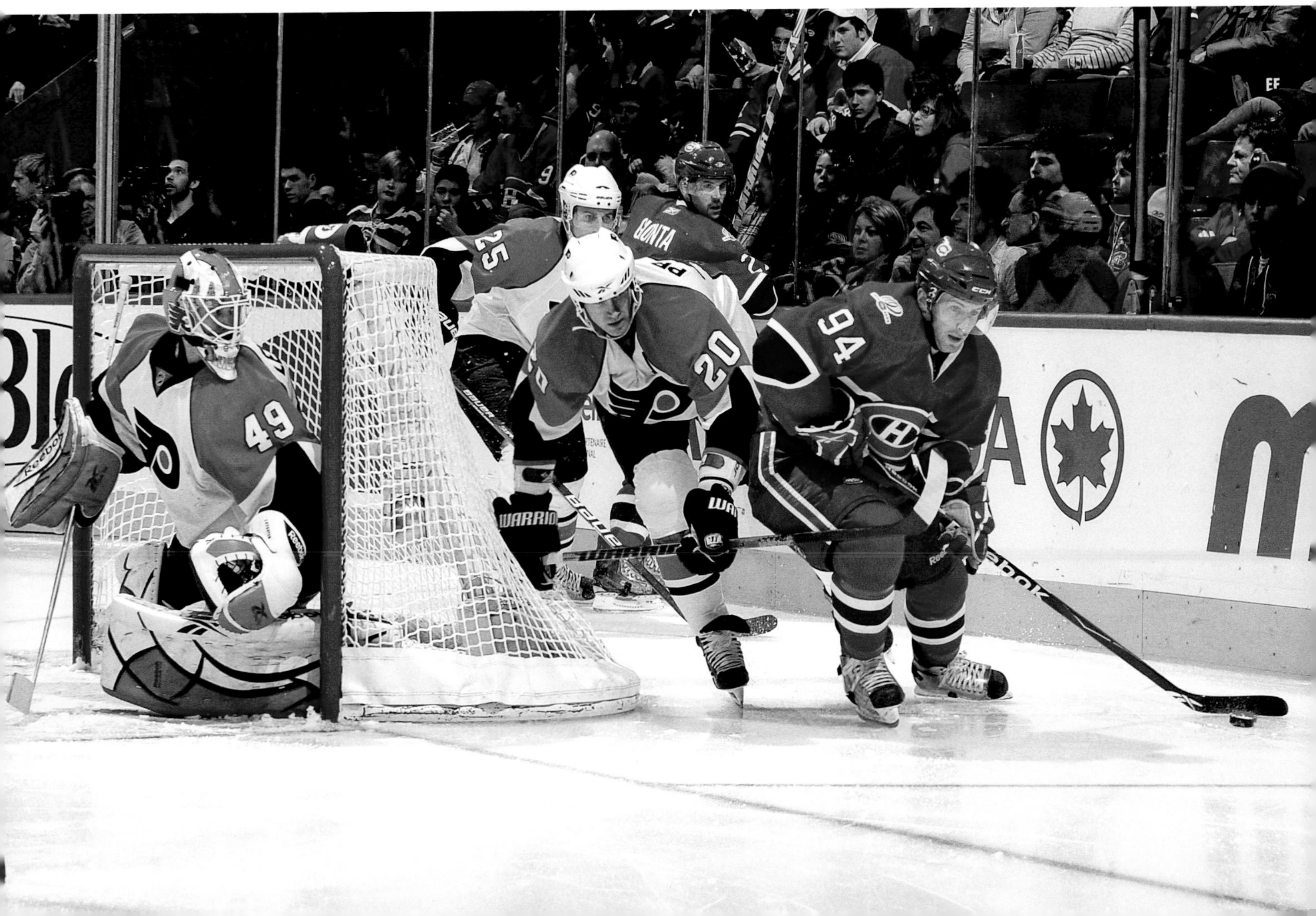

There are times when a GM gets fired because he is made a scapegoat for organizational errors. Then there are times when a GM is let go and it is the absolute right thing to do. Many pundits felt the latter was the case when John Ferguson, Jr. was let go by the Toronto Maple Leafs. A glorified scout in the eyes of many, Ferguson's trading record as GM of the Leafs was largely abysmal, but no deal was worse than the one that sent goaltender Tuukka Rask to the Boston Bruins in exchange for netminder Andrew Raycroft. Toronto had drafted Rask 21st overall in 2005 with the hopes he would develop into a top goaltender during the next few years. Instead, the desperate Ferguson used Rask to acquire Raycroft (selected 135th overall by Boston in 1998), a goalie the Bruins didn't want anymore. In effect, Ferguson flipped a first round pick (Rask) for a third round selection (Raycroft) and eventually the Leafs had nothing to show for the deal. Raycroft flopped badly in Toronto during two seasons, while Rask was thriving in Boston by the end of 2009–10. There was really no need for Ferguson to pay such a steep price, but that is why some teams are successful, while others never seem to get anywhere.

Rask was born in Savonlinna, Finland, and played his entire junior career in his native country. He stayed in Finland, a country known for producing top goalies, until he was 20. He also did some military service in his home country, which gave him exposure to a variety of people of all ages. Rask was assigned to the Providence Bruins of the American Hockey League for the 2007–08 season, posting a 27–13–2 record in his first season as a North American professional. He played 57 games the following season with Providence and won 33 times in the regular season and another nine times in the playoffs. Rask also made a favorable impression when he played in five games for the big-league Bruins the same two seasons (winning three times), but there was no sense of urgency to get him to the NHL. The Bruins had veteran Tim Thomas doing very well as a Vezina Trophy winner as the league's top goalie in 2008–09.

But Rask was hot on Thomas' skates and when the Vezina winner faltered somewhat during the 2009–10 campaign, Rask jumped at the opportunity to be Boston's No. 1 netminder. He got into 45 games for Boston and posted a great record of 22–12–5, while leading the league in save percentage (.931) and goals-against average (1.97) to go along with five shutouts. As much as the Bruins thought they had a gem, even they had to be a little surprised when the 6-foot-3, 169-pound Rask took over the B's starting job and never let it go. The calm, cool and collected Rask plays a style much different than that of the frenetic Thomas; he inspires confidence in teammates with a controlled butterfly style, positioning himself just right for every shot. The beefier Thomas, on the other hand, flips and flops all over the ice and relies on his very athletic reflexes to survive. Only a good shot will beat Rask most of the time, because he is so prepared for each drive. He also shows great bounce-back ability, rarely losing focus after giving up a goal, a trait every top goalie needs. While Rask has said that he holds no grudges against the Maple Leafs, it is interesting to note that he has won four of five games against Toronto.

Rask was very strong in his first NHL playoff appearance, getting his team past the Buffalo Sabres while posting a 7–6 post-season record. The Bruins faltered badly in the second round after taking the first three games of the series against Philadelphia. Rask and the rest of the Bruins lost the next four games to the Flyers, which is just the third time in NHL history a team has lost a series after leading three games to none. The young netminder looked worn down from all the pressure. Rask also had let downs in the AHL playoffs, so there is something of a pattern developing that might be of great concern.

However, it is just as likely that Rask will learn from his post-season failures and get the Bruins further into the playoffs as time passes and he gains more experience.

ICE CHIPS Recorded his first NHL win against the team that drafted him, the Toronto Maple Leafs, on November 20, 2007

- Originally drafted 21st overall by Toronto in 2005
- Led the NHL in both save percentage (.931) and goals-against average (1.97) in 2009–10
- Has six career shutouts in only 50 career games played
- Had 22 wins in 45 games in 2009–10

CAREER HIGHLIGHTS

Brad Richards liked playing hockey in Tampa Bay for the Lightning. He had enjoyed great success, winning the Stanley Cup in 2004 and winning the Conn Smythe Trophy for his brilliant playoff performance (12 goals, 26 points in 23 games). He also loved playing alongside his best friend, Vincent Lecavalier, who Richards had teamed with through prep school in Saskatchewan and major junior in Quebec, and with Martin St-Louis, one of the top-producing forwards in the NHL at the time. Richards re-signed with the Lightning hoping the trio could lead Tampa back to the Cup, but it was soon clear that too much money was going to be spent keeping this group together under the new salary cap rules. In need of a goaltender and having to move a large contract, Tampa traded Richards to the Dallas Stars in 2008 with stopper Johan Holmqvist for netminder Mike Smith and forwards Jussi Jokinen and Jeff Halpern. Richards was clearly the best player in the deal (although Jokinen did score 30 goals for the Carolina Hurricanes in 2009–10), but he had a hard time adjusting to his new environment.

The trade was a shock for Richards, who had excelled from the minute he arrived in the NHL in 2000–01 after a stellar junior career. Despite his excellent play in junior and being named the Canadian major junior player of the year and MVP of the Memorial Cup in 2000, Richards was expected to take some time to adjust to the NHL, but the 20-year-old developed quickly. He did not play any minor pro — impressive for a player drafted 64th overall — and was named to the NHL's All-Rookie Team after scoring 21 goals and 62 points in 82 games. He had another 62-point performance in 2001–02, but the next two seasons saw him post 74 and 79 points, including a career-high 26 goals in 2003–04, and add the Lady Byng Trophy for gentlemanly play to his impressive haul of awards in the same year the Lightning became Cup champions for the first time. Most figured Tampa would challenge for more championships, but they started to make frequent first round playoff exits. Richards did play for Canada at the 2006 Olympics, but significant change was unavoidable and soon Richards found himself deep in the heart of Texas.

When he first arrived in Dallas in February of 2008, Richards did quite well with 11 points in 12 regular season games and 15 points in 18 playoff games for the Stars. However, during his first full season with Dallas, Richards played in just 56 games due to wrist and hand injuries, although he posted a very respectable 48 points. In addition, Richards did not feel comfortable on a team that included Brenden Morrow, Mike Modano and Marty Turco as its established leaders. They were long-time members of the team and Richards was an outsider. Richards' meteoric rise had seemed to crash loudly.

The 2009–10 season included a big rebound for Richards. After not being invited to Team Canada's Olympic orientation camp in August, Richards' strong, two-way play and ability to once again post a lot of points had him shooting up Canada's depth chart. Centering a line featuring young wingers Loui Eriksson and James Neal seemed to rejuvenate Richards, who finished the year with 67 assists and tied a career high with 91 points, good for seventh spot in the NHL scoring race. The 29-year-old's chemistry with his new linemates was noticeable to all who saw Richards taking advantage of Eriksson's smarts and Neal's size to form a dynamic trio — even rivaling what he had in Tampa Bay with Lecavalier and St-Louis. The line combined for 80 goals and 217 points, although the Stars fell short of the playoffs.

A native of Murray Harbour, P.E.I., the 6-foot, 196-pound Richards has shown that his NHL career is now back on track and that he is worth his $7.8 million cap hit. With Turco now gone and Modano considering retirement, Richards is more comfortable and once again a team leader, this time in Dallas.

BY THE NUMBERS Set an NHL record with seven game-winning goals in the 2004 playoffs

- Tied a career-high with 91 points in 2009–10
- Won the 2004 Conn Smythe with Tampa Bay en route to a Stanley Cup
- Member of the NHL's All-Rookie Team in 2001
- Played for Canada in the 2006 Olympics
- Has 639 points in 700 career games

CAREER HIGHLIGHTS

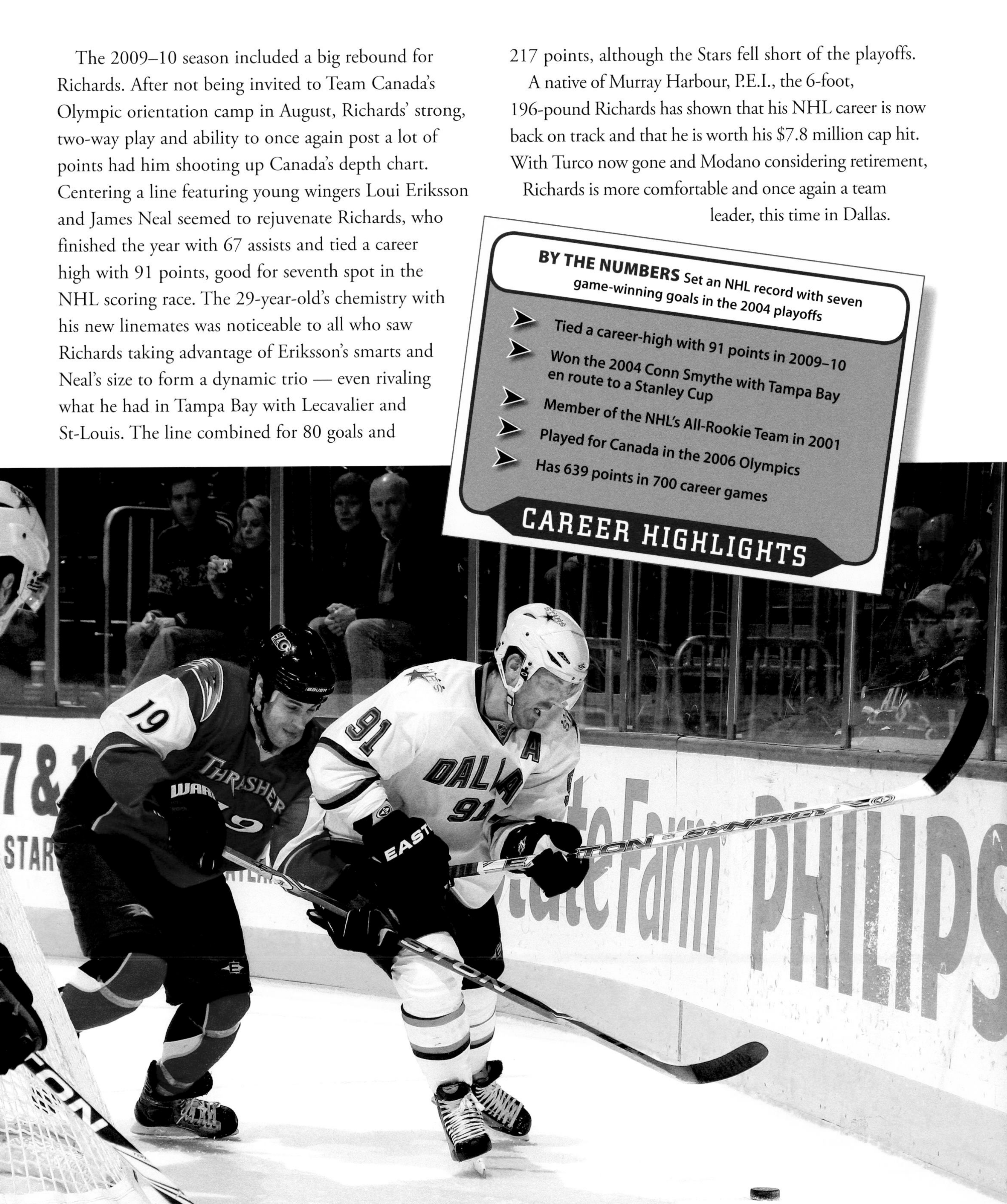

When the Sedin twins played out their contracts with the Vancouver Canucks, it was assumed by many they would test the free agent market. Other NHL teams were ready to pry away the brothers, who have only played for Vancouver since they entered the league in 2000, but the Canucks quickly moved to secure both to new deals just before they could go to the open market in 2009. Vancouver GM Mike Gillis gave $6.1 million a season to both Daniel and Henrik, locking up the brother act until 2014. It was believed the agent for the twins was looking for a contract in the 10-year range, but Gillis wasn't going that far to get them signed. It was clear the Sedins were going to be signed in a package deal and it was evident the best way to stay together was to re-sign in Vancouver. In addition to hockey, the twins also share a love of horses, golf, drinking coffee and have the same fashion sense. How could they even think about playing apart?

Daniel Sedin was drafted second overall, one spot ahead of his brother, in 1999 by the Canucks. He has scored 209 goals and 547 points in 705 career games and has proven to be a very consistent performer. Sedin has led the Canucks in goals for the last four seasons, including the 2009–10 campaign when his brother tied him for the lead with 29 markers, and has scored more than 30 goals twice in his career. Sedin has a pair of very soft hands and is an exceptionally smart player on the attack. He does a great job of keeping the puck away from the opposition with good body positioning and he will go to the net, but not as often as he should. Sedin is perhaps best known for the great on-ice chemistry he has with his brother and they sometimes look like they are reading each other's minds. They are extremely dangerous down low and can make opposing defenders look totally out of position. With their 30th birthday set for the eve of the 2010–11 season, the twins are squarely in their prime years, but questions still remain as to the ultimate effectiveness of both players.

Doubts about the Sedins go as far back as the 1999–00 season, when they decided to finish high school at home in Sweden rather than come to the NHL. While they played for Modo in the Swedish Elite League, former Vancouver GM Brian Burke decided to see a game in person and wasn't very impressed, to say the least. There was nothing in their play that night that suggested either one would be an NHL star. Burke was rather furious and hoped to hear that the flu or some other malady caused their bad play. Instead Burke was told the twins had stayed up all night trying to figure out how to solve a math problem for school! Once he heard the reason for their uninspired play, Burke was happy to know the players he drafted showed such good

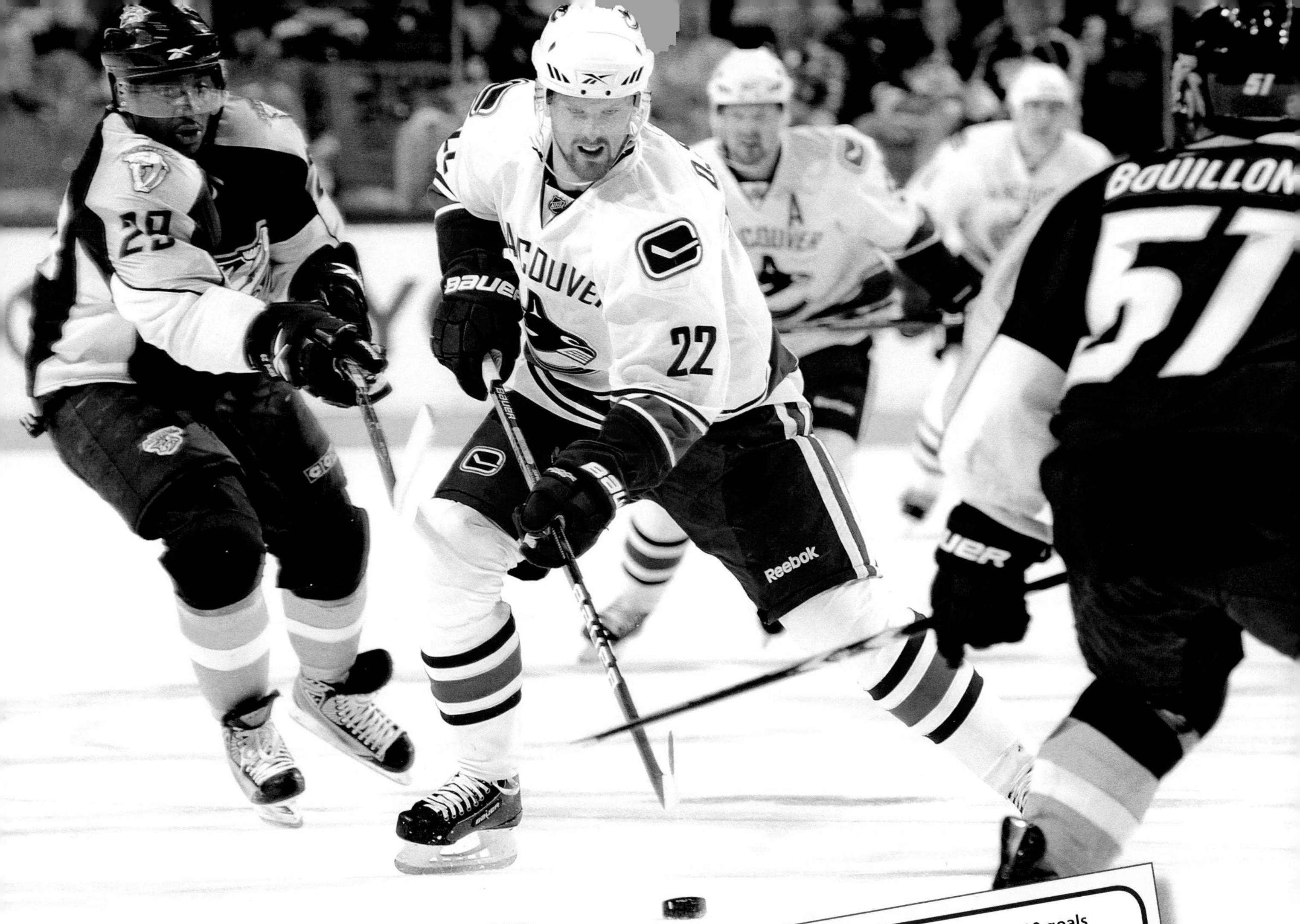

character and a commitment to doing as well as they possibly could. No wonder Burke was willing to sign them for the Toronto Maple Leafs in the summer of 2009.

The major question about the Sedins' overall effectiveness centers on their playoff performances. Daniel has but 42 points in 65 post-season games and was as invisible as his brother in two second round defeats at the hands of the Chicago Blackhawks in 2009 and 2010. Part of the reason for the lack of playoff success might be that each Sedin is a little too easy to play against, with Daniel only recording 292 penalty minutes over his career. At times the criticism has become very derisive — the twins were nicknamed the 'Sedin Sisters' at one point by commentators who hide behind microphones — yet neither brother has ever complained, although both were sensitive to the issue. They have also never been seen arguing in the Vancouver dressing room or anywhere else for that matter.

Vancouver has reached the point where it will be judged solely on how it performs in the playoffs. It is unlikely that Daniel or Henrik will be battered and bruised if the Canucks ever make a deep run, so Vancouver fans better hope other players like Ryan Kesler, Alex Burrows, Mason Raymond and Alexander Elder do the dirtier work. If properly supported, the Sedins can be difference-makers, but only under those conditions.

BY THE NUMBERS Has recorded at least 20 goals and 45 assists in each of the past five seasons

- Had a career-high 85 points in only 63 games in 2009–10
- Scored a career-high 36 goals in 2006–07
- Won gold with Sweden at the 2006 Olympics
- Was a career-high plus-36 in 2009–10
- Named to the Second All-Star Team in 2010

CAREER HIGHLIGHTS

The Pittsburgh Penguins built their team around a tried and true method — strength down the middle. Typically, Sidney Crosby and Evgeni Malkin take up the first two center slots, while the third line is anchored by 6-foot-4, 220-pound Jordan Staal — the perfect player for this role on the Penguins. Like Crosby and Malkin, Staal landed in Pittsburgh after the Penguins took him very high — second overall in 2006, to be exact — in the draft. Staal came to the attention of the hockey world when the native of Thunder Bay, Ontario, played his final season of junior hockey with the Ontario Hockey League's Peterborough Petes. He produced 28 goals and 68 points in 68 games for the Petes, but his stock was also helped by his terrific family pedigree. His older brother, Eric, was already a star with the Carolina Hurricanes by 2006, while another older sibling, Marc, was taken 12th overall by the New York Rangers in 2005. All that encouraged the Pens to take Staal so high in the draft.

The Penguins were still a fairly weak team when Staal cracked the lineup as an 18-year-old. He scored 29 times in his first year and made a very noticeable impact with seven shorthanded goals — the most in the league during the 2006–07 season and an NHL rookie record. Staal scored his first hat trick when the Penguins came to the Air Canada Centre to play the Toronto Maple Leafs, a team Staal watched on television as a kid. He also scored a goal on a penalty shot and his first three markers were scored with the Penguins a man short. Staal had 18 even-strength goals and four game-winners for a team on the rise. He also showed he was a dependable two-way player with a plus-16 rating. His great year was recognized with a nomination for the Calder Trophy and a place on the NHL's All-Rookie Team.

Pittsburgh was a contending team by the 2007–08 season, but Staal took a slight step back with only 12 goals and 28 points in 82 games to go along with a minus-5 rating. The Penguins were not alarmed since many players have a difficult time in the second season and Staal redeemed himself somewhat in the playoffs when he scored six times in 20 post-season contests as Pittsburgh made it to the Stanley Cup final. Staal was much better in 2008–09 when he scored 22 goals and added 27 assists during the regular season. He was very important in the playoffs, recording nine points in 24 games. While his offensive production was not overwhelming, he scored a significant goal in the playoffs during the fourth game of the Cup final. Pittsburgh was playing Detroit for the second consecutive year and the Red Wings got the early jump by winning the first two games at home. Many predicted Detroit would romp to a second straight Cup, but the Penguins won their first home game to get back into the series. They were in a tough spot in the fourth contest when Staal scored a shorthanded marker — a goal that highlighted his power, speed and ability to finish — that tied the game halfway through the second period. The Penguins went on to win the game 4–2 and ultimately took the Cup with a Game 7 win on the road.

Staal does not score enough to be considered an elite power forward, though he fills every other aspect of that role. He is able to ward off big defensemen with his large frame and has the quick hands to steal pucks and get the attack going in the Penguins' favor. He is excellent on face-offs and rarely out of position. He can play in traffic without any difficulty and his forechecking skills lead to plenty of chances for him and his teammates. His offensive totals will likely be in the 45- to 55-point range (he had another 49-point season in 2009–10), but his full value can't be measured in those statistics. Pittsburgh was hoping to defend its championship, but Montreal ended the Pens' season in the second round of the 2010 playoffs. Staal contributed five points in 11 games, while missing two contests with a foot injury.

The Penguins believe Staal is a big part of their team and backed it up by signing him to a deal that pays $4 million annually through 2013. With Crosby and Malkin also under long-term contracts, Pittsburgh has shown that building a team the old-fashioned way is still quite effective.

BY THE NUMBERS Is the youngest player in NHL history to score a hat trick at 18 years and 153 days

- Scored a career-high 29 goals in his rookie season (2006–07)
- Led the NHL in shorthanded goals (7) and shooting percentage (22.1) in 2006–07
- Has only missed one game in his four-year NHL career
- Named to the NHL All-Rookie Team in 2006–07
- Was nominated for the Selke Trophy in 2009–10

CAREER HIGHLIGHTS

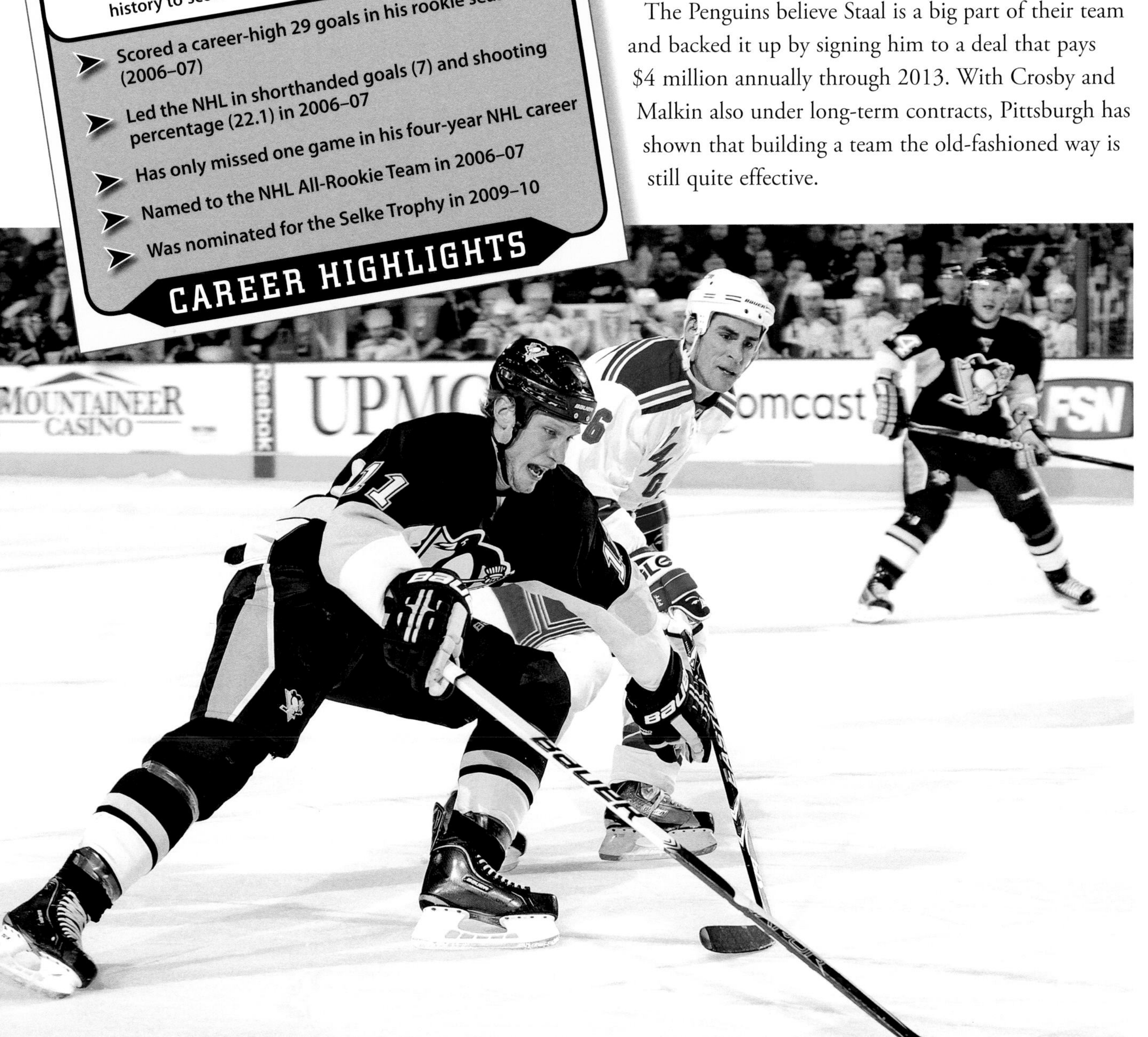

When Martin St-Louis first went to Tampa Bay for the start of the 2000–01 season, he was hoping for an opportunity that had eluded him with the Calgary Flames. An undrafted free agent many considered simply too small to play in the NHL (he's listed as 5-foot-9 and 177 pounds), St-Louis signed with the Flames in 1998, but played just 69 games for them, scoring four goals and 20 points. But he made the most of his opportunity with Tampa, tallying 18 goals and 40 points in 78 games that first season; St-Louis showed he could play in the NHL and from that point on has accomplished more in his career than most even dream of. In 2004, he won the Stanley Cup with Tampa along with the Hart and Art Ross Trophies, and the Pearson Award. He's also played for Canada at the 2006 Olympics and has been named a First Team All-Star and a Second Team All-Star. He's played on the best Lightning teams in franchise history and on some of the club's best lines, although he's also played on some of the worst Lightning squads. Through it all, the courageous 35-year-old winger has been one of the best players in the NHL.

If everyone was waiting for St-Louis' play to begin fading with age (and a little grey hair), they were certainly disappointed after his stellar 2009–10 performance. Playing on a line with Steven Stamkos — still a teenager when the season began — St-Louis recorded a remarkable 29 goals and 94 points to finish sixth in NHL scoring, one spot behind Stamkos. St-Louis' 94 points equaled the second-best mark of his career (he scored 102 points in 2006–07); he looked rejuvenated playing with the young Stamkos, flying around the ice like he was in his mid-20s, not his mid-30s. Like any Canadian, he hoped to be selected to Team Canada for the 2010 Olympic Games. He attended the orientation camp in August '09, where he worked on a line with Jarome Iginla and Sidney Crosby, but the invitation to play for his country never came. Many were surprised at St-Louis' omission since his statistics at the time were among the best in the NHL. He had also played well for Canada at the 2006 Olympics, scoring three points in six games and had been outstanding with Stamkos at the previous year's World Championship. But whatever his level of disappointment, it did not affect his post-Olympics play with the Lightning.

Being a team leader, St-Louis is not afraid to speak his mind. An example came during a dismal 2008–09 season that saw the Lightning finish 29th overall. St-Louis called out teammates after a difficult loss in Atlanta, saying there were too many players too interested in seeing the clock run out on games and not giving it their all every shift. He is a very proud player, one who sets an excellent example by being one of the Lightning's hardest workers — something that has not escaped the eye of Stamkos, who has indicated he learned a great deal from the veteran. More recently, St-Louis was upset that teammate, captain and face of the franchise Vincent Lecavalier was rumored to be on the trade block. The Lightning had to trade Brad Richards in 2008 and the loss of Lecavalier might have been more than St-Louis was willing to take. While he was pleased with the make-up of the Lightning as the 2009–10 season was starting, he was less than pleased when the year ended and Tampa Bay was out of the playoffs once again.

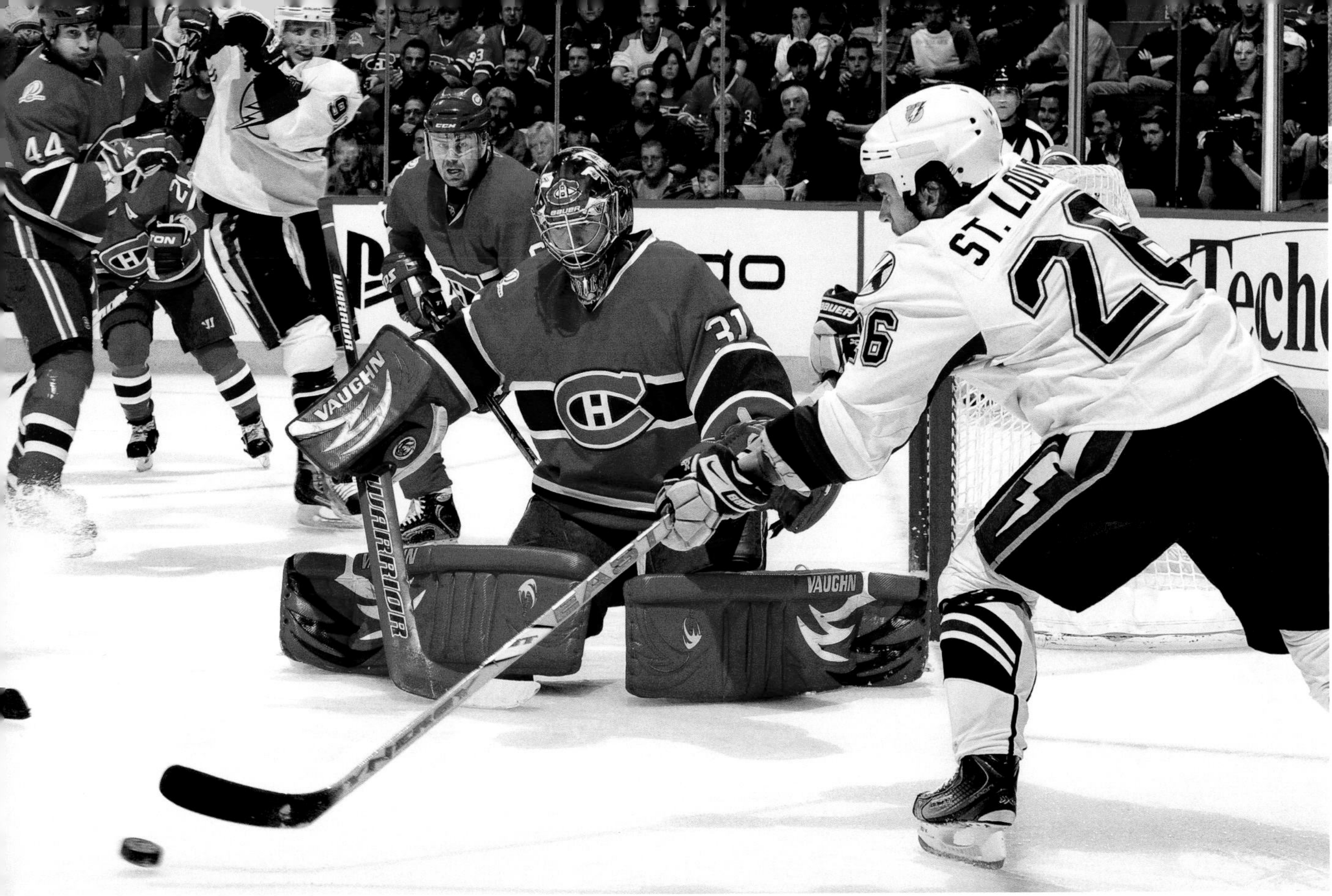

The Lightning have a new owner, Jeff Vinik, once again as Tampa's boardroom has had a revolving door since entering the league in 1992 and changes were quickly made at the end of the season. Vinik dismissed GM Brian Lawton along with coach Rick Tocchet and his staff. St-Louis said that the Lightning's past "two or three years" had been depressing from a team point of view with no play-off berths and he sensed that Vinik was going to make changes. One of the first moves made was to bring in Steve Yzerman as GM, and the first major player decision made by the Red Wings legend was to sign St-Louis to a four-year, $22 million extension. Yzerman believes St-Louis is vital to the Lightning franchise, both on and off the ice.

St-Louis is a father of three boys, the eldest of whom is named Ryan and is just getting his skates wet in hockey. It is certain that the right winger took into account what was best for his youngsters in his decision to stay in Tampa Bay. St-Louis likely envisions playing for four more seasons and with the numbers he posted in 2009–10, who could argue with him?

BY THE NUMBERS

Has only missed two games in the past seven seasons

- Won the Hart and Art Ross Trophies in 2004
- Tallied 24 points in 23 post-season games en route to the Stanley Cup in 2004
- Recorded career highs with 43 goals and 102 points in 2006–07
- Has played in five NHL All-Star games
- Won the Lady Byng Trophy in 2010

CAREER HIGHLIGHTS

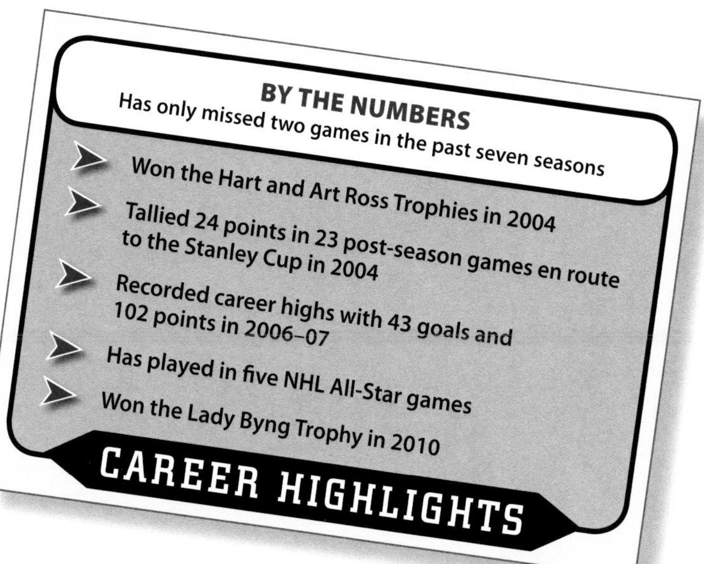

116 Nicklas Backstrom – Washington Capitals
118 Dustin Brown – Los Angeles Kings
120 Jeff Carter – Philadelphia Flyers
122 Pavel Datsyuk – Detroit Red Wings
124 Shane Doan – Phoenix Coyotes
126 Ryan Getzlaf – Anaheim Ducks
128 Dany Heatley – San Jose Sharks
130 Tomas Kaberle – Toronto Maple Leafs
132 Patrick Kane – Chicago Blackhawks
134 Miikka Kiprusoff – Calgary Flames
136 Vincent Lecavalier – Tampa Bay Lightning
138 Milan Lucic – Boston Bruins
140 Roberto Luongo – Vancouver Canucks
142 Evgeni Malkin – Pittsburgh Penguins
144 Andrei Markov – Montreal Canadiens
146 Zach Parise – New Jersey Devils
148 Brent Seabrook – Chicago Blackhawks
150 Jason Spezza – Ottawa Senators
152 Henrik Zetterberg – Detroit Red Wings

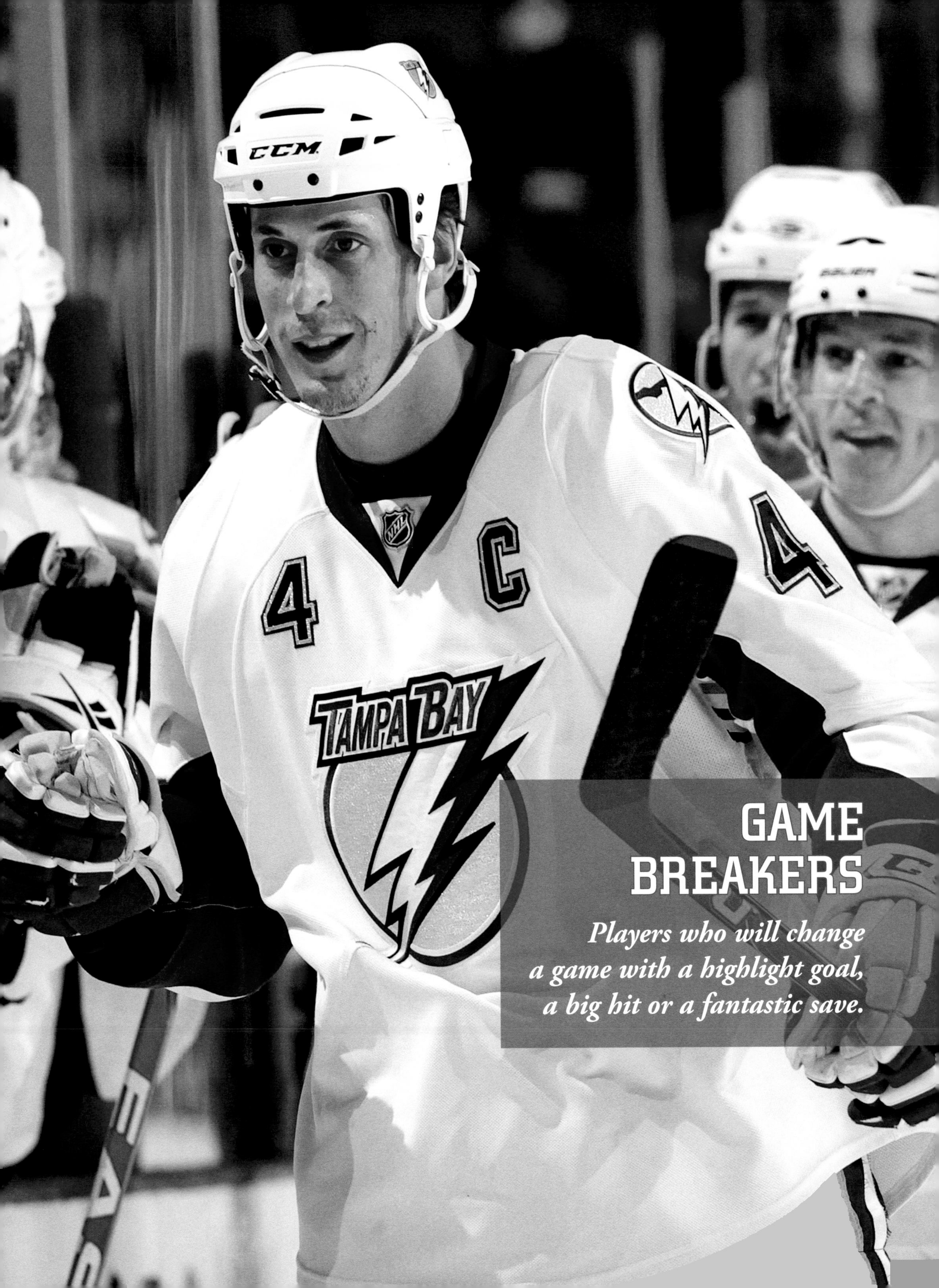

GAME BREAKERS

Players who will change a game with a highlight goal, a big hit or a fantastic save.

It seems the best teams in the NHL like to have at least two main forwards they can count on for scoring. In Pittsburgh, Sidney Crosby and Evgeni Malkin take on the role, while Patrick Kane and Jonathan Toews pair up nicely in Chicago. Joe Thornton and Dany Heatley are fixtures up front for the San Jose Sharks and the Detroit Red Wings like having Pavel Datsyuk and Henrik Zetterberg locked up to long-term deals. The Washington Capitals became the latest team to go in this direction, first signing Alex Ovechkin to a 13-year deal in 2008 and then inking center Nicklas Backstrom to a 10-year contract in the spring of 2010. The Capitals have made it clear they have faith in these players to be the top two forwards on a team that hopes to win the Stanley Cup very soon. Both are young enough to be around for some time, so they should get a number of chances to win a championship.

Based on his performance over his first three years in the NHL, it is easy to see why the Capitals wanted to hang on to the 21-year-old Backstrom. He has not missed a single regular season game since entering the NHL in 2007–08 and has produced at a remarkable pace, with 258 points in 246 games. He had his best year in 2009–10 with 33 goals and 101 points, placing him fourth in NHL scoring. The native of Gavle, Sweden, had a little trouble adjusting to life in North America after playing his entire junior career in his homeland, but the Capitals had Michael Nylander, a fellow Swede, on their roster and he was very helpful to Backstrom in his first two years. The 6-foot-1, 210-pound Backstrom is now comfortable hanging out with other young Washington stars like Ovechkin, Alexander Semin, Mike Green and Brooks Laich.

Backstrom's skill set is of All-Star caliber. He is especially adept at passing the puck and reading the play on the attack. Backstrom's assist totals are very impressive, climbing from 55 his first season to 68 by his third season. His 66 assists in 2008–09 were the most in the NHL and showed he had a great imagination for setting up goals. He is not afraid to hold onto the puck and his patience leads to him feeding his teammates with perfect passes. His reliable and creative offensive play was a big reason why the Capitals led the entire NHL in goals-scored in 2009–10 with 318. He has a good, hard shot, which his increasing goal totals indicate he's more willing to use. That said, Backstrom has a pass-first mentality which might be hard to change. When a player like Ovechkin is on your wing it is certainly tempting for a center like Backstrom to hit the speedy, hard-shooting Russian with a pass. Backstrom is only now just starting to adjust to his fully developed body, which can only mean he will get better in the future.

The Capitals have rebuilt their team primarily through

the draft. Backstrom was selected fourth overall in 2006 and he has met all expectations. Backstrom has also produced in the playoffs with 30 points in 28 games, but after leading the league with 54 wins and 121 points in 2009–10 there was tremendous disappointment in Washington when the team was ousted in the first round of the playoffs by the surprising Montreal Canadiens. Like many of his teammates, Backstrom has to increase his intensity in the post-season and play at a little higher level than in the regular season. The Capitals did not hesitate to give Backstrom a lucrative contract worth a total of $67 million almost as soon as the playoffs were over, but now have to face the fact that a great deal of their salary cap space is spent on a few players. It is a conundrum each club faces in this new era of hockey, especially when the team has some success. Managing a budget properly is a bit of a poker game, but you can bet every team would like to have a pair of aces like Ovechkin and Backstrom on its side.

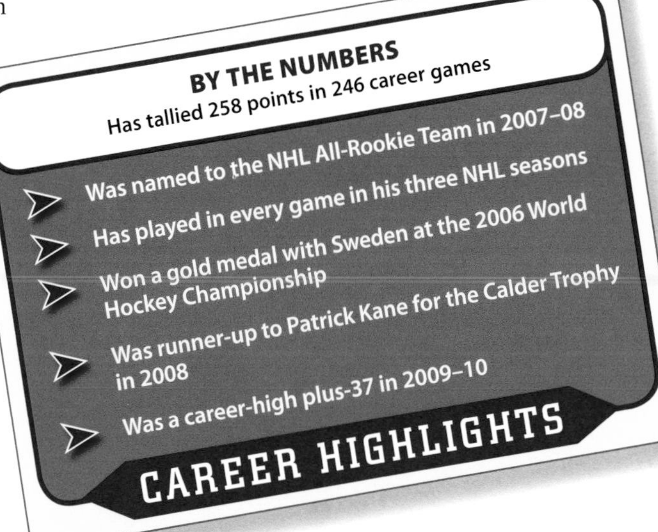

BY THE NUMBERS
Has tallied 258 points in 246 career games

- Was named to the NHL All-Rookie Team in 2007–08
- Has played in every game in his three NHL seasons
- Won a gold medal with Sweden at the 2006 World Hockey Championship
- Was runner-up to Patrick Kane for the Calder Trophy in 2008
- Was a career-high plus-37 in 2009–10

CAREER HIGHLIGHTS

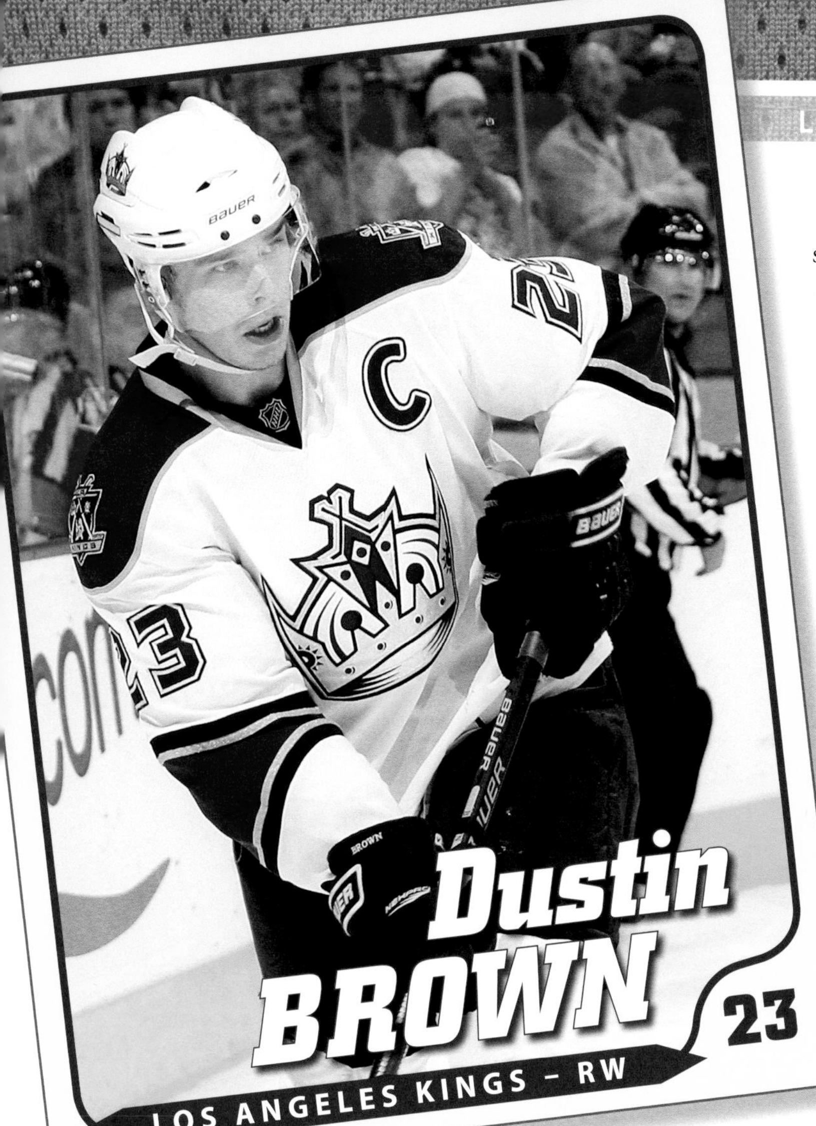

Anyone who visits the website of the Los Angeles Kings will see the words 'Pride, Passion and Power' prominently displayed on the welcoming page. Those three words could also be used to describe team captain Dustin Brown, who exudes those characteristics to near perfection. Brown was first given the coveted 'C' on his sweater back on October 8, 2008, and he's a natural fit for the role of team leader. The 25-year-old plays a very physical and emotional style of game and his teammates react well to his leadership. He is the 15th captain in team history and, as a native of Ithaca, New York, is the first one to be born in the United States. He was very proud to be named the youngest captain in Kings' history and his alternates, center Anze Kopitar and defenseman Matt Greene, were also new to their roles, so they all learned how to do these jobs together. With veterans like Ryan Smyth and Sean O'Donnell also in the mix, the Kings entered the 2009–2010 season in search of their first post-season berth since 2002 and accomplished that goal by finishing sixth in the Western Conference with 101 points. As for Brown, he may not be the most talented player on his team, but he is definitely the guy who makes the Kings go.

Los Angeles expected a great deal from Brown when it selected him 13th overall in 2003. After playing a couple of years of high school hockey in Ithaca, Brown made the jump to the Ontario Hockey League with the Guelph Storm. In 174 career games with the Storm, Brown scored 98 goals and totaled 194 points. He played 31 games for the Kings as a 19-year-old in 2003–04, then played in the American Hockey League during the 2004–05 season when NHL players were locked out. He had an outstanding year with the Manchester Monarchs, recording 29 goals and 74 points in 79 games, a strong indication he was ready for the NHL. Brown started slowly with the Kings, scoring 14 goals in his first year and 17 in his second season, although he did establish a physical presence with 80 penalty minutes as a rookie. His third season was a breakthrough year, as Brown posted a career-high 33 goals and 60 points. His tenacious play didn't go unnoticed, either, helping lay the groundwork for the team giving him the 'C.' Brown has yet to get back to the 60-point plateau in either of his two seasons as captain, but 2009–10 saw him cut his plus-minus rating down to a more respectable minus-6 and he trimmed his penalty minutes down to 41.

In January 2010, Brown was made a member of Team U.S.A. for the Winter Olympic Games. He was named as one of the four alternate captains for the team and simply being on the squad was a dream come true. He could not get untracked at the tournament, failing to register a point in six games, but it was still a great honor to be part of the silver medal-winning team. It was not the first time Brown had worn the red, white and blue sweater in international competition, having captained the American side during the 2009 World Championship.

One of Brown's best games in the regular season came in Toronto when he had three assists against the Maple Leafs in a 5–3 Kings' victory. He hit everything in a blue uniform and stole the puck from a Leaf with a good defensive play to set up Jarret Stoll for a goal. His team followed his strong, power forward lead and picked up a valuable two points. Brown would have liked to see his squad win a playoff round in 2010, but some poor team defense and spotty goaltending cost the Kings in their first round series versus the Vancouver Canucks. Brown scored once and had four assists in the six games, not to mention the fact he was all over the ice getting in the face of many Canucks. If the Kings are to advance in the playoffs in the future, Brown has to be a noticeable, physical force on the ice with offensive production thrown in for good measure.

BY THE NUMBERS Has been in the top three in the NHL in hits in each of the past four seasons

- Had a career-high 33 goals and 60 points in 2007–08
- Drafted 13th overall by Los Angeles in 2003
- Ranked eighth in the NHL with 292 shots on goal in 2008–09
- Won silver with the U.S. Olympic Team in 2010
- Is the 15th captain in Kings' history

CAREER HIGHLIGHTS

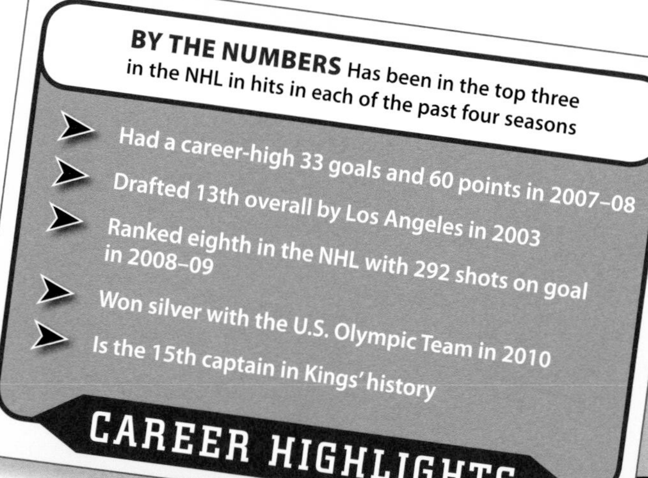

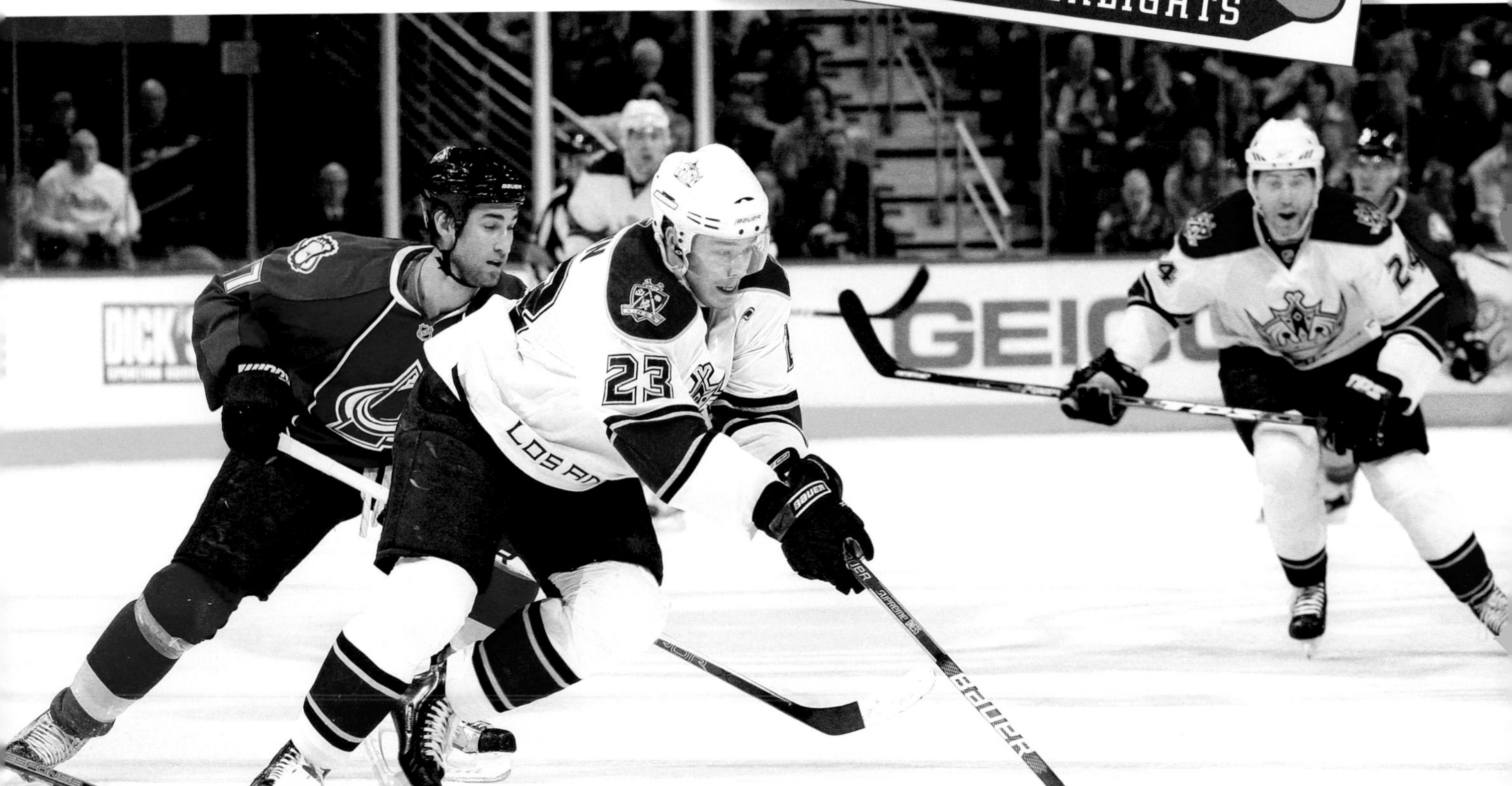

Jim Carter knew his son Jeff was something of a special hockey player when the youngster was just 10 years old. The senior Carter had played major junior hockey himself, but decided a career in the game wasn't going to work out for him so he went to work in a mill instead. Jim coached his son from the time Jeff could first skate until the age of 16. He was not a father who pushed his son into hockey and stressed having fun whenever Jeff played a game. He also emphasized the fundamentals of the game, particularly skating. Jeff learned his lessons well and started scoring at a goal-a-game pace when he turned 10. His father could see the game came naturally to Jeff and he was soon pursued by the Sault Ste. Marie Greyhounds of the Ontario Hockey League. Unlike his father, Jeff excelled in junior and had 35 goals and 71 points in 61 games during his draft year of 2002–03.

The Philadelphia Flyers had their eye on Carter and rated him as the ninth-best player available in the 2003 draft. Philadelphia held the 11th pick and believed they would have no chance of getting the 6-foot-3, 200-pound center. It was thought the Montreal Canadiens were going to select Carter, but they instead took Andrei Kostitsyn in a move they would love to have a mulligan on. Meanwhile, Greyhounds coach Craig Hartsburg had given Carter a strong recommendation to the Flyers. Despite some questions about his consistency, Philly was happy to make the rangy pivot their top choice. Then, just a little while later with the 24th pick, the Flyers took another center named Mike Richards. What a great day for the Philadelphia franchise, which seems to make great picks no matter when it's selecting.

Carter returned to 'the Soo' for a couple more seasons and actually teamed with Richards as part of the Canadian squad that won gold at the 2005 World Junior Championship. The pair also won the Calder Cup together later that same season after making the jump to the American Hockey League's Philadelphia Phantoms as Carter potted 23 points in 21 playoff contests. As an NHL rookie in 2005–06, Carter scored 23 goals and 42 points in 81 games. The next season was a difficult one as injuries held him to 62 games and only 14 goals. Expecting more out of him, the Flyers nearly traded Carter away on two occasions, but luckily for Philadelphia, neither transaction materialized. A 29-goal season in 2007–08 got Carter's career back on track and he followed it up with a break-out year in 2008–09 when his 46 goals were the second highest total in the entire NHL, behind only the 56 put up by Washington Capitals superstar Alex Ovechkin. His 12 game-winning goals were the most in the league.

The strongest part of Carter's game is that he can play both ways. He has long strides and can make moves at top speed. Defenders have to watch him carefully because they never know when he is going to unleash his terrific wrist shot. Carter's drive is good enough that he can score from virtually any part of the attacking zone and he developed this skill by listening to his father, who always urged him to shoot the puck. He is deadly on the power play and knows how to take risks while killing penalties, giving him more opportunities to create offense.

Now that he is established as an NHL star, Carter only needs to improve on his playoff performances. He has faced injuries in the post-season, which would account for his rather dismal playoff production of 19 points in 41 games. If Carter had been at full capacity in the 2010 Stanley Cup final, the Flyers might have been sipping champagne instead of the Chicago Blackhawks.

The Flyers' glory days came when the team won back-to-back championships in the mid-1970s, but they have yet to claim another title in six return trips to the final since. At just 25 years of age, Carter has plenty of time to rectify his playoff record and get the Flyers that elusive third championship.

BY THE NUMBERS Ranked first in the NHL with 12 game-winning goals in 2008–09

- Played in 2009 NHL All-Star Game
- Was second in the NHL in goals in 2008–09 with a career-high 46
- Drafted 11th overall by Philadelphia in 2003
- Won the CHL sportsman of the year in 2005

CAREER HIGHLIGHTS

To put it simply, Pavel Datsyuk of the Detroit Red Wings is a great hockey player. The 5-foot-11, 194-pound Russian center is not only a league All-Star and a multiple award winner, he is also one of the best players in Detroit's long and storied history. The Red Wings were fortunate to select Datsyuk 171st overall in 1998, taking the underrated player late in the draft because his smaller stature and the fact he had never played major junior scared some teams away. Datsyuk's only really productive year playing second division hockey in Russia came when he potted 44 points in 35 games for Dynamo. Much like fellow European center Henrik Zetterberg, the Red Wings were not sure what they had in Datsyuk, but the highly skilled forward never spent a day in the minors after coming to North America.

Datsyuk tasted success early when he joined the Red Wings for the 2001–02 campaign. He played 70 games as a rookie and recorded 11 goals and 35 points. He also chipped in three goals and six points in 21 playoff games as Detroit won the Stanley Cup. The Wings started to undergo some changes after their championship in '02 and Datsyuk was in the right spot to assert himself as a top-six forward. Starting with the 2003–04 season, when he and Brett Hull led the team with 68 points, Datsyuk has either led or been tied for the lead in team scoring for six straight years. In four of those seasons, Datsyuk had 87 or more points, topping out at 97 in both 2007–08 and 2008–09. He has never scored more than 32 goals in a season, but his assist totals over those six years include 38, 59, 60, 66, 65 and 43 helpers, a clear indication of consistent play.

As much as Datsyuk has excelled on the attack, he is perhaps the best defensive forward in the league. A three-time winner of the Selke Trophy as the league's top defensive forward, Datsyuk goes about his duties in a clean manner, which is why he's also won four Lady Byng Trophies for his sportsmanlike play. He's a great example of how the game should be played and the fact you don't need imposing size to excel in hockey. Datsyuk also earned a spot on the NHL's Second All-Star Team for his play in 2008–09 and would get additional recognition if he scored more goals. Datsyuk was integral to the Red Wings winning another Cup in 2008, netting 23 points in 22 post-season games, as well as a return trip to the final in 2009.

Datsyuk's superb puckhandling and outstanding work ethic continue to serve him well. He has improved all aspects of his game since arriving in the NHL as a 23-year-old. The slick pivot is aware of everyone on the ice and is exceptional at spotting the open teammate. Datsyuk's diversity means he's on the ice whether his team is in desperate need of a goal or if it is trying to keep the opposition at bay. He can win 1-on-1 battles

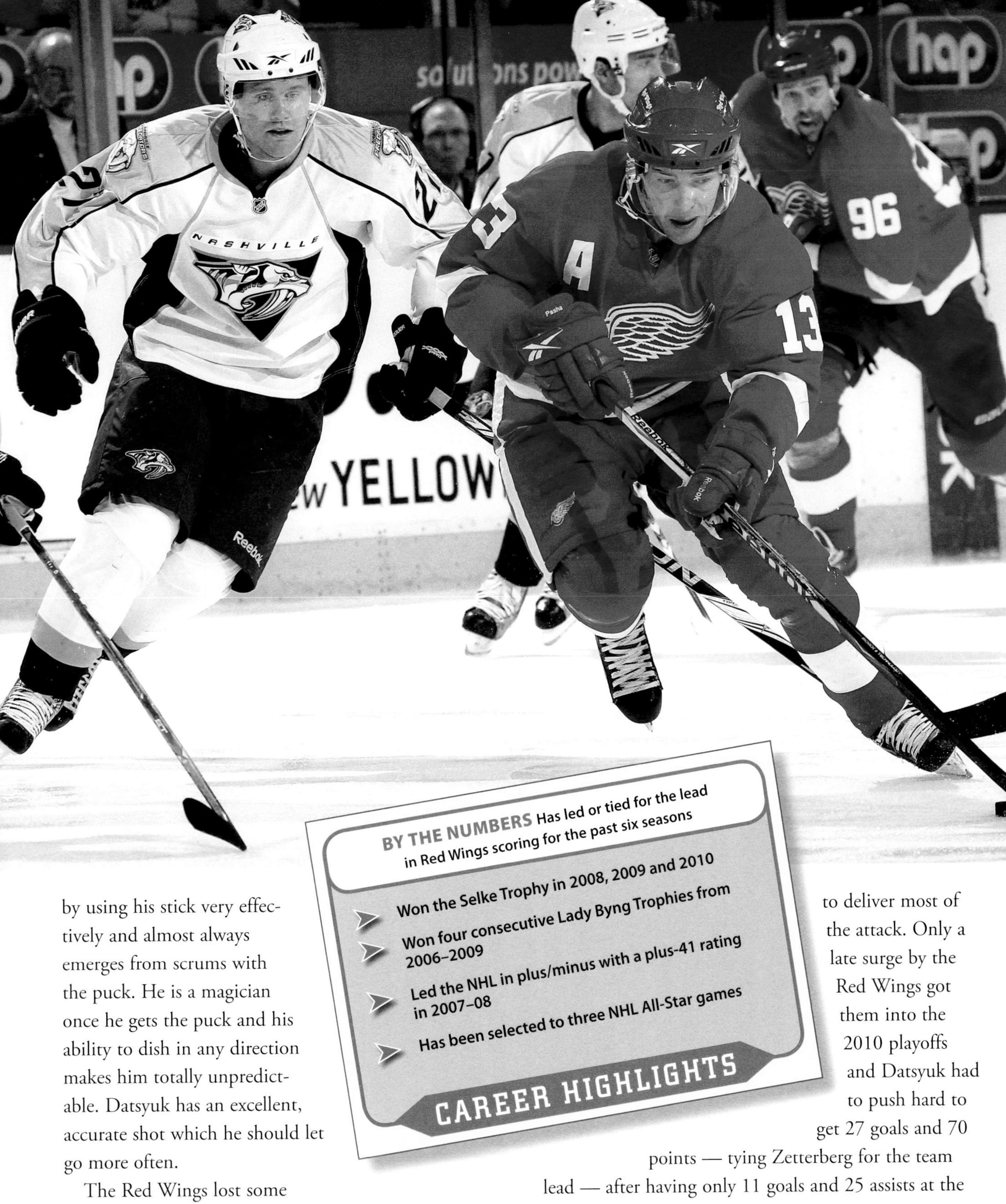

CAREER HIGHLIGHTS

BY THE NUMBERS Has led or tied for the lead in Red Wings scoring for the past six seasons

- Won the Selke Trophy in 2008, 2009 and 2010
- Won four consecutive Lady Byng Trophies from 2006–2009
- Led the NHL in plus/minus with a plus-41 rating in 2007–08
- Has been selected to three NHL All-Star games

by using his stick very effectively and almost always emerges from scrums with the puck. He is a magician once he gets the puck and his ability to dish in any direction makes him totally unpredictable. Datsyuk has an excellent, accurate shot which he should let go more often.

The Red Wings lost some key players like Marian Hossa, Mikael Samuelsson and Tomas Kopecky after their Cup final loss to Pittsburgh in '09. Some senior players like Nicklas Lidstrom, Kris Draper and Tomas Holmstrom are still effective, but are also aging rapidly, leaving Datsyuk and Zetterberg to deliver most of the attack. Only a late surge by the Red Wings got them into the 2010 playoffs and Datsyuk had to push hard to get 27 goals and 70 points — tying Zetterberg for the team lead — after having only 11 goals and 25 assists at the halfway mark.

While Datsyuk's numbers were not up to his usual standards in 2009–10, it is still quite likely he will be very effective for the foreseeable future and add to his Red Wing legacy.

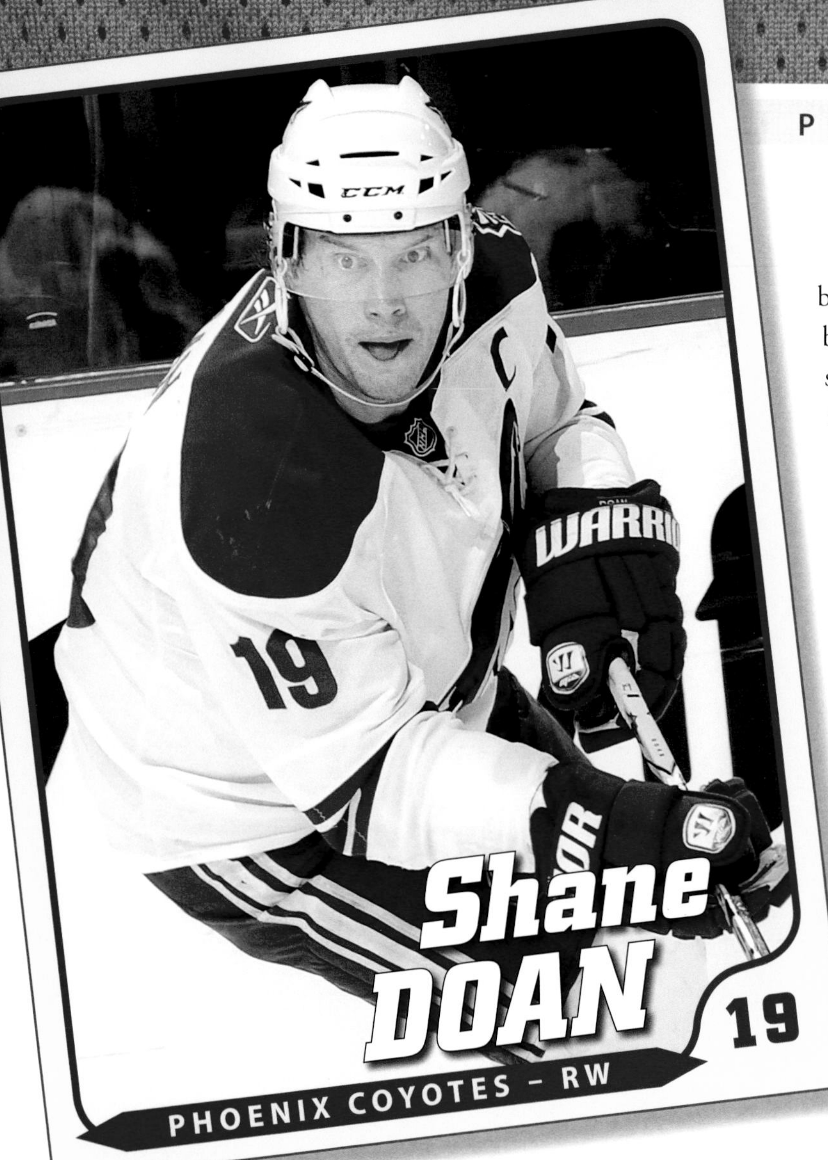

Shane Doan had not played in an NHL playoff game since 2002 and was looking forward to leading his team into the 2010 post-season. Just three games into the first round matchup between Phoenix and Detroit, his season came to a sudden stop after crashing into the end boards. Doan had scored one goal and picked up one assist in the three contests he dressed for, but the Coyotes captain could not get himself back into the lineup for the rest of the series, which went the full seven games. His veteran leadership was noticeably absent on the Phoenix side, while the Red Wings relied on their most experienced players to take the series with a 6–1 win in Game 7 right in Phoenix. Had Doan been able to play every game of the series, there's a chance he could have been the difference-maker for his team.

Doan's hockey abilities were no doubt influenced by his father, Bernie, who was drafted 80th overall by the St. Louis Blues in 1971 as a defenseman. The senior Doan gave up on playing hockey one year later in favor of attending Bible college. Bernie and his wife, Bernice, then decided to operate a Christian summer camp in Halkirk, Alberta, where Shane was born. His parents' values were a very strong influence on Doan, as was the fact almost everyone in his family was in athletics. His sister excelled at track and field and basketball, while one uncle was a hall of fame rodeo performer. Two other uncles played professional hockey, while two cousins made it to the NHL for a brief time. Carey Price of the Montreal Canadiens is a second cousin and Keaton Ellerby, a Florida Panthers prospect, is a first cousin. Doan has joked that he was not tough enough to be a cowboy, so he chose hockey instead. He obviously made the right decision.

In 1991–92, at the age of 15, Doan had a whopping 80 goals and 164 points in just 56 games playing bantam hockey for the Killam Selects. The rugged right winger then went off to play major junior with the Western Hockey League's Kamloops Blazers. His last season in Kamloops saw him score 94 points in 71 games and helped him get selected seventh overall by the Winnipeg Jets in the 1995 NHL draft. He made the Jets as a 19-year-old and recorded 17 points in 74 games during the last season an NHL team existed in Winnipeg. When the franchise moved to Phoenix and was renamed the Coyotes for the 1996–97 season, Doan played 63 games, notching just 12 points. He split the 1997–98 campaign between Phoenix and Springfield of the American Hockey League and his minor league stint saw him produce 42 points in 39 games. Doan finally established himself as a full-time NHL player with 26 goals in 1999–2000. In total, Doan has scored 20 or more goals nine times, including a career-best 31 in 2008–09. He has also led the Coyotes in scoring six straight years, indicating he is a consistent and reliable producer. Doan also holds the team record for most game-winning goals with 44.

The 6-foot-2, 204-pounder is a nice blend of brawn and finesse. He never shies away from the rough stuff and will drop the gloves to fight on occasion. Doan is the type of player who will battle in the corner, come out with the puck, then put a shot past the goalie. He is not a player who carries the puck on end-to-end rushes, but he can keep up with the play and finish with a strong drive on net. He has strong leadership skills and has been selected to play for Team Canada on many occasions, including the 2004 World Cup tournament, which saw the Canadian side emerge victorious.

The 2009–10 season was trying in Phoenix since the team was constantly in flux thanks to an ongoing, public ownership squabble. Although Doan failed to hit the 20-goal mark for the first time in a decade, he still led his club with 55 points. The Coyotes dedicated themselves to being a good defensive team and that led to a 50-win, 107-point season — both team records. Doan now needs to find a way to help Phoenix rise once the playoffs begin.

BY THE NUMBERS

Had a career-high 31 goals in 2008–09

- Only member of the Coyotes left who also suited up for the Winnipeg Jets
- Captained Canada's 2007 gold medal-winning World Championship team
- Has played in two NHL All-Star games
- Selected seventh overall by Winnipeg in 1995

CAREER HIGHLIGHTS

Ryan Getzlaf hasn't always been viewed as a hockey player with huge potential. For example, the Calgary Hitmen of the Western Hockey League selected him 54th overall in the bantam draft despite the fact he had 81 points in 49 games during the 2000–01 season, when he played both bantam and midget hockey in his hometown of Regina, Saskatchewan. It appeared Getzlaf's upside was indeed limited when he potted just nine goals as a WHL rookie. However, he recorded 68 points in 70 games in the 2002–03 campaign and that got him noticed by the Anaheim Ducks. To the surprise of Ducks scouts, he was still available when their turn to pick came around and they snapped him up with the 19th selection at the 2003 NHL draft. The Ducks hesitated momentarily, wondering if there was some sort of problem with the 6-foot-4, 220-pound center, but quickly dismissed any lingering doubts and made the pick.

Getzlaf returned to junior hockey for two more seasons and never quite hit the 30-goal barrier, then began his pro career with the Portland Pirates of the American Hockey League in 2005–06. He got off to a terrific start, netting 33 points in just 17 games and that quickly earned him a promotion to Anaheim, where he finished out the year. In his first full year with the Ducks, Getzlaf scored 25 times and added 33 assists. He saved his best for the playoffs, when he led the team in scoring with 17 points in 25 contests, taking the Ducks to their first-ever Stanley Cup victory. His point totals continued to climb, culminating with a 91-point season in 2008–09 that was good for sixth in league scoring. He also set a team record that year with 66 assists.

When Anaheim couldn't repeat as Cup champs in 2008, Getzlaf joined Canada's entry at the World Championship, where he won a silver medal that added to an international collection that already consisted of gold and silver medals from the World Junior Championship.

Even before the 2009–10 season began, Getzlaf got some good news when he was invited to Canada's Olympic orientation camp in August. However, he was recovering from surgery to repair a tear in his abdominal muscle and could not participate. He was ready for the start of the NHL season, but was plagued with more injuries throughout the year. He was only able to play 66 games and produced a very impressive 69 points, though even that wasn't enough to get the Ducks into the playoffs. Selected to the final roster for the 2010 Winter Games, Getzlaf suffered an ankle injury a few days before the Canadian team was going to assemble in Vancouver. He missed some action, but played a game in Edmonton prior to the break and showed Team Canada management he was ready to go with two goals and two assists in the contest. Getzlaf had an outstanding tournament, scoring three goals and seven points in seven games as Canada reclaimed the gold medal it had lost at the 2006 Games. The triumph was just another great accomplishment for Getzlaf, who was still only 24 years old.

Getzlaf is a big man who plays an impressive power game. His great hands allow him to distribute the puck very effectively and his shot is rocket-like when he lets it go, something he should probably do more often. He has teamed very well with right winger Corey Perry since the two arrived together in Anaheim, but both players could stand to curb their penalty minutes. Getzlaf wants to be a consistent two-way force and that means staying out of the penalty box. He would also like to be a team captain one day and he needs to show a good example to his teammates if the 'C' ever lands on his sweater.

Getzlaf has a contract with Anaheim which pays him $5.3 million a year until 2013, giving the robust center plenty of time to refine his game and keep adding to his success story.

BY THE NUMBERS

Had a career-high 91 points in 2008–09

- Has played in two NHL All-Star games
- Won gold with Canada at the 2010 Winter Olympic Games
- Holds the Ducks' record for assists in a season with 66 in 2008–09
- His brother is a slotback for the Saskatchewan Roughriders of the Canadian Football League

CAREER HIGHLIGHTS

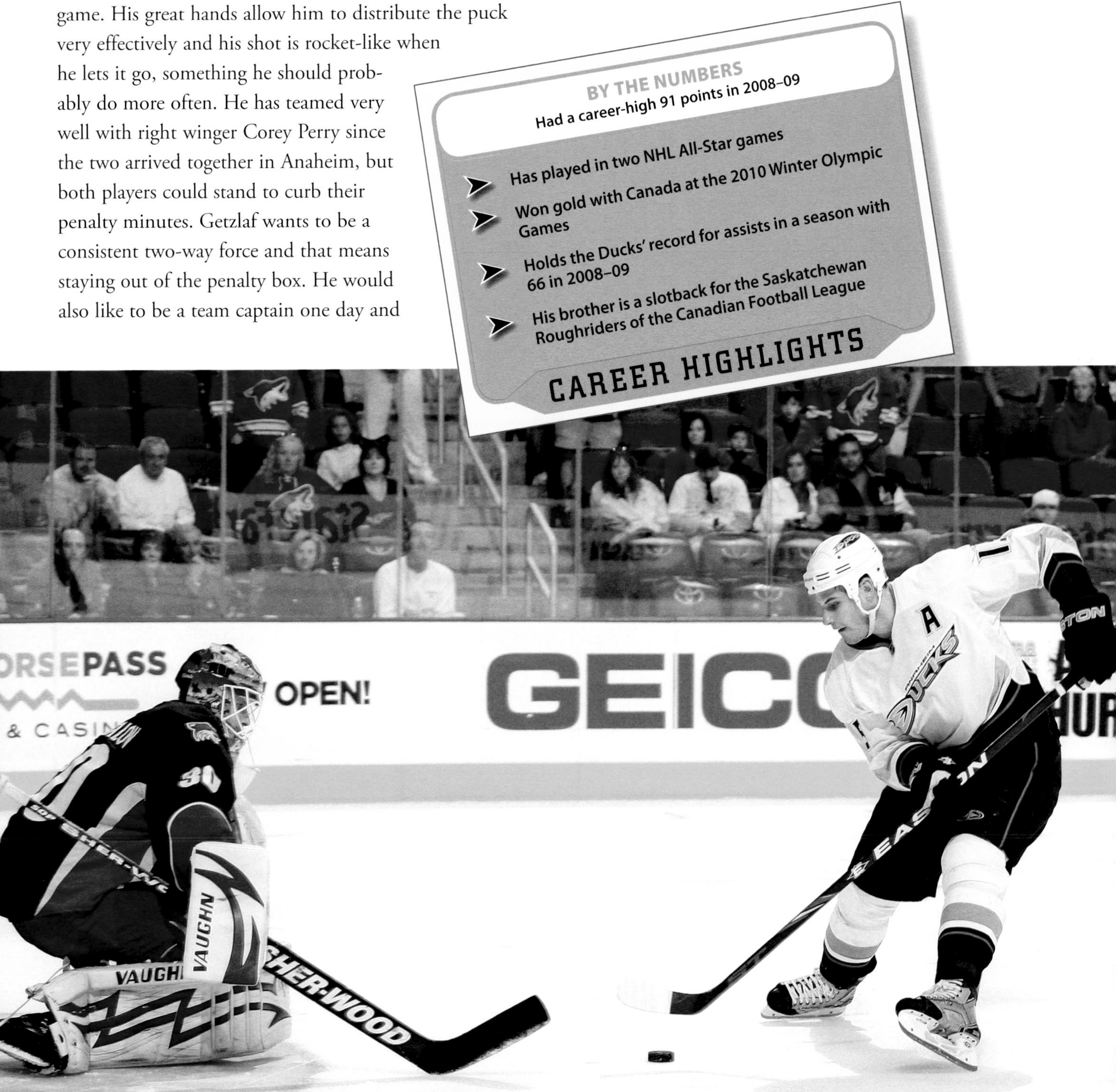

When the San Jose Sharks were eliminated by the Anaheim Ducks in the first round of the 2009 playoffs, GM Doug Wilson promised there would be changes to his roster before the start of the next season. Many Sharks fans called for a complete makeover of the team, but Wilson was much more calculating than those who simply wanted him to 'blow up' a very talented club. Wilson deleted some bottom-of-the-roster players and moved out a couple of veteran defensemen. However, his main move was to add a gifted goal-scorer in the hopes of giving his team an added boost at playoff time. After careful consideration, the Sharks completed a deal to pick up sharp-shooting winger Dany Heatley. For most of the year and for a good portion of the playoffs, Wilson's adjustments worked very well, but when he was needed most, Heatley was not able to deliver a clutch performance.

Controversy just seems to follow Heatley around — he cannot avoid it no matter how hard he tries. It started in Atlanta, where he was the driver in a terrible accident that claimed the life of teammate Dan Snyder in the summer of 2003. Drafted second overall by the Thrashers in 2000, Heatley requested a trade out of Atlanta, unable or unwilling to cope with the scrutiny of the accident aftermath. He was accommodated with a deal to the Ottawa Senators and he excelled in the Canadian capital city for the next four seasons. He posted 50 goals in each of his first two seasons with the Sens and Ottawa made it all the way to the Stanley Cup final in 2007. Heatley tied linemates Jason Spezza and Daniel Alfredsson for the post-season scoring lead with 22 points in 20 games, but Ottawa was dropped in a five-game final by the Anaheim Ducks.

Heatley's output dipped a bit over the next two seasons and he had a hard time getting on the same page as new Sens coach Cory Clouston late in the 2008–09 campaign. In the summer of 2009, Heatley asked Ottawa for a trade, citing personal and hockey reasons as the incentive for the move. Ottawa worked out a transaction with the Edmonton Oilers, but Heatley invoked his no-trade clause to nix the deal, stating he wanted to go to a contender. He was, however, happy to take a $4 million bonus from the Sens when it was due. Furious with Heatley for refusing to go to the Oilers, the Sens wouldn't move him to the Sharks until San Jose agreed to include two-way player Milan Michalek in the swap. Many in the Ottawa organization were glad to see the enigmatic Heatley gone.

While he was certainly aware of the anger being directed his way, Heatley turned his attention to joining a team that was considered a legitimate threat to win the Stanley Cup. He was put on a line with stars Joe Thornton and Patrick Marleau, and got off to a great

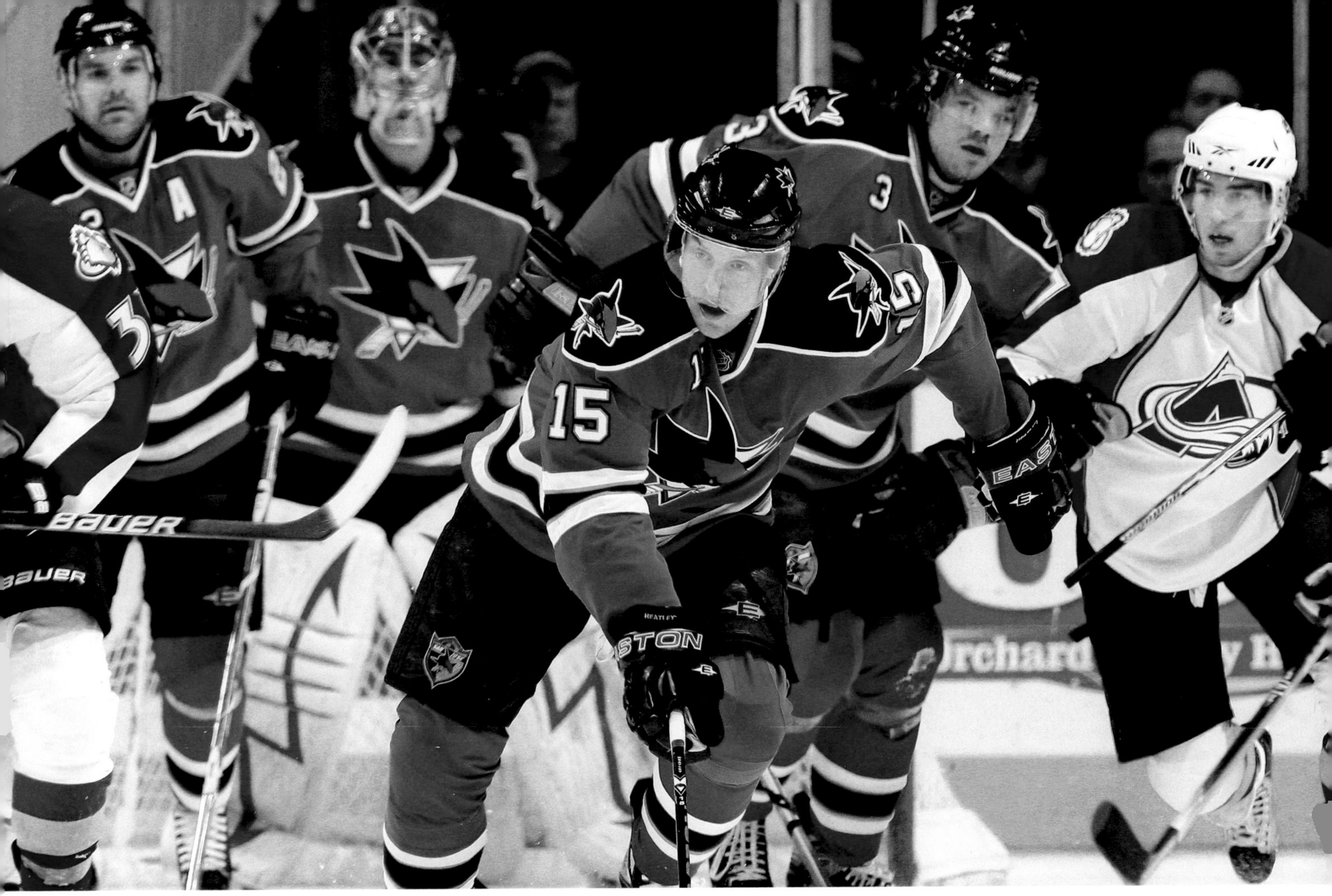

start by scoring three goals in the Sharks' first home game versus Columbus, a 6–3 San Jose victory. He averaged a point a game for the first half of the year as the line became one of the most feared in the NHL. Their excellent performance got all three named to Team Canada for the 2010 Winter Olympics and Heatley played very well with four goals and seven points in seven games. With their gold medal victory, all three Sharks players had won a major championship for the first time, giving San Jose fans hope for the playoffs.

Heatley finished the regular season with 39 goals and 82 points, good for third in team scoring just behind Thornton and Marleau. As soon as the playoffs began, the Sharks were swimming in troubled waters. The Colorado Avalanche were a formidable first round opponent, but the Sharks were able to subdue them in six games. San Jose then handled the Detroit Red Wings in five games and just when it looked like the Sharks were finally going to go all the way to the final, the Chicago Blackhawks burst their hopes in four straight games. Another year, another disappointment.

Heatley had just two goals in 14 playoff games and it was revealed afterwards that he was playing through a groin injury. He did record 11 assists, but he was brought to San Jose to score key goals and his minus-7 rating in the post-season was hardly the stuff of Conn Smythe Trophy winners. As a result, many still question whether Heatley has the right make-up to help a team become a champion.

BY THE NUMBERS
Has 625 points in 589 career games

- Won the Calder Trophy in 2002
- Named to four NHL All-Star games
- Had back-to-back 50-goal seasons from 2005–07
- Was named a First Team NHL All-Star in 2006–07
- Won gold with Canada at the 2010 Olympics

CAREER HIGHLIGHTS

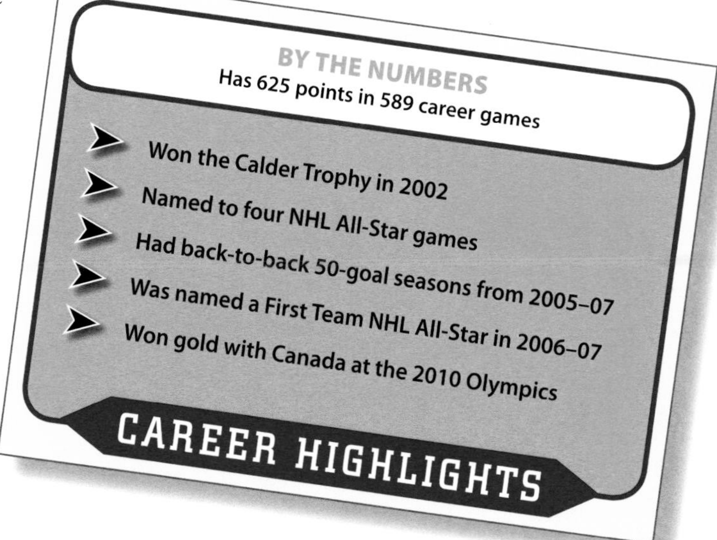

No matter what happens to defenseman Tomas Kaberle in the future, his place in Toronto Maple Leafs history is assured. A member of the Leafs since the 1998–99 season, Kaberle has passed every other defenseman on the club's all-time point list except for Borje Salming. The 2009–10 season saw the smooth-skating blueliner pass the legendary Tim Horton when he recorded his 459th point during a game against Montreal. He ended the season with 49 points to bring his career totals to 402 assists and 482 points. He still has a ways to go to catch Salming, who recorded 768 points as a Maple Leaf. At the age of 31, Kaberle has ample time to reel in the Hall of Fame Swede, but the big question has become whether he'll continue the pursuit in Toronto.

The Maple Leafs have not been a very good team since NHL hockey returned after the 2004–05 lockout, but Kaberle has still managed to be a fairly consistent performer. He had a career-best 67 points in 2005–06 and followed that up with seasons of 58 and 53 points, respectively. His production declined in 2008–09, when he finished with just 31 points in a 57-game, injury-shortened season. He began the 2009–10 campaign superbly and led the team in scoring over the first half of the season. However, after he returned to the Leafs at the conclusion of the Olympics, he was never able to get back to being a point-producer. His assist total was still the highest on the team, but he could not hit the 50-point mark when it looked like he was going to be well beyond that number.

Kaberle's paltry finish to the year was typical of the enigmatic Leaf. At times he can look like one of the best defensemen in the NHL and make long, accurate passes that spring teammates for a clear shot on goal. He can command a power play with a great set of skills that include pinpoint passes and an underrated shot he uses far too infrequently. Other nights, Kaberle is much more invisible, making himself conspicuous only when he commits giveaways in his own end. He has never been a physical player, relying on his sublime skating skills to survive. His ability to spin with the puck at full speed is marvelous to watch and when he joins the attack, Kaberle can be a dangerous player.

Before GM Brian Burke took over the Maple Leafs, a trade to Philadelphia that would have benefited Toronto greatly was arranged by interim GM Cliff Fletcher in 2008, but was turned down by Kaberle. That made the defender part of a group of players who invoked no-trade clauses in their contracts to veto potential deals. All those players are now gone and, as of the end of the 2009–10 campaign, Kaberle was the only one still toiling in Toronto. One of the new players to join the Leafs during recent wide-scale turnover is defenseman Dion Phaneuf, who is expected to take Kaberle's place driving

ICE CHIPS Has 482 career points as a Maple Leaf, which ranks him second on the Leafs all-time list for defensemen, trailing only Hall of Famer Borje Salming (768)

- Has played in four NHL All-Star games
- Recorded a career-high 67 points in 2005–06
- Drafted 204th overall by the Leafs in 1996
- His brother Frantisek is also a professional hockey player

CAREER HIGHLIGHTS

the Leafs' power play. Phaneuf has already been named Toronto's captain and is taking a prominent role in the team's rebuilding process.

Burke has said that he would not ask Kaberle to waive his no-trade restriction, but that has not stopped the chatter about the Czech-born defender's future as a Leaf. His contract, at $4.2 million, is very reasonable and he should be attractive to many teams, yet none have come forth to make Burke a solid offer. Kaberle has repeatedly stated that he would like to stay in Toronto, but that may or may not happen. If a trade cannot be worked out in the off-season when the no-trade clause is not in effect (because the Leafs failed to make the playoffs), it might be a good idea for Burke to offer up a new contract and take advantage of the defenseman's vast experience and hope he can keep up the pace of 40 to 60 points a year. The summer of 2010 began with all kinds of talk that Kaberle would be traded to a team where he would have a better chance to win, while the Leafs could beef up their rather thin crew of scoring forwards by moving one of their most desired assets. While it remained unclear whether or not Kaberle would continue his career with the only NHL club he's ever known, there's no doubt he's capable of contributing valuable blueline minutes to any team that employs him.

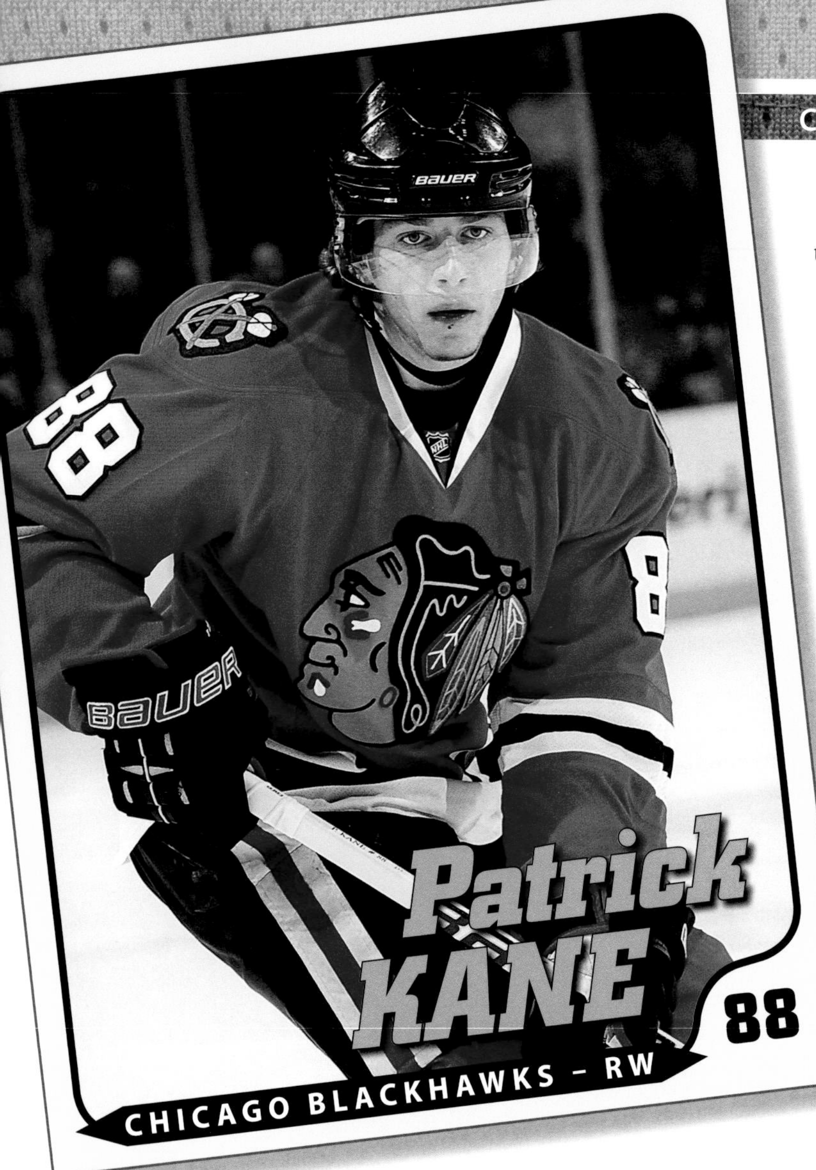

Patrick Kane took a pass from teammate Brian Campbell and steamed past Philadelphia defenseman Kimmo Timonen. The Blackhawks' 5-foot-10, 178-pound winger was at such a sharp angle that a shot on goal did not seem like a viable option. However, top goal-scorers know every attempt on net has a chance to end well. Kane let go a quick snapshot and it went past Flyers netminder Michael Leighton. It should not have gone in and the arena was frozen for a moment as Kane celebrated wildly since he had just scored the Stanley Cup-winning goal. Even his Chicago teammates did not know how to react, but it became evident very quickly that the puck did indeed get past Leighton and rested under the padding that rims the bottom of the net. The Philadelphia crowd was silenced, sad at the thought their team's incredible playoff run was over. Kane and his teammates began flinging their gloves and sticks all over the ice as the Blackhawks captured their first Cup since 1961. For Kane, scoring a goal when it mattered most was not only a great moment of triumph, but also a time of vindication.

A Buffalo native, Kane began his hockey career playing in the house leagues close to his home and would attend Sabres games with his family. Patrick Sr. and Kane's mother, Donna, soon came to realize their son had a great deal of talent and dedicated time and money to developing Patrick's skills. When he was just 14 years old, Kane had become too good for the local teams he was playing on, so the decision was made to get him better competition in the Detroit area. The Kanes made sure to attend as many games as possible, footing the steep cost of lodging and driving in the name of making their homesick son a little more comfortable. The father was able to join his son on many occasions because he ran a jeep dealership and, as the boss, he could set his own work schedule. The business eventually had to be sold as rising gas costs undermined its value. The cost of hockey was spiking, too, but the Kanes always found a way. The U.S. national team development program finally took Kane at the age of 16, just when it looked like it was going to ignore his prodigious talent. He could score at roughly a goal-per-game pace, but was still unknown until he played one year for the London Knights of the OHL.

Kane scored 62 goals and 145 points in just 58 games for the Knights during the 2006–07 season. He added another 31 points in 16 playoff games and then saw the Blackhawks select him with the first choice of the 2007 NHL draft. It was thought Chicago GM Dale Tallon was going to select James van Riemsdyk or maybe Kyle Turris, but Kane was the man the Blackhawks thought had the most offensive potential. Kane was given a three-year entry level deal that assured him $875,000 per year and more if he hit certain bonuses over the last two seasons of the pact. In December 2009, Kane signed a five-year contract extension totaling $31 million. All the sacrifices made by Kane and his family had paid off handsomely.

In his first year with Chicago, Kane took the Calder Trophy as the NHL's best rookie when he scored 21 goals and 72 points in 82 games. The improving Blackhawks saw their young sniper up his goal total to 25 the next year and the team made it to the Western Conference final for the first time since 1995, re-invigorating a long-suffering fan base. Kane's first playoff appearance saw him record 14 points in 16 games, but the Detroit Red Wings were far too experienced for the Blackhawks to challenge seriously.

The 2009–10 season was a special one for Kane. First, he helped Team U.S.A. take the silver medal at the Winter Olympics, then he finished the season atop the Chicago scoring charts with 30 goals and 88 points — matching his sweater number. He continued his strong play in the post-season, but was drawing some heat for not performing in the final. However, his total of four goals and nine points in the last series indicate the maturing Kane was still pretty effective. Kane's overtime Cup-winning tally, while not as beautiful as some others, will keep his name forever prominent when the biggest goals in hockey history are discussed.

BY THE NUMBERS Has had at least 20 goals and 70 points in all three of his NHL seasons

- Won the Calder Trophy in 2008
- Played in the 2009 NHL All-Star Game
- Selected first overall by Chicago in 2007
- Was the CHL Rookie of the Year in 2007

CAREER HIGHLIGHTS

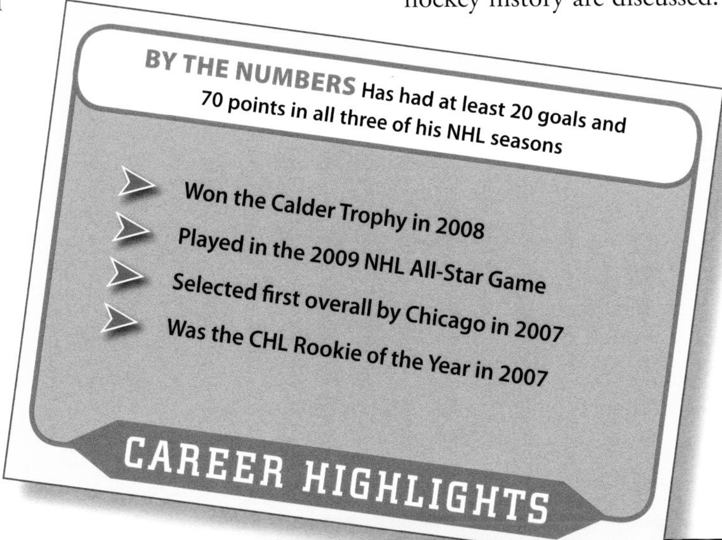

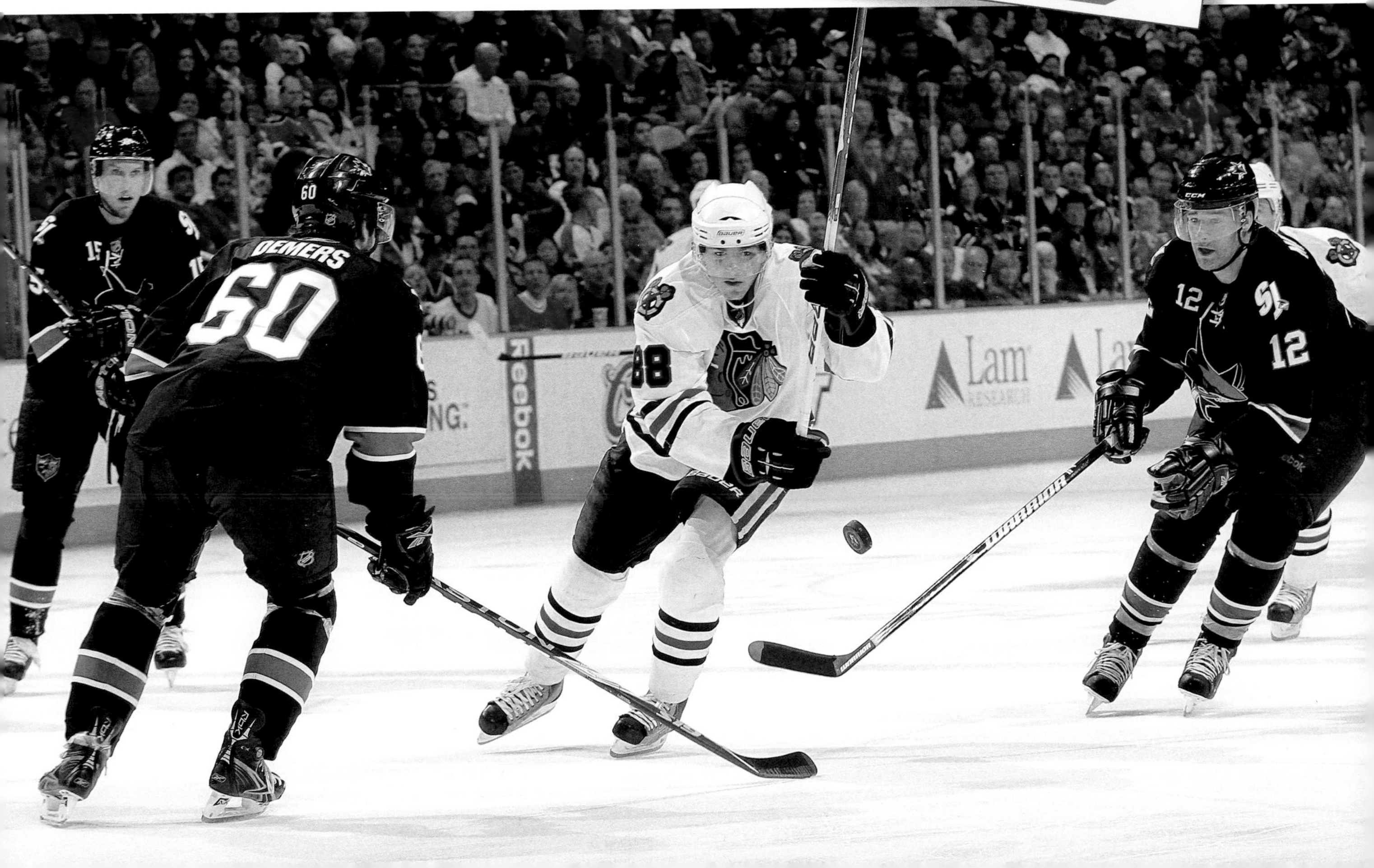

A quick glance at Miikka Kiprusoff's career numbers in the NHL is enough to demonstrate he is no ordinary goalie. For the last five seasons — all in a Calgary uniform — he has played at least 73 games and has never recorded a save percentage under .903, his best mark coming in 2005–06 at .923. Over that same five-year span he has won at least 35 games each season and has had over 40 wins on three occasions. And those numbers don't even include the 2003–04 season when the Finn's brilliant play backstopped Calgary to within one win of the Stanley Cup. Expectations on Kiprusoff are high and it seems like each year the Flames' go-to goalie gets less and less support and more criticism.

When Darryl Sutter took over as coach-GM of the Flames, one of his first moves was to look to his previous team, the San Jose Sharks, for a netminder. He actually asked for Vesa Toskala, but — luckily for Flames fans — was offered Kiprusoff instead in exchange for a second round draft choice in 2005 (the Sharks used the pick on defenseman Marc-Edouard Vlasic). Kiprusoff was a virtual unknown at the time, but he appeared in 38 games for the Flames in 2003–04 and won 24 times to gain some positive reviews. The Flames were giant-killers in the 2004 post-season with wins over Vancouver, Detroit and San Jose to make it to the final, before Tampa Bay edged them out in seven grueling games despite Kiprusoff's heroics. That performance got everyone thinking Kiprusoff could carry the Flames on his back every year, but that was very unrealistic and Calgary has not won a playoff round since. In 2009–10 the Flames did not even make the playoffs and Kiprusoff couldn't escape shouldering some of the ample blame.

Once the season ended, many of the Calgary players, including captain Jarome Iginla, believed Kiprusoff had played well enough to earn a second Vezina Trophy as the NHL's best goaltender, an award he won in 2006 along with being named a First Team All-Star. Night after night, 'Kipper' did his best to keep the Flames in the game, but a lack of offense was their ultimate undoing. At least Sutter recognized where his team was deficient and traded for a variety of new players, mostly forwards, but none of the moves worked well enough to get the attack ignited. Kiprusoff will turn 34 in October 2010 and while he's not getting any younger, he should still have some good years left. However, the question needs to be asked if there will be anything left of the 6-foot-1, 185-pounder if the Flames continue to rely so heavily upon him.

Even though Kiprusoff looks worn down by the end of the year, he still manages to keep the Flames competitive. He moves very well across his crease and is very agile, usually making a few highlight-reel saves every season. Kiprusoff can be on his stomach or back and still manage to kick out a leg or get his glove on a puck when it looks all but impossible to do so. He blocks the lower part of the net as well as any butterfly goalie in the NHL, but he is on occasion susceptible to the high shot, especially on the glove side. However, Kiprusoff does not focus on any goals that beat him — good or bad — but rather on getting his team a victory. He can also make the timely save, rarely giving up the goal that breaks his team's back.

One-time Flames coach Mike Keenan said Kiprusoff could get his rest on off days, but that can only work for so long. Calgary either needs to get a competent backup who can spell Kiprusoff for 15 to 20 games a year or at the very least, increase his margin for error by scoring more goals. If that is the case, Kiprusoff may be able to become more effective and stay fresher for the playoffs should the Flames get back there.

BY THE NUMBERS Has had at least 35 wins in each of the past five seasons

- Won the Vezina Trophy in 2006
- Originally drafted 116th overall by San Jose in 1995
- Led the NHL with 46 wins in 2008–09
- Led the NHL in goals-against average (2.07) and shutouts (10) in 2005–06
- Won a bronze medal with Finland at the 2010 Winter Olympics

CAREER HIGHLIGHTS

The Tampa Bay Lightning have always needed Vincent Lecavalier to be something special. From the moment he was drafted and labeled 'hockey's Michael Jordan' by an overzealous Tampa Bay owner, Lecavalier has been the straw that stirs the drink for the Florida-based franchise. The 2009–10 season was supposed to be no different, but at the ripe old age of 29 in the second season of an 11-year, $85 million contract, Lecavalier's performance flopped for the Lightning. A one-time 52-goal scorer and Rocket Richard Trophy-winner in 2006–07 and a vital cog in Tampa Bay's only Stanley Cup victory in 2004, the Lightning captain got off to a horrid start in 2009–10. He scored just one goal in October and finished the campaign with just 24 total, disappointing considering he had scored 30 or more five times in his career. He did post a respectable 70 points and appeared in all 82 Lightning games, which is a great achievement considering he was recovering from shoulder surgery and a chronic wrist problem, but the Lightning missed the playoffs once again, leading to questions about Lecavalier's future in Tampa Bay.

Actually, the questions surrounding Lecavalier's long-term future with the Lightning first arose when the Montreal Canadiens made serious inquiries about the big center's availability. The Habs desperately wanted to bring the Quebec-born star back to his home province and give Montreal fans the French-Canadian hero they have lacked since Patrick Roy left town. A deal could not be worked out and Lecavalier now has the benefit of a no-trade clause in his contract. Perhaps all the talk affected Lecavalier and his performance suffered as a result. The 90- to 100-point season the Lightning were hoping to see from their best player never materialized. Tampa Bay lurked around a playoff spot, but in the end finished with just 34 wins, eight points out of the final post-season position. If that was not enough, second-year center Steven Stamkos became the team's leading scorer (95 points, including 51 goals) and solidified his place as the Lightning's best player as well — a title once the sole domain of Lecavalier.

Stamkos will need a new contract and a huge raise after the 2010–11 season and the Lightning may have to prepare for his contract by moving Lecavalier's similarly massive deal. It will be hard to find another team willing to take on such obligations, but Lecavalier's positives should still prove enticing. The 6-foot-4, 223-pound center has the size to compete effectively and his on-ice vision is still great. His playmaking skills are as good as any in the league and with the right linemates he is good for 40 to 50 assists. If that were not enough, Lecavalier is a competitive player with a great wrist shot who does not hesitate to get physical if necessary. He has paid good attention to strength and conditioning issues (something he ignored in the past) and is a much better defensive player than when he first entered the NHL.

If Lecavalier's on-ice talent is not enough, consider that his off-ice behavior was rewarded with the King Clancy Memorial Trophy in 2008 for best exemplifying leadership qualities both on and off the ice. He has also made a noteworthy humanitarian contribution in his community. He was the first Tampa Bay player to win the Clancy after, among other things, donating $3 million to a local hospital. Such actions solidified Lecavalier's hero status to all Lightning fans. It's never easy to trade a legend, but that might be just what the Lightning's new owner, Jeff Vinik, and GM Steve Yzerman have to consider. A big-market locale might be just the landing place for Lecavalier should the Lightning — and Lecavalier himself — decide he would be better off moving on.

Whatever Lecavalier's future holds, he has shown himself to be a classy individual, something no one expects to change, no matter where he plays.

BY THE NUMBERS

Has scored at least 20 goals in 10 straight seasons

- Scored a career-high and led the NHL with 52 goals in 2006–07
- Received the King Clancy Trophy for humanitarian efforts in 2008
- MVP of the 2004 World Cup with Team Canada
- Has played in four NHL All-Star games

CAREER HIGHLIGHTS

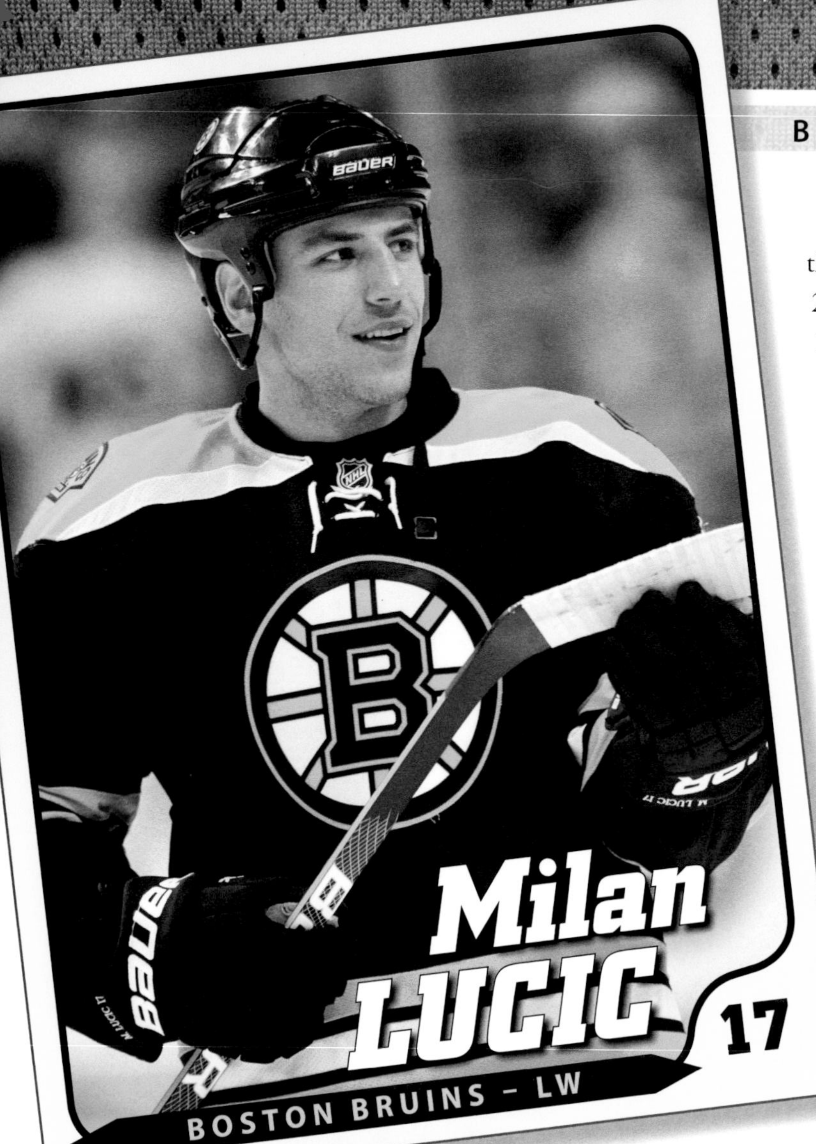

Boston Bruins winger Milan Lucic has a very noticeable, thick build at 6-foot-4, 220 pounds, but it's a good thing he also has thick skin. Born in Vancouver on June 7, 1988, Lucic was set to quit hockey when the Western Hockey League decided he was not worth drafting in 2003. Cut at rookie camp by a Jr. A team, he ended up playing Jr. B hockey for a while, but then moved up to play for the Coquitlam Express of the British Columbia Hockey League in 2004–05. He scored just nine times in 50 games, but registered 100 penalty minutes as a 16-year-old, which got him promoted to the WHL's Vancouver Giants the following season. He scored just nine goals and 19 points in 62 games and recorded 149 penalty minutes as a WHL rookie, but the Bruins liked what they saw in the developing winger and took him 50th overall in the 2006 NHL draft. Lucic returned to Vancouver for the 2006–07 season and scored 30 goals and 68 points in 70 games to lead the team in scoring. He then added 19 playoff points as the Giants marched to the Memorial Cup championship; Lucic was named MVP of the tournament. The Bruins were not really expecting Lucic to stick with them as a 19-year-old the next season, but his NHL-ready body gave him a leg up; he scored eight goals and 27 points, and added 89 penalty minutes in 77 contests.

Lucic's style of play is reminiscent of the 'Big, Bad Bruins' of the 1970s. He is more likely to run over someone or put them into the first few rows than score a goal, but he does have a soft pair of hands, scoring 17 times as an NHL sophomore. He will not hesitate to fight and will defend a teammate when necessary. It has been suggested that Lucic reminds Bruins fans of Cam Neely and Terry O'Reilly from Boston's glorious past, but Lucic has a long way to go if he is to match the achievements of those two superb wingers. He can be a mean, driven player, but at times he finds himself out of position after going out of his way to lay a crushing bodycheck. Lucic is most effective when he forechecks smartly and causes jumpy defenders — leery of the big, bruising winger bearing down on them — to turn the puck over. He does not have the speed to cause havoc with his skating, but he does handle the puck well enough to go to the net with some effectiveness. His shot is better than average, but he must use it more to be a feared goal scorer. He was a surprise invitee to Team Canada's Olympic orientation camp in the summer of 2009.

Along with his physical play, Lucic tends to thrive in big-game situations and relishes the chance to do well when it counts most. He does so in part because he is a responsible defensive player, which puts him in a position to be on the ice at the key moments of a game. In his past 23 post-season games, Lucic has recorded eight goals and 18 points. He had his best playoff —

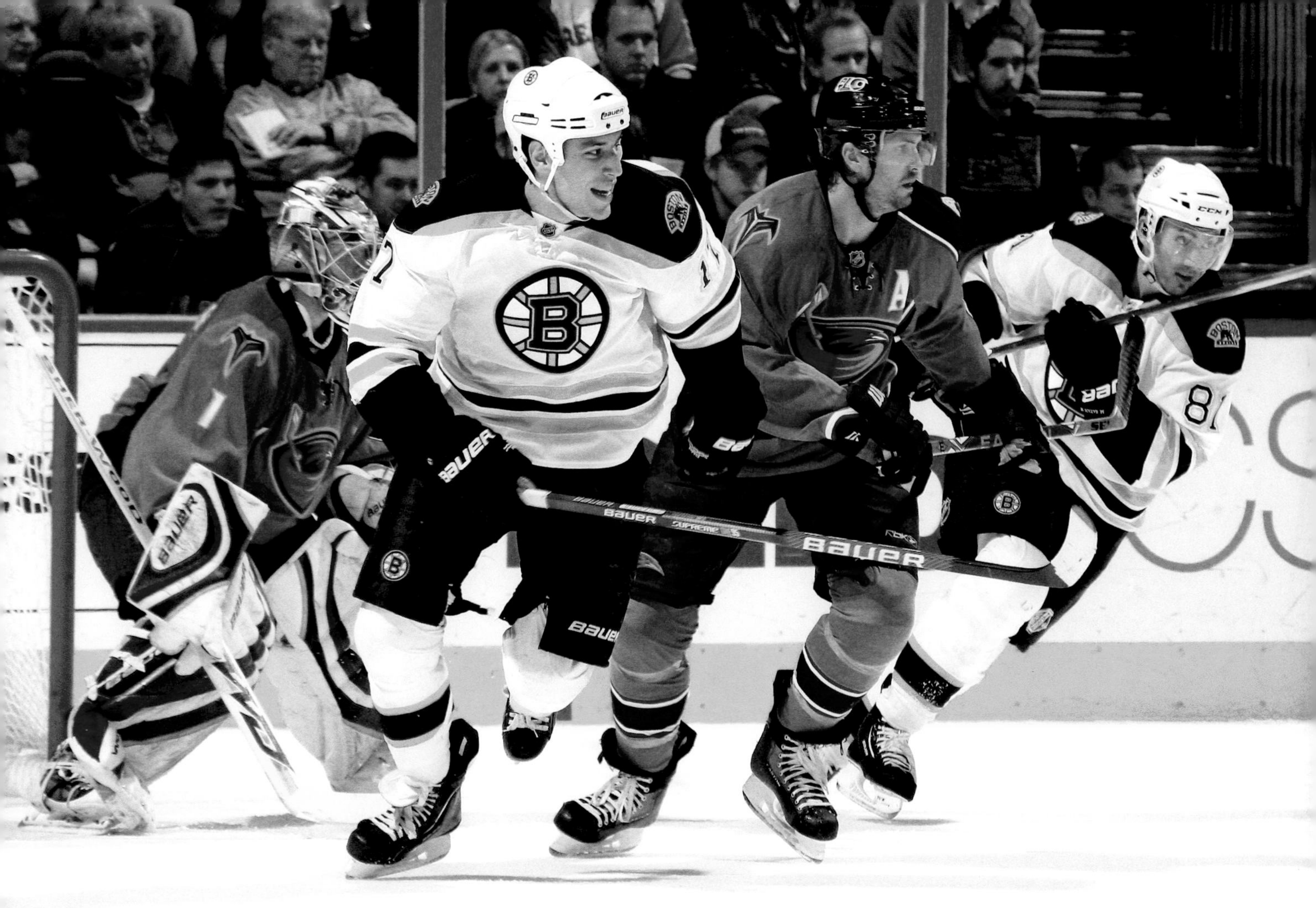

in terms of points-per-game average — in 2009 when the Bruins knocked off Montreal before losing a close conference semifinal in seven games to Carolina (the last game between the Bruins and Hurricanes was 3–2; Lucic scored the tying goal for Boston in the third period). He had five goals and nine points in 13 games during the 2010 post-season, but the Bruins lost to Philadelphia in the second round.

Lucic's style of play creates many enemies, none bigger than veteran defenseman Mike Komisarek who first started jousting with the Bruins winger when he was with Montreal. Lucic got the better of the Habs blueliner in a fight that eventually led to shoulder surgery for Komisarek. The Bruins strong man played to the Boston crowd as he celebrated his obvious win. Komisarek signed with Toronto as a free agent in the summer of 2009, but it was Maple Leafs tough guy Colton Orr who evened the score by beating Lucic severely during a fight in Boston. Lucic was criticized for calling in the linesmen when Orr was clearly winning. If a player fights often enough he will get beaten at some point — a lesson well learned by Lucic who must play it smarter and be effective night in and night out.

BY THE NUMBERS

Has 20 points in 30 career playoff games

- Was sixth in the NHL with 262 hits in 2008–09
- MVP of the Memorial Cup in 2007
- Had a career-high 17 goals and 42 points in 2008–09
- Selected 50th overall by Boston in 2006

CAREER HIGHLIGHTS

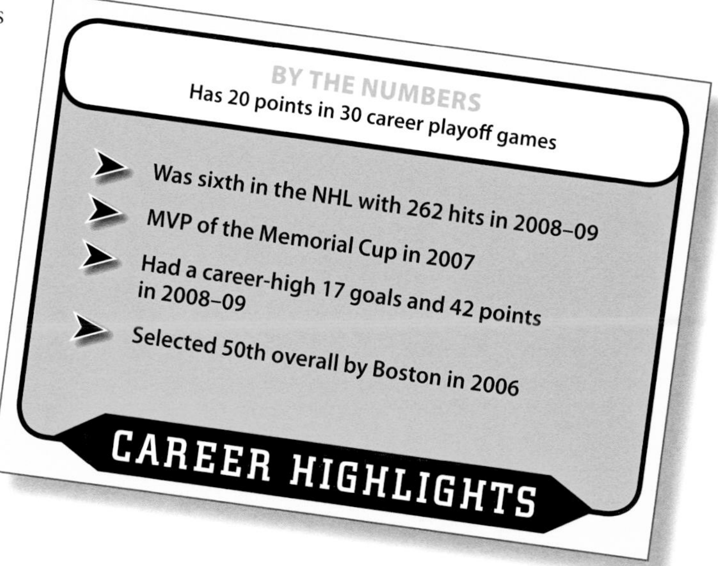

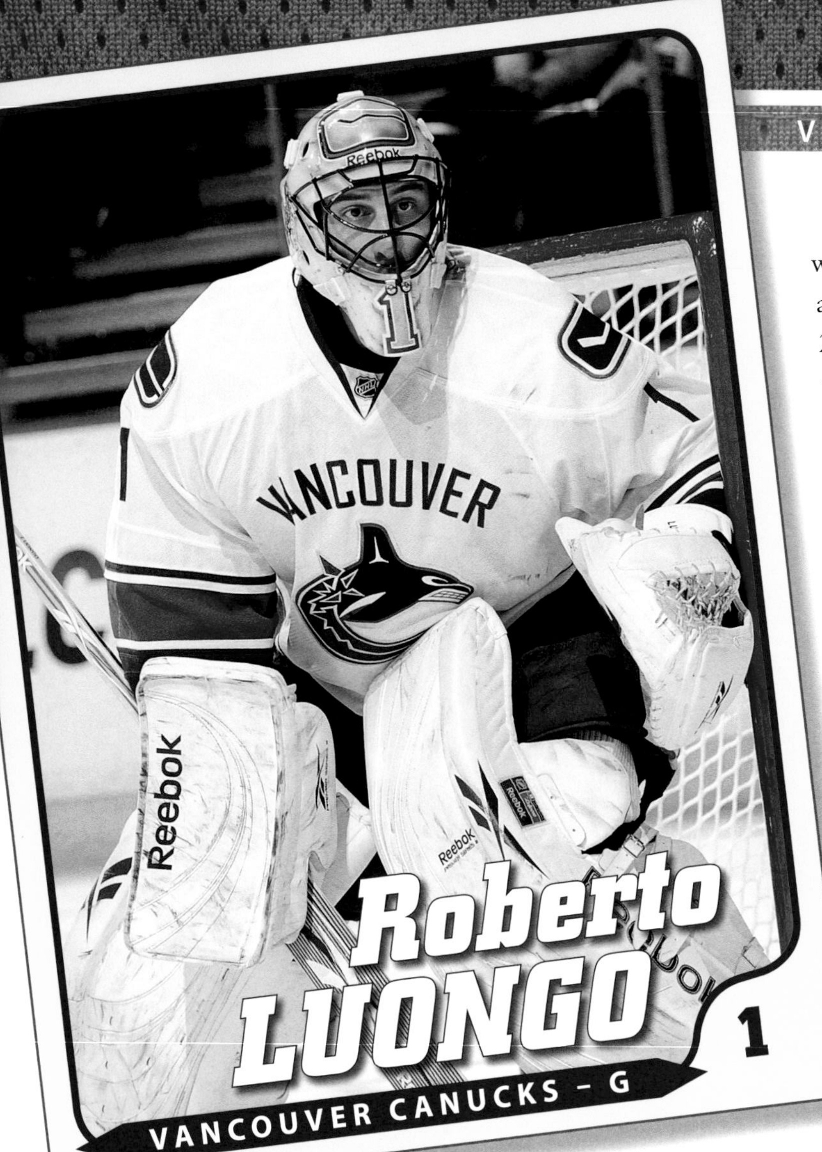

When the Vancouver Canucks named goaltender Roberto Luongo team captain in September of 2008, it surprised many people. It had been 60 years since a goalie — Bill Durnan of the Montreal Canadiens — last held that distinction with his team and the NHL has a rule that prohibits puckstoppers from wearing the 'C' on their sweater. In many ways, Luongo would be the captain in name only, limited to an off-ice leadership role. But the Canucks said they wanted someone who showed a good example to his teammates with a high work ethic and who had the respect of everyone in the dressing room. Vancouver might also have used the captaincy as a way to keep Luongo interested in staying with the Canucks since his contract was expiring after the 2009–10 season. If that was the case, the ploy worked because Luongo signed a 12-year extension with the team in October of 2009. For a while, everything seemed to work pretty well as Luongo loved being captain and the Canucks excelled during the regular season with 45 wins and 100 points in 2008–09 and 49 wins in 2009–10 with 103 points. However, consecutive playoff failures have caused questions surrounding his captaincy to be raised again. It's tough enough playing the lonely, pressure-packed position of goaltender without having to answer for the team's failures as captain. Is it a good idea to have a team captain acknowledge it was his fault the squad lost because he let in bad goals?

The Canucks were thrilled when they stole Luongo away from the Florida Panthers for aging left winger Todd Bertuzzi, marginal defenseman Bryan Allen plus backup netminder Alex Auld in a June 2006 trade. Luongo had been very good during his time as a Panther, but had never taken the team to the playoffs. Since his arrival in Vancouver, Luongo has won 47, 35, 33 and 40 games in his four seasons with the Canucks and the team has made the playoffs three times. Drafted fourth overall by the Islanders in 1997, Luongo has been considered a top goalie in the league for a number of years now. Benefiting from ample size at 6-foot-3 and 217 pounds, Luongo is at his best when he uses his chest to cover a large portion of the net. Even though he uses the butterfly technique, Luongo works very hard to cut down the angles and give the shooter nothing to see. He has long arms and legs and uses both effectively to block many drives, especially down low. His aggressive nature is very noticeable when he is doing well, but it is just as plain that he sits a little too far back in his net when he is beaten with a shot he might have stopped.

The Canucks have come to rely on Luongo almost exclusively for all their netminding needs, with their backup being almost irrelevant unless there is an injury. He set a club record with nine shutouts in 2008–09 and

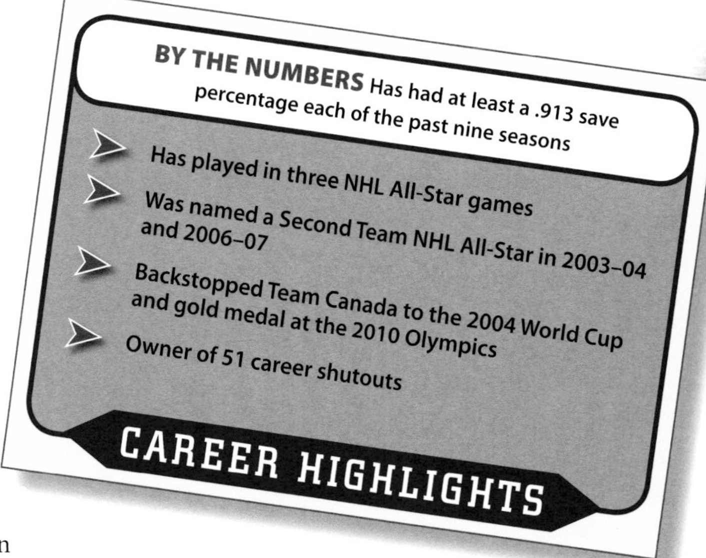

BY THE NUMBERS Has had at least a .913 save percentage each of the past nine seasons

- Has played in three NHL All-Star games
- Was named a Second Team NHL All-Star in 2003–04 and 2006–07
- Backstopped Team Canada to the 2004 World Cup and gold medal at the 2010 Olympics
- Owner of 51 career shutouts

CAREER HIGHLIGHTS

has twice been named to the NHL's Second All-Star Team. The biggest moment of his career came when he replaced Martin Brodeur as Team Canada's goalie partway through the 2010 Olympics and went 5–0 as the starter, leading his team to gold. Luongo did not have to steal the show, but was good enough to stymie the opposition in key moments to get Canada all the important wins. The tournament was played before the same Vancouver fans who are used to Luongo's heroics when the hometown Canucks are rolling and they showed their appreciation for his Team Canada efforts with loud cheers.

When he returned to NHL play after the Olympics, Luongo did not seem like his usual self. The Canucks did get past Los Angeles in the first round of the playoffs, with Luongo clearly better than counterpart Jonathan Quick in the Kings net. But the Chicago Blackhawks bounced Vancouver in Round 2 for the second consecutive year and Luongo looked shaky, as he had the previous year.

Luongo has trouble dealing with big players who clog his crease, even though he has the size to deal with large opponents. In fairness to Luongo, Vancouver has never had much in the way of stars on the blueline. The team took strides to upgrade the defense corps in the summer of 2010, something that could have a very positive effect on the club and its goalie.

Evgeni Malkin made an instant impact in the NHL. Drafted second overall in 2004, the 6-foot-3, 195-pound Russian center has produced at more than a point-a-game pace since entering the league in 2006–07, won three major awards and been part of a Stanley Cup championship. Still just 24 years old, Malkin has enough talent to be the best player in hockey, but must focus on bringing his best game every time out. The 2010 playoffs showed he can get worn down and lose his effectiveness. It was just as evident that the Pittsburgh Penguins need him to be at the top of his game if they want to recapture their recent glory.

Malkin's importance to his team's success was punctuated when the Pens won just two of seven games he missed with a shoulder injury early in 2009–10. Upon his return, Malkin immediately helped the Penguins defeat Boston 6–5 in overtime with three assists. The previously stagnant Sidney Crosby came alive with a goal and two assists as well. Many of the Pittsburgh players said their team needed the man they affectionately call 'Geno' back and producing. When Crosby was out for 29 games with an ankle sprain during the 2007–08 season, it was Malkin who picked up the team and carried them with 20 goals and 46 points during that period of time. The Penguins went 16–9–4 under Malkin's leadership and were also undefeated over a five-game stretch when Crosby was out during the 2008–09 campaign. Team captain Crosby was terrific in the '08 playoffs, when the Penguins lost to Detroit in the Cup final. But it was Malkin who won the Conn Smythe Trophy with a 36-point performance in the 2009 post-season when the Cup returned to Pittsburgh. Both players are vital to the Penguins' attack and for as much as Malkin has accomplished in his relatively brief NHL career, there is little doubt Crosby is the man who stirs the drink in Pittsburgh. Malkin, however, might be the league's best wingman — even when he's playing center.

Even if he is No. 2 in Pittsburgh, Malkin has all the physical tools to take a team and make it a winner on his own, as his awards indicate. He recorded 33 goals and 85 points in 78 games as a rookie to take home the Calder Trophy in 2007 and two years later claimed the Art Ross Trophy when he led the league with 113 points in 82 games. He became the first player to win the Art Ross and Conn Smythe Trophies since Mario Lemieux produced the same results in 1992. Unlike Crosby, Malkin has yet to win the Hart Trophy as the league MVP, but that might be in his immediate future.

Malkin is a player who competes hard most nights and is an explosive skater when he is on his game. He has a wicked shot that he can unleash at any point and is not afraid to challenge defensemen with a variety of highly skilled moves. Malkin can score spectacular goals and has no trouble driving to the net with the puck. He is not a fighter by any means, but is very willing to use his body to create space for himself and will battle opponents physically. Malkin is one of the best players in the league on the power play, especially when he and Crosby have found their rhythm together.

Injuries held Malkin to just 67 games in 2009–10, but he still managed to record 28 goals and 77 points, and the Penguins were again one of the better teams in the NHL with 47 wins and 101 points. Malkin contributed 11 points in 13 playoff games, but never came close to matching his MVP performance from a year earlier as the Pens' season ended earlier than they hoped for with a second round loss to the Montreal Canadiens.

For $8.7 million a season, the Penguins need to see Malkin raise his intensity level and team with Crosby to perform as the best 1-2 punch in hockey.

BY THE NUMBERS

Has 381 points in 309 career games

- Put up back-to-back 100-point seasons in 2007–08 and 2008–09
- Led the NHL with 113 points in 2008–09
- Won the Calder Trophy in 2006–07
- Won the Conn Smythe Trophy by scoring 36 points in 24 games in the 2009 playoffs
- Named a First Team NHL All-Star twice

CAREER HIGHLIGHTS

It seemed like such an innocent play, but it cost the Montreal Canadiens their best defenseman for much of the 2009–10 season. After just 17:42 of play at the Air Canada Centre in the very first game of the year versus Toronto, Montreal goalie Carey Price collided with blueliner Andrei Markov as they were trying to kill off a penalty. Somehow Price's skate blade sliced a tendon in Markov's left foot, forcing the star defender to hobble off the ice. After the game was over, the Habs were shocked to learn the injury would keep Markov out for an estimated four months since surgery was required to reattach the tendon. Most of the hockey world thought Markov's absence would spell the end of any hope the Canadiens had of making the playoffs.

Not only did the Habs lose a great player on the ice, they lost one of their team leaders. Montreal had let go of many respected veterans in the off-season and was looking to players like Markov to assume new roles. New coach Jacques Martin had designated Markov as an alternate captain before the season began and though Montreal did not anoint a captain, everyone knew the Russian defenseman was the Habs' true leader. Most of Markov's teammates believe he would be an excellent choice for the captaincy, especially at this point in his career when he is now more comfortable speaking English. The 31-year-old defender is not one to promote himself, but he seems much more comfortable with the idea of assuming the team captaincy, which has a long and rich tradition in the hockey-mad city of Montreal. There were reports later in the season that Markov had taken Price to task when he felt the young goalie wasn't concentrating enough on his job and although Markov denied the incident took place, it was clear he was starting to play a more prominent role within the Canadiens' dressing room.

Markov's strength is that he can play a very efficient two-way game. He finished the 2008–09 season with 12 goals and 64 points in 78 games, just one point behind the team's leading scorer, Alex Kovalev. He averages around 24 minutes per game for a team that is rather thin in talent on the blueline. He has great on-ice vision and his ability to make long or short passes is what separates him from other defensemen in the NHL. He is very good in even-strength situations in his own end and is well above average when he commands the Canadiens' power play. The 6-foot, 209-pound Markov has a knack for sneaking in from the point and letting go a blast that few goalies can handle. Having a defenseman who can move the puck quickly and efficiently is essential to the success of any team in the NHL today and Markov is a prime example of how such players are important to their respective clubs.

Markov worked extremely hard to rehabilitate his injury and returned to the Canadiens lineup much

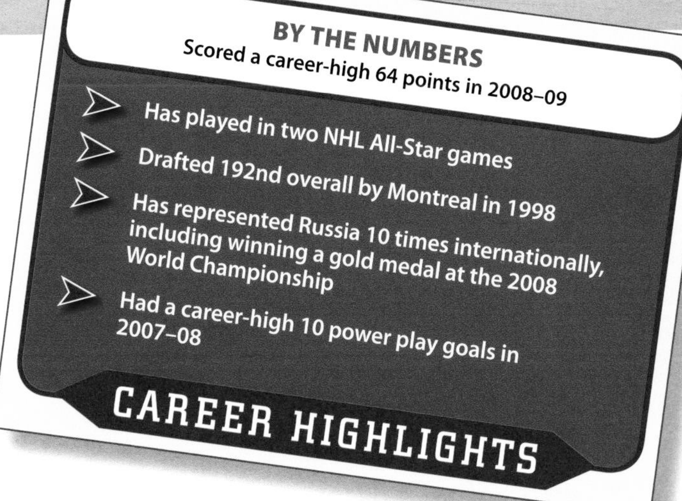
CAREER HIGHLIGHTS

BY THE NUMBERS
Scored a career-high 64 points in 2008–09

- Has played in two NHL All-Star games
- Drafted 192nd overall by Montreal in 1998
- Has represented Russia 10 times internationally, including winning a gold medal at the 2008 World Championship
- Had a career-high 10 power play goals in 2007–08

earlier than expected, making a great impact in his first game back against the New York Islanders less than three months after he sustained the cut. Montreal scored three power play goals in their 3–0 win over the Islanders with Markov popping two of them. It took Markov only 7:44 to score his first goal by finding the puck in a scramble in front of the New York goal. His second tally was a Markov classic as he fired a laser beam from the top of the face-off circle. Martin commented on how good it was to have a top player back on the ice. It had been 35 games since Markov had last played, but he stepped in without missing a beat. Markov played 45 games in 2009–10 and managed six goals and 34 points. The Habs played better with him in the lineup and snared the last playoff spot in the Eastern Conference with a 39–33–10 record, good for 88 points. It is highly unlikely they would have been in such a position if Markov had not returned so soon.

Markov was a big part of Montreal's first round upset of the Washington Capitals in the 2010 playoffs, but another serious ailment — this time a knee injury — sustained in Game 1 of Montreal's second round series versus Pittsburgh knocked him out of the season for good. Another operation followed, but if Markov's quick healing powers kick in again, he won't miss much of the 2010–11 campaign. Markov could use some help on the blueline and adding defenseman P.K. Subban is a step in the right direction for a team in need of a youthful injection.

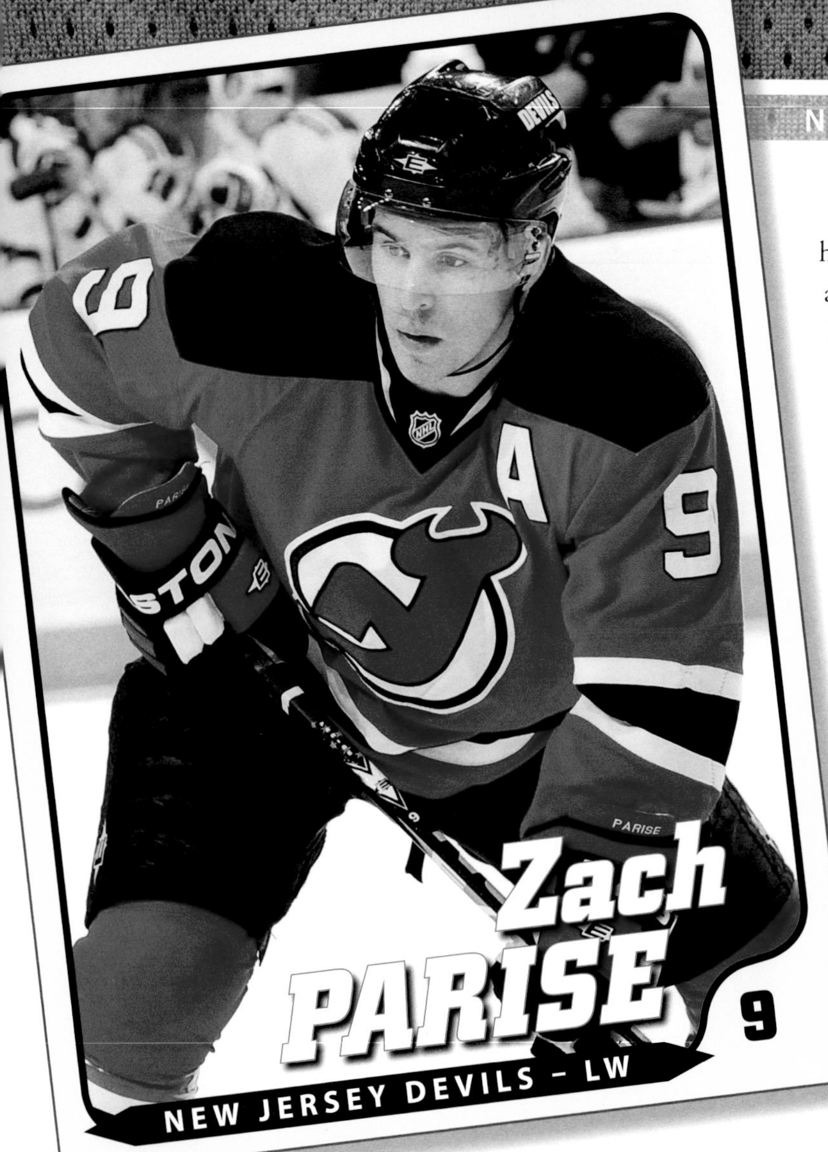

Even though Zach Parise's father Jean-Paul played in the National Hockey League, Parise-the-younger has had nothing handed to him and works very hard to become a better player every season. Zach was skating as early as the age of two, but actually was not good at hockey. He was cut from a squirt team he tried out for and thought he might excel at other sports such as baseball, golf or tennis. But he could not resist the frozen ponds in his native state of Minnesota (J-P was a North Stars player for parts of nine seasons) and stayed with the game that interested him the most. He attended Shattuck-St. Mary's prep school in Fairbault, Minnesota, whose hockey program is famous for alumni such as Parise, Sidney Crosby, Jonathan Toews and Ryan Malone. In two seasons at Shattuck, he recorded 146 goals and 340 points in 125 games and earned a scholarship to the University of North Dakota. He scored 49 times in 76 college games, but it was his first season at North Dakota scoring 61 points in 39 games that put him into a position to be a first round draft choice.

The New Jersey Devils have a habit of drafting kids out of U.S. colleges and the team's scouts rarely make first round mistakes. When Parise was still available when the Devils selected 17th overall in the 2003 NHL draft, they were delighted to take the left winger with the great pedigree. The Devils are also very smart about not rushing their players into the NHL; they sent Parise back to school for one more year before assigning him to the Albany River Rats of the American Hockey League. In 73 games with the Rats in 2004–05, Parise picked up 58 points, scoring 18 times and adding 40 assists. When play resumed following the NHL lockout, Parise made the Devils and had a decent rookie year with 14 goals and 32 points in 81 games. Each year since then Parise has improved his overall play and his goal totals went from 14 as a rookie to 31, 32, 45 and 38 in subsequent seasons. His dedication to hard work in practice has really paid off (for example, he has a teammate fire shots from the point while Parise stands in front of the net trying to tip them in, but only after he has skated out from the corner of the rink to re-create game conditions) and he knows where to go to score goals.

Parise's father had a much more stocky build, good for digging pucks out of the corner and playing a robust game with a bit of a fiery temper. But the younger Parise is only 190 pounds and does not look that heavy with his 5-foot-11 body. His skill set was considered more than adequate to be a good NHL player, but there were those who believed his body would not be strong enough to handle the actions of hard-edged defenders once they keyed on him. Parise has proven he can deal with the toughest defensemen in the league and still thrive. He has a special knack for spinning and churning his body in whatever way necessary when he gets in front of the net. A great number of Parise's goals are scored in close, often in the crease area where others fear to tread. He has a deft touch and is also deceptively fast when he gets a chance to break down the wing. His performance in 2008–09 saw him score 45 times and notch a career-high 91 points, good for fifth in league scoring and a spot on the Second All-Star Team. Parise does not seem to have inherited his father's sometimes explosive nature and has never recorded more than 32 penalty minutes in a season.

His cool on-ice demeanor belies the fact that Parise is ultra-competitive and driven to succeed. He seems to take it personally when the Devils lose (as they did to Philadelphia during the 2010 playoffs) and did his best to get the United States the gold medal at the 2010 Winter Olympics. His dramatic last-minute goal to tie the gold medal game against Canada was typical of his never-say-die attitude. When the Canadians won the game in overtime, it was clear on television that no American player was more upset than Parise during the post-game ceremonies, despite being handed the silver medal.

Parise is only going to get better in the future and may yet become the Devils' first-ever 50-goal scorer.

ICE CHIPS Parise led the Americans to their first-ever gold medal in the World Junior Championship in 2004 when he had 11 points. Parise was also named the Most Valuable Player in the tournament

- Ranked third in the NHL with a career-high 45 goals in 2008–09
- Named a Second Team All-Star in 2009
- Has scored at least 30 goals in each of the past four seasons
- Has led the Devils in scoring the past three seasons

CAREER HIGHLIGHTS

When Brent Seabrook was a youngster, the native of Richmond, B.C., would attend Vancouver Canuck games. After going to one playoff contest, he told his father on the way home he would one day play in that building. He was a junior player at the time, suiting up as a defenseman for the Lethbridge Hurricanes of the Western Hockey League. But the Canucks never drafted Seabrook, who was instead selected by the Chicago Blackhawks 14th overall at the 2003 NHL draft. If Seabrook was disappointed at not being taken by his hometown team, he sure didn't show it. In 2009 and 2010, Chicago ended the Canucks' playoff hopes and Seabrook celebrated a Stanley Cup win in '10, something Vancouver has yet to achieve.

Seabrook played minor hockey for the Pacific Vipers, a team that also featured future Chicago teammates Troy Brouwer, Colin Fraser and Andrew Ladd. When he was 15, Seabrook played for the Delta Ice Hawks scoring 42 points in 54 games during the 2000–01 season. He then joined Lethbridge for the next three seasons and his all-around game produced 176 points in 264 career contests as a Hurricane, which impressed many NHL scouts. His career in Lethbridge also had Seabrook play alongside Kris Versteeg, another future teammate in Chicago. He was captain of the Hurricanes and they made it to the WHL final under his leadership before losing to the Calgary Hitmen. Seabrook played for the gold medal-winning Canadian 'dream team' at the 2005 World Junior Championship during the NHL lockout. After a very brief time with Norfolk of the American Hockey League, Seabrook made the Blackhawks in his first attempt when he was just 20 years of age. He has never looked back.

Like many of his young Blackhawk teammates, Seabrook has steadily improved since his rookie year, which saw him score five goals and add 27 assists in 69 games during the 2005–06 campaign. Over the next four seasons, the sturdy 6-foot-3, 220-pounder has averaged just below 30 points a season, which is not a high number, but he is the perfect complement to defensive partner Duncan Keith who likes to go more on the attack. Seabrook may not be a flashy attacker like Keith, but he does have a heavy, accurate shot. He provides Chicago with stability on the back end and although he is not overly aggressive, woe to any player who gets hit by Seabrook. He is very strong on his skates and even though he is not extremely fast, opposition forwards still have a difficult time getting by him.

One of Seabrook's main goals in the 2009–10 season was to be named to the Canadian Olympic team. The Games were going to be played in Vancouver and Seabrook wanted very much to be on the team. He was thrilled to receive a phone call from associate manager

Kevin Lowe telling him he had indeed been selected, along with his buddy Keith. He had to repeat every word Lowe said just to be sure he had heard everything correctly. Seabrook was by no means a star at the Olympics, recording one assist in a mostly supporting role, but it was his first major victory as a professional and winning gold in Vancouver made it extra special for the rugged blueliner.

Chicago finished the 2009–10 regular season with a 52–22–8 record, good for 112 points and second place in the overall Western Conference standings. The playoffs proved to be a shining moment for Seabrook, who saw a ton of ice time with Keith, making the pair the most important and reliable defensemen on the Blackhawks. The dynamic duo is the best shutdown pair in the NHL, but they can also score. Seabrook had four goals and 11 points in 22 post-season games, while posting a plus-8 mark.

Provided they can both be retained under the salary cap, Keith and Seabrook will provide leadership on the blueline in Chicago for years to come. Many will consider Keith the more talented of the two, but Seabrook's style of game allowed Blackhawks coach Joel Quenneville to run his team in the manner that saw them become Stanley Cup champions.

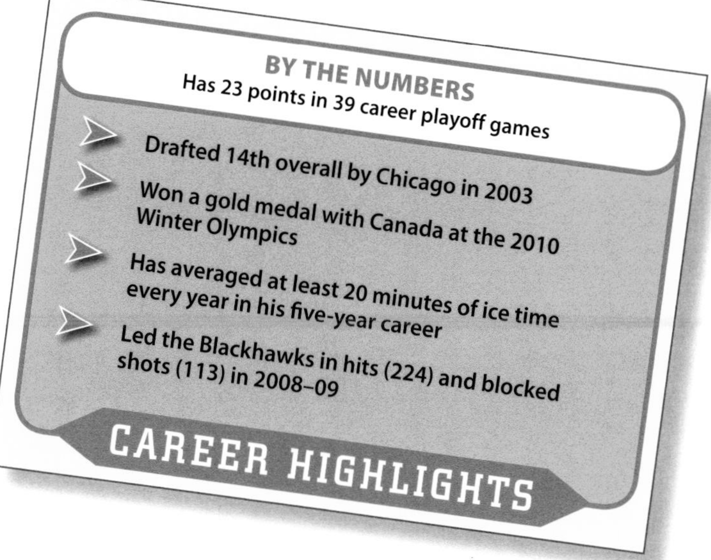
BY THE NUMBERS
Has 23 points in 39 career playoff games

- Drafted 14th overall by Chicago in 2003
- Won a gold medal with Canada at the 2010 Winter Olympics
- Has averaged at least 20 minutes of ice time every year in his five-year career
- Led the Blackhawks in hits (224) and blocked shots (113) in 2008–09

CAREER HIGHLIGHTS

If there is one play that epitomizes the frustration the Ottawa Senators and their fans have with the play of star center Jason Spezza, it occurred at the hands of Sidney Crosby. During Game 2 of the Ottawa-Pittsburgh 2010 opening round playoff series, the Penguins superstar put on a puck-control clinic at Spezza's expense. Chased along the endboards by Spezza, Crosby was able to control the puck with one hand and fend off the larger Senator with the other, while wheeling around the Ottawa goal. Crosby was even able to double back without letting Spezza get body position on him. At one point the Penguins superstar fell to his knees, but still managed to get the puck back to the blueline for a point shot that ended up in the Senators' net for the game-winner. Losing a battle to the best player in the game is nothing to be ashamed of, but that lets Spezza off the hook rather easily. On too many occasions the 6-foot-3, 215-pounder is too easy to play against in his own end and does not show enough interest in getting the puck out himself. He does not relish using his good size to initiate body contact and has a tendency to over-handle the puck, which causes turnovers. Like it or not, the Senators have become used to their No. 1 center playing in such a way. And with a $7 million cap hit until 2015, there is little chance he will leave Ottawa.

Despite his shortcomings, nobody denies that Spezza has produced at every level of hockey. It started when he was 14 playing for the minor hockey Toronto Marlboros; he recorded 53 goals and 114 points in just 54 games. His impressive performance meant Spezza was able to play major junior a year earlier than normal and he produced more than a point per game his first two Ontario Hockey League seasons. Spezza played in Brampton as a 15-year-old and began his second OHL season in his hometown of Mississauga, but was traded twice during his junior career, unusual for such a skilled player who notched 131 goals and 353 points in 228 OHL games. The Senators stepped up to take Spezza second overall at the 2001 NHL draft with a selection they had acquired from the New York Islanders for Alexei Yashin, also a one-time Ottawa center who never lived up to expectations. Spezza split his first year as a pro between Ottawa and Binghamton in the American Hockey League, playing well in each league. His most impressive performance early on in his career came during the NHL lockout in 2004–05 when he was named the AHL's most valuable player with a league-leading 117 points. When the NHL resumed play in 2005–06, Spezza was tagged as a major cog in the Senators' future.

For most of his time in Ottawa, Spezza has put up good numbers, including three 30-plus goal seasons and three seasons of 87 or more points, but he has also had trouble staying healthy. In the 2007 playoffs, Spezza tied

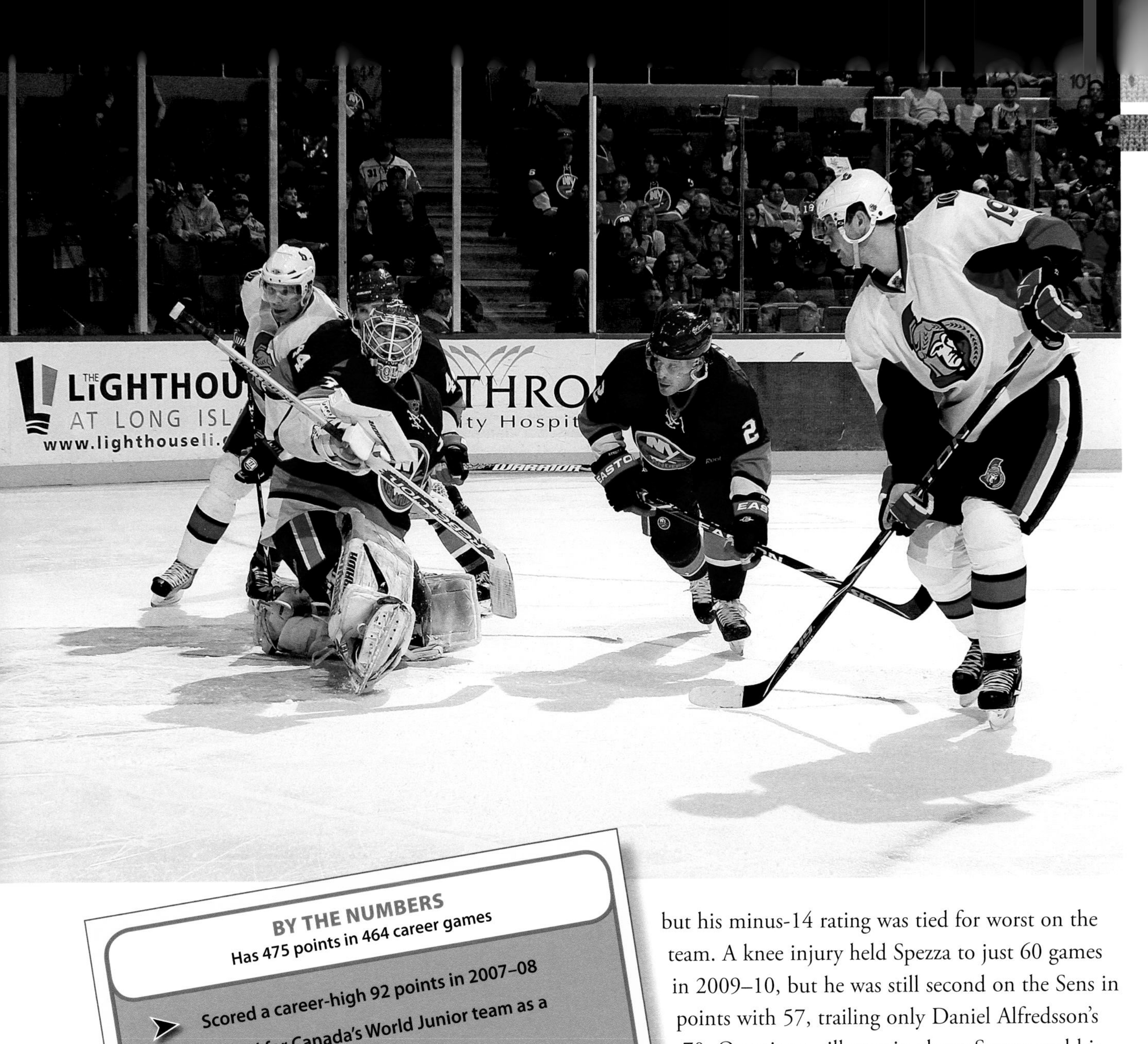

CAREER HIGHLIGHTS

BY THE NUMBERS
Has 475 points in 464 career games

- Scored a career-high 92 points in 2007–08
- Played for Canada's World Junior team as a 16-year-old
- Played in the 2008 NHL All-Star Game
- Has the Ottawa Senators record for most assists in a single season with 71 in 2005–06

teammates Daniel Alfredsson and Dany Heatley for the league scoring lead with 22 points (seven goals, 15 assists). But like many of the other Ottawa players, Spezza failed to impress during the Stanley Cup final versus Anaheim. He played in all 82 games in 2008–09, which is the only time he's played an entire regular season schedule, and recorded 73 points, but his minus-14 rating was tied for worst on the team. A knee injury held Spezza to just 60 games in 2009–10, but he was still second on the Sens in points with 57, trailing only Daniel Alfredsson's 70. Questions still remain about Spezza and his ability to be a more complete player. Even GM Bryan Murray could only muster a 'he is what he is' response when asked about Spezza's tenure in Ottawa. Coach Cory Clouston said the 27-year-old Spezza did about as well as could be expected in 2009–10 considering his long-time winger, the high-scoring Heatley, was traded away by the Senators.

Spezza certainly understands that as long as he is making millions of dollars on a long-term contract he is expected to be a more complete player. He wants to be the 'go-to' guy, but has yet to perform to lofty expectations in Ottawa. He might be better suited for another team at this stage of his career, but he will likely wear the Senator uniform for a long time to come.

By playing in his 500th career game during the 2009–10 season, Detroit Red Wings center Henrik Zetterberg proved many hockey experts wrong. When Zetterberg was drafted 210th overall in 1999, it was expected the native of Njurunda, Sweden, would need time in the minors if he had any chance of making it to the NHL. He was on the small side at 5-foot-11 and under 180 pounds, which in part accounts for him being selected so low in the draft. Detroit first had him pegged as a third- or even fourth-line player, but the Red Wings were pleasantly surprised to learn Zetterberg could play a great two-way game. He has become one of the top players in the NHL and has a 12-year, $73 million contract to prove it.

Part of the reason Zetterberg was given a chance to show what he could do was based on Detroit's need to find offense when forwards like Steve Yzerman, Sergei Fedorov and Brendan Shanahan were declining in effectiveness and about to leave the team. Zetterberg joined the Red Wings for the 2002–03 season, just as the squad was coming off its third championship in six years. He quickly showed he belonged with a 22-goal, 44-point season as a rookie. After a slight decline as a sophomore, Zetterberg really arrived in the first season of the post-lockout era in 2005–06, bagging 39 goals and 85 points. Any questions about him being able to play in the NHL were totally erased.

Since his breakout campaign, Zetterberg has produced seasons of 68, 92, 73 and 70 points, indicating he is a very consistent performer. The only remaining question was his ability to play at his best in the playoffs. After a few disappointing appearances in the post-season, Zetterberg had 13 goals and 27 points in 22 contests during the 2008 playoffs to earn the Conn Smythe Trophy as Detroit claimed the Cup for the first time since '02. It was a stellar performance that saw Zetterberg score the championship-clinching goal. He also blocked a Pittsburgh Penguins drive taken by Sidney Crosby that preserved a victory for his team and did a wonderful job all series long of thwarting the young star. His playoff performance capped a great year for Zetterberg, who scored a career-high 43 goals, earning him a berth on the NHL Second All-Star Team — a first for the slick Swede.

Zetterberg and the Red Wings nearly repeated as champions in 2009, but an early 2–0 lead in the final evaporated against the determined Penguins. Detroit coach Mike Babcock once again assigned Zetterberg to check Crosby and he held 'Sid the Kid' to just one goal in the final. However, that meant Evgeni Malkin was free of the pesky Zetterberg and that killed Detroit's chance for a second straight title as Malkin skated off with the Conn Smythe Zetterberg had won the year before. That didn't happen before Malkin got some frustration out by fighting

Zetterberg at the end of Game 2, as the Pens fell behind early in the series. It was hardly a scrap for the ages, but showed Zetterberg could get under the skin of one of the best players in the league through his hard work.

Although he may be somewhat undersized, Zetterberg is a very determined player who has some flash to his offensive abilities. His superb instincts make him difficult to deal with at both ends of the ice and his stick work to gain control of the puck can be mesmerizing. Once he has the frozen rubber, Zetterberg's tremendous puck-handling skills make him a threat to score every time. His playmaking talents are sublime and his assist total will almost always outnumber his goal tally. Zetterberg has made his body bigger and stronger since landing in the league and that has helped him to become a top defensive forward.

Zetterberg has now played 506 career games and has recorded 475 points, and he could make his numbers even higher if he focused solely on offense. The Red Wings were somewhat concerned about his lack of production in 2009–10, but a strong finish got him up to 70 points. There is little doubt he could put up higher numbers, but Zetterberg is most effective when he's backchecking as hard as he attacks.

BY THE NUMBERS Has had at least 70 points in each of the last five seasons

- Established career highs with 43 goals and 92 points in 2007–08
- Won the Conn Smythe Trophy in 2007–08 by accumulating 27 points in 22 games
- Has 475 points in 506 career games
- Won a gold medal with Sweden at the 2006 Winter Olympics and the 2006 World Championship

CAREER HIGHLIGHTS

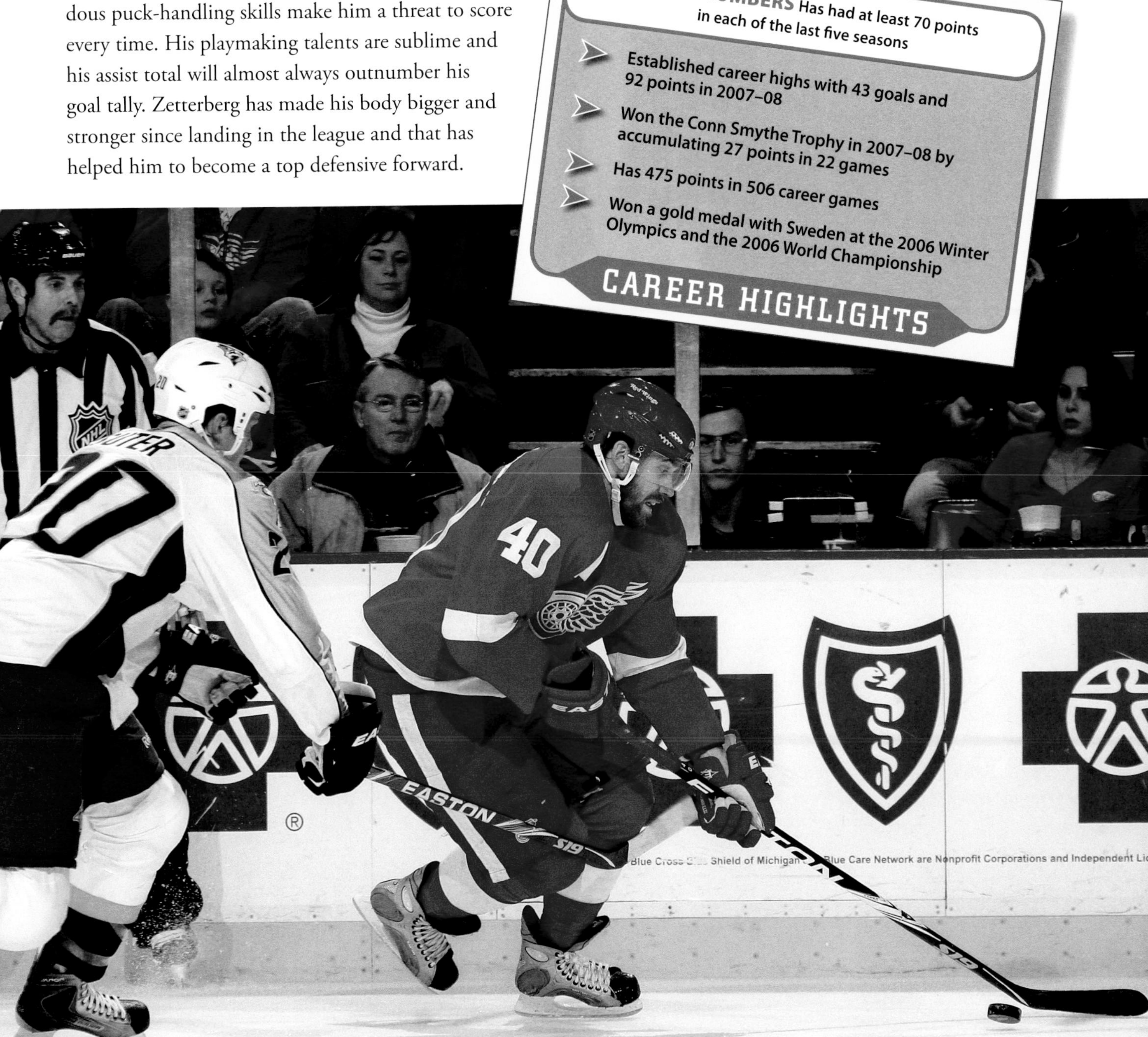

156 Tyler Bozak – Toronto Maple Leafs
158 Michael Del Zotto – New York Rangers
160 Drew Doughty – Los Angeles Kings
162 Steve Downie – Tampa Bay Lightning
164 Matt Duchene – Colorado Avalanche
166 Jimmy Howard – Detroit Red Wings
168 Evander Kane – Atlanta Thrashers
170 Tyler Myers – Buffalo Sabres
172 James Neal – Dallas Stars
174 Bobby Ryan – Anaheim Ducks

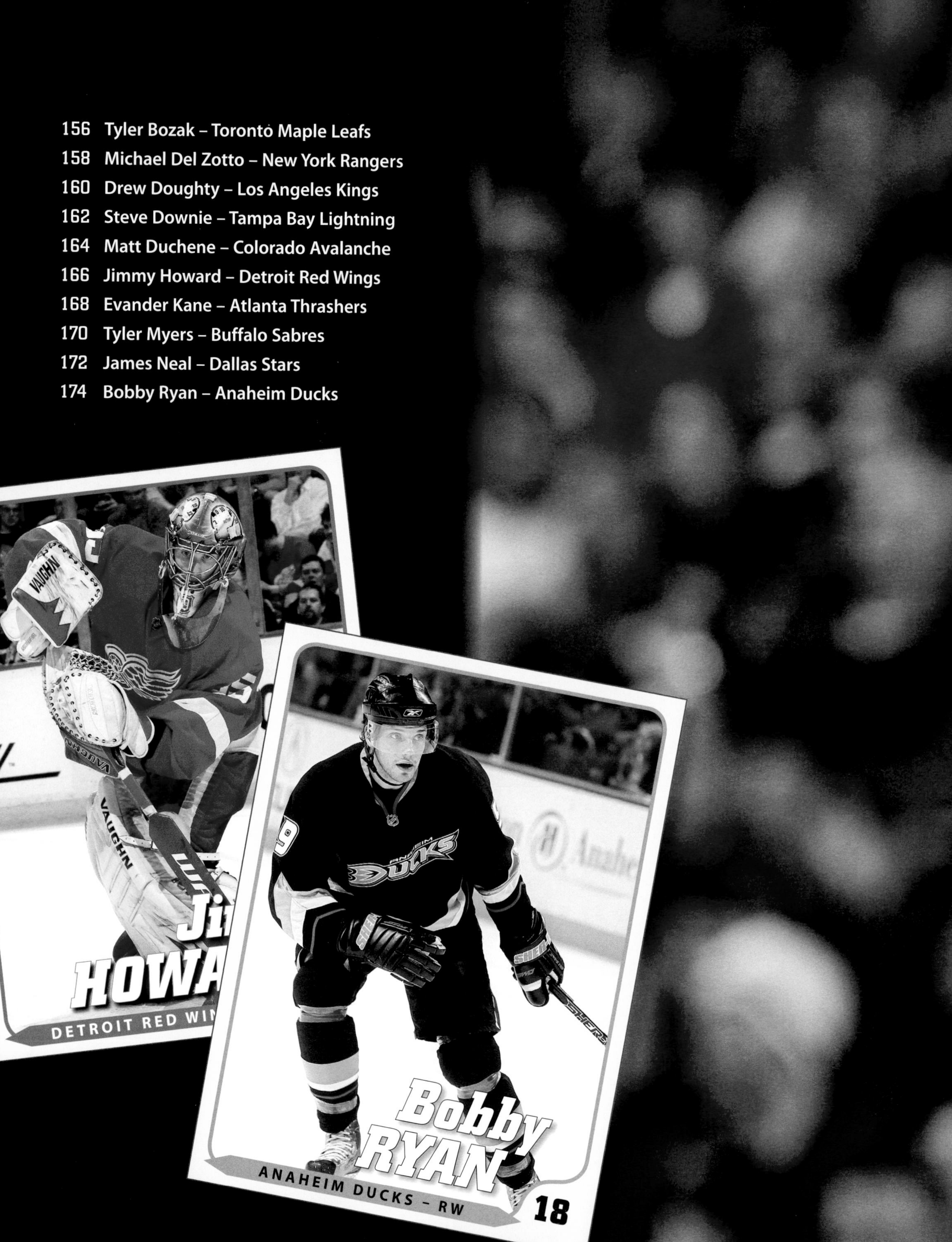

ON THE RISE

Young players ready to dominate.

The Toronto Maple Leafs needed to find new players to augment their rather mediocre talent level after missing the playoffs for a number of years. One player they pursued vigorously was center Tyler Bozak. Bozak was not the big type of player Toronto GM Brian Burke usually likes to put on his roster, but this youngster had too much potential to be ignored. Pursued by a number of teams since he was a free agent coming out of college hockey, Bozak thrilled the Maple Leafs when he agreed to a contract with them in the spring of 2009. A native of Regina, Saskatchewan, Bozak had a productive two-year career at the University of Denver, but no one was quite sure what to expect in his first season of professional hockey.

Bozak had a very good training camp with the Leafs in September of 2009, but could not be kept on the roster due to financial commitments the team had made to veteran players. It was also thought best if Bozak got some pro experience by starting out with the Toronto Marlies of the American Hockey League. It would have been a much better plan had Bozak not come down with a version of the H1N1 flu. He lost weight and missed significant time before he was able to get back in the lineup. It took time for Bozak to recover, but he still managed to record a respectable 20 points (including 16 assists) in 32 AHL games. He was not burning up the American League, but the Leafs saw enough to consider Bozak for promotion. The slick center earned an assist during his NHL debut in an October call-up versus the Colorado Avalanche, but did not stick with the big team until the month of January.

His first goal was very memorable as it came on a pretty play on home ice against the Philadelphia Flyers. Bozak took the puck down the wing and then cut across the ice, sliding the puck through the legs of a Flyers defender. Now in alone on Michael Leighton, he got the Philadelphia netminder to fall to his knees before roofing the puck over his glove. The crowd at the Air Canada Centre gave him a rousing ovation and it led the Leafs to a 4–0 victory. It was the kind of skilled play the Leafs had hoped to see from the prized prospect.

Bozak first began playing hockey for the Regina Canadians in 2003–04 and notched 36 points in 42 games. He then moved to play in the British Columbia Hockey League (BCHL) for a team in Victoria and in his final season there, he recorded 45 goals and 128 points in 59 games, earning himself the Brett Hull Trophy as the top scorer in the league for the 2006–07 season. He then decided to attend the University of Denver for the 2007–08 campaign and notched 18 goals and 34 points in 41 games. He won a number of rookie awards for his performance, but his second season was

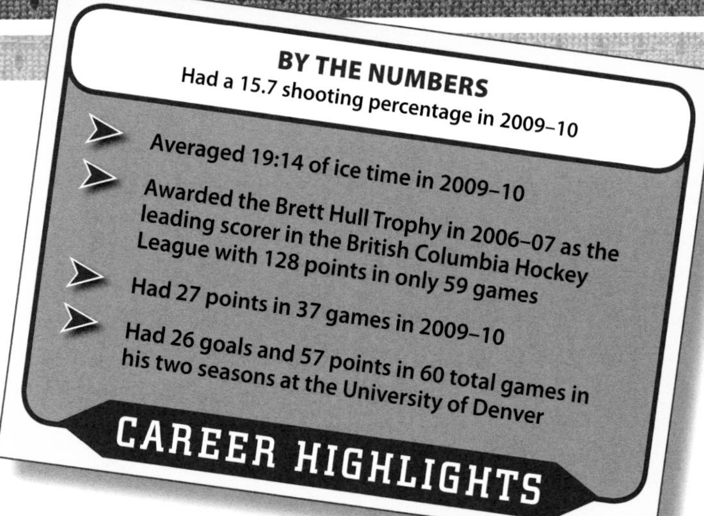
BY THE NUMBERS
Had a 15.7 shooting percentage in 2009–10

- Averaged 19:14 of ice time in 2009–10
- Awarded the Brett Hull Trophy in 2006–07 as the leading scorer in the British Columbia Hockey League with 128 points in only 59 games
- Had 27 points in 37 games in 2009–10
- Had 26 goals and 57 points in 60 total games in his two seasons at the University of Denver

CAREER HIGHLIGHTS

marred by a serious knee injury. He missed about half the season, still managing to get 23 points in 19 games. Despite the lack of games played, his performance caught the eye of many NHL scouts. He decided to sign a two-year deal with the Maple Leafs and was very impressive in recording eight goals and 27 points in 37 games, leaving little doubt he will begin the 2010–11 season in Toronto.

Bozak displayed many of the skills the Leafs had hoped for when he signed with the team. He showed a strong willingness to use his body and his on-ice vision proved to be very impressive. Bozak was surprisingly strong on faceoffs, a skill he developed at the insistence of his father when he was a youngster, and was a hard worker at both ends of the ice. Still, like many young players, he needs to work on his defensive play without the puck and the 24-year-old needs to bulk up to be able to compete over an 82-game schedule.

Bozak played center on the Leafs' top line alongside sniper Phil Kessel and they proved to be an effective combination. He also played in the middle beside two other young college-trained players in Viktor Stalberg and Christian Hanson. When the trio was playing together they were known as the 'Frat Pack' and they produced some moments of great success. The NCAA grads seem to have a special chemistry, but the line will not be together again since Stalberg is now in Chicago. One thing that is certain: the Leafs are glad they pursued and landed Tyler Bozak.

The 2008 NHL draft was loaded with defensemen who showed great potential. After star forward Steven Stamkos was selected by the Tampa Bay Lightning with the first pick, rearguards made up the next four selections. Drew Doughty went to Los Angeles with the second choice, followed by Zach Bogosian to Atlanta, while St. Louis chose Alex Pietrangelo and Toronto took Luke Schenn with the fifth choice. Another wave of D-man selections started when Buffalo chose Tyler Myers with the 12th pick. Colten Teubert went next to the Kings and then Zach Boychuk was drafted by Carolina. The New York Rangers were looking to nab a blueliner and their prospects of landing a good one seemed damaged when Anaheim took Jake Gardiner at No. 17 and Philadelphia grabbed Luca Sbisa with the 19th pick. However, the Rangers were not going to be denied their high-quality defender and with the 20th pick, they chose Stouffville, Ontario, native Michael Del Zotto.

The 6-foot-1, 200-pound Del Zotto played for the Markham Waxers in 2005–06 and recorded a whopping 30 goals and 120 points in 73 games. He then played for the Oshawa Generals of the Ontario Hockey League and posted seasons of 57 and 63 points, which got him noticed by NHL scouts. He returned to the Generals for one more season after he was drafted and was traded mid-season to the London Knights, where he played two playoff rounds, notching 19 points in 14 contests. He also got to play with another quality blueliner in John Carlson, who was selected by the Washington Capitals in the second round of the '08 draft. It was thought Del Zotto would return to junior for one more year, but he made the Rangers after their 2009 training camp and stayed with the big club for the whole season. He appeared in 80 games during 2009–10 and scored nine goals and 37 points — not bad for a kid who was just 19 years old and the youngest defenseman to ever make the Rangers' opening night roster.

Del Zotto scored his first NHL goal in his first appearance at home on Madison Square Garden ice against the Ottawa Senators. But his biggest thrill may have come the night of October 17, when he played against the Maple Leafs at the Air Canada Centre on *Hockey Night in Canada*. His entire family was in attendance and he scored a goal in a Rangers' victory. His father, Steve, talked about how his son was very determined, even at the tender age of four, to be a hockey player. As Del Zotto progressed up the various levels of minor and junior hockey, his father noticed his level of desire would rise just as high. Del Zotto was determined to make the Rangers and not return to junior, and he largely did so on the strength of his

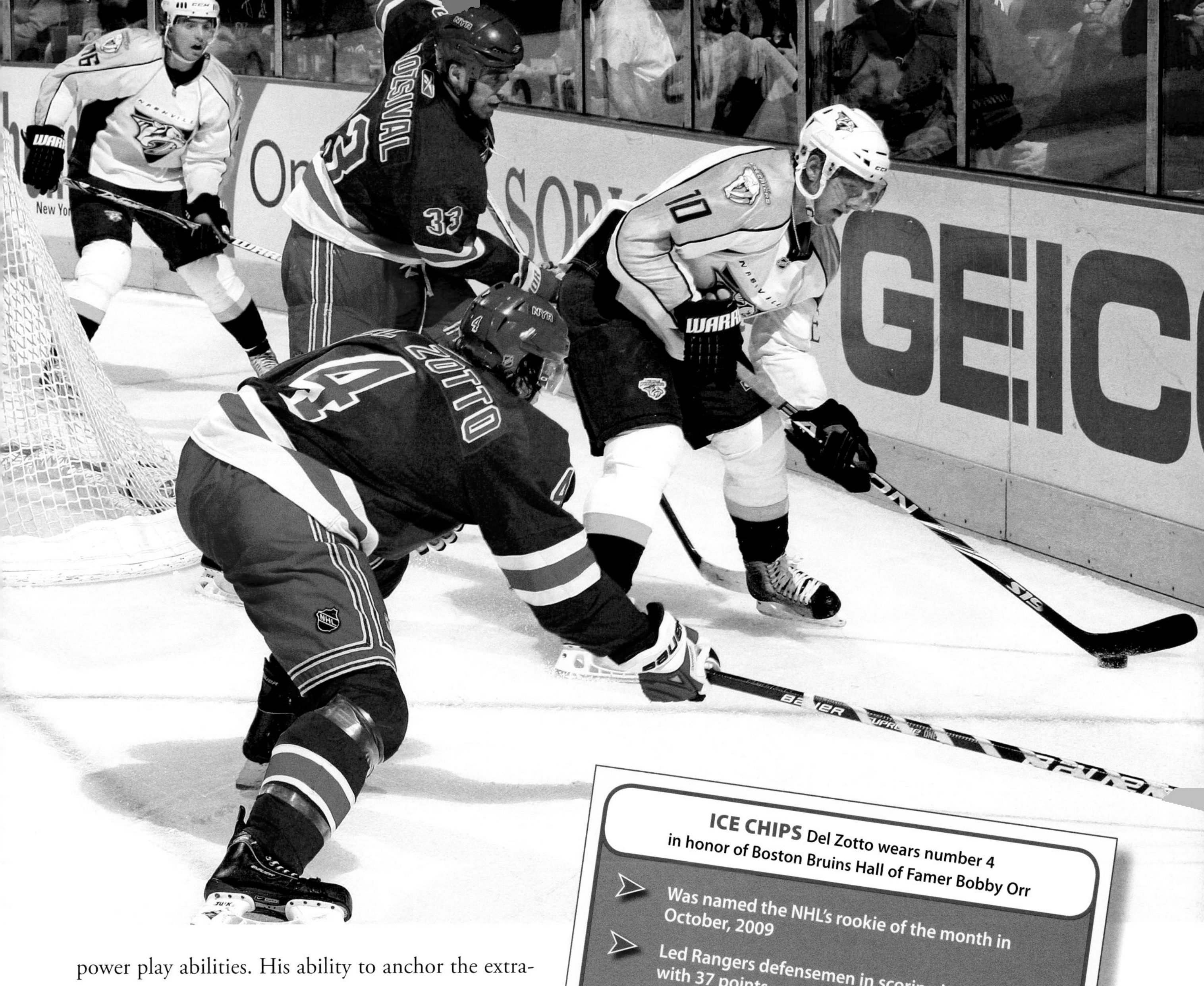

ICE CHIPS Del Zotto wears number 4 in honor of Boston Bruins Hall of Famer Bobby Orr

- Was named the NHL's rookie of the month in October, 2009
- Led Rangers defensemen in scoring in 2009–10 with 37 points
- Named to the 2009–10 NHL All-Rookie First Team
- Second among NHL rookie defensemen in points in 2009–10

CAREER HIGHLIGHTS

power play abilities. His ability to anchor the extra-man unit drew rave reviews, especially early in the year. However, every season is long and Del Zotto made his share of mistakes. He ended up minus-20 on the season, a fact that did not endear him to coach John Tortorella, who never hesitated to let the rookie know of his displeasure.

Del Zotto's main assets are his soft hands and his ability to move the puck quickly. He can deliver a sharp pass and can let go of a hot shot from the point. Del Zotto likes the offensive game, which leads to him taking chances when he thinks he can start the attack or keep the pressure on in the other team's end. A gambler's mentality and inexperience no doubt led to his poor plus-minus rating and he must learn to use his size more if Del Zotto is to become more effective, especially in his own end. His skating may not be the best in the NHL, but he should be able to make up for any deficiency with more playing time and attention to the defensive side of the game.

The Rangers are banking on a group of youngsters to lead this team to the playoffs. Ryan Callahan, Brandon Dubinsky, Marc Staal, Matt Gilroy, Artem Anisimov and a few other notables are part of the group the Rangers hope to build around. Del Zotto is sure to be a key building block and may yet prove to be one of the best defensemen to come out of the 2008 draft.

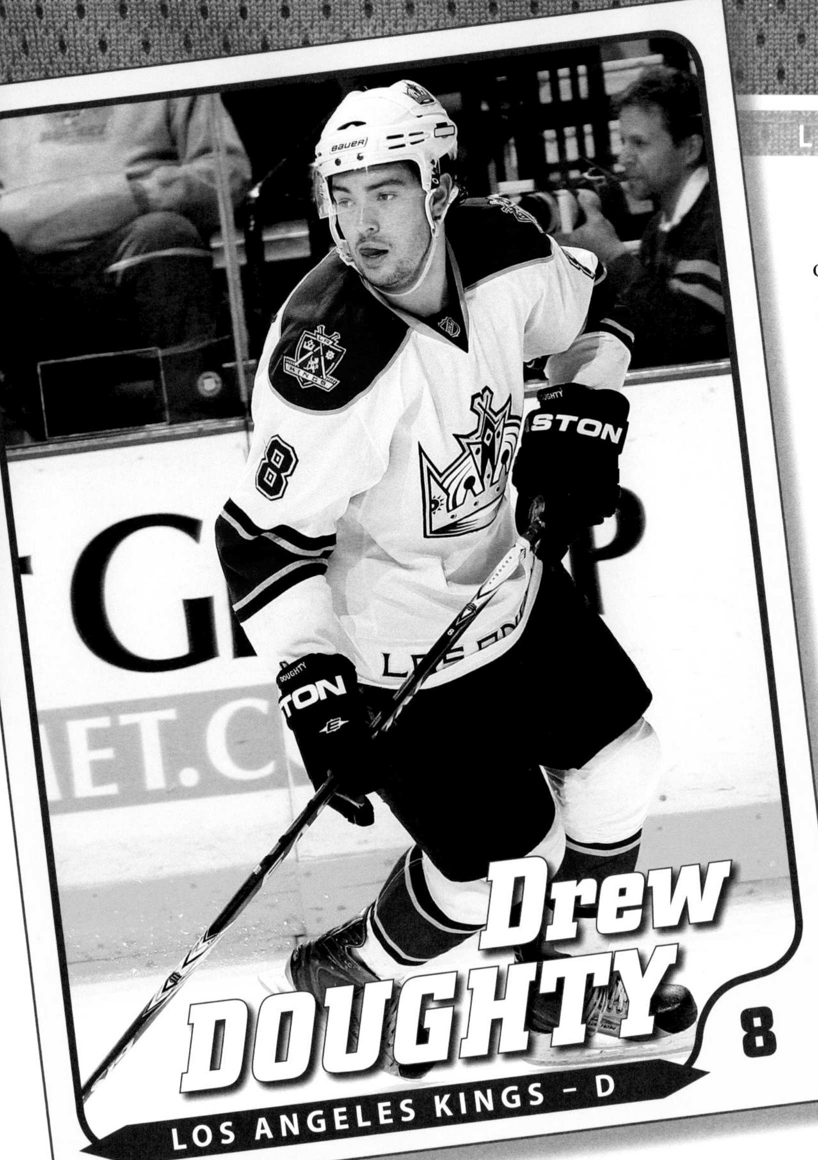

When Drew Doughty was just a year old, he was given a mini hockey stick as a birthday present. As soon as he saw the stick Doughty began playing hockey with a great passion. He was skating by the age of two and a little more than a year later, was playing on a house league team. His mother wrote a fan letter (twice) to Wayne Gretzky just before Doughty turned six and got a response from 'The Great One.' That event turned Doughty into a Los Angeles Kings fan and he got a team sweater to wear and an official Kings phone for his room. Even when he played video games, Doughty imagined himself as a member of the Los Angeles team. He spent many hours in the basement of his home shooting pucks and by the age of 15 he had advanced to the point where he was selected fifth overall by the Guelph Storm in the Ontario Hockey League draft.

Although he loved hockey first, Doughty also played soccer as a goalie and excelled at that sport, to the point he nearly tried out for a provincial under-14 club. However, he decided to give up soccer around the same time and devote himself to hockey. The native of London, Ontario, had a coach in his hometown who saw Doughty's great potential to play defense and moved him to the blueline from forward. Brad Ostrom told his star player that he was too good with the puck to simply chip it off the glass as many defensemen focus on doing. Ostrom told Doughty he should be carrying the puck and joining the attack, and when the youngster joined the Storm, it was more of the same. Doughty made the Guelph coaching staff stand up and take notice because he was toying with players two and three years his senior as a 15-year-old. In 190 career games with Guelph, Doughty recorded 39 goals and 157 points and was a member of the 2008 Canadian team that won gold at the World Junior Championship. He was named top defenseman at that prestigious tournament, which proved to be good timing since the '08 NHL draft was just around the corner.

The Los Angeles Kings had the second overall choice and wanted to be sure about the player they were going to select. Kings GM Dean Lombardi went to visit the Doughty household and was shown Drew's room, which was adorned with plenty of Kings souvenirs. While the Los Angeles merchandise caught Lombardi's attention, so did the fact that Team Canada sweaters Doughty had worn when representing his country as a junior had the front of the uniform showing in the frame and not the back with the player's name and number. Lombardi also noted team pictures were displayed as opposed to individual shots of Doughty himself. Convinced this player was meant to be a King, Los Angeles was pleased to know Tampa Bay would select Steven Stamkos first overall, leaving Doughty at No. 2.

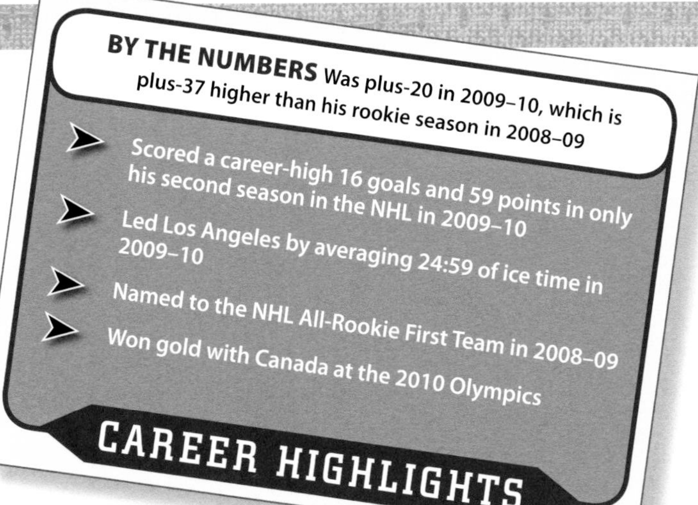

BY THE NUMBERS Was plus-20 in 2009–10, which is plus-37 higher than his rookie season in 2008–09

- Scored a career-high 16 goals and 59 points in only his second season in the NHL in 2009–10
- Led Los Angeles by averaging 24:59 of ice time in 2009–10
- Named to the NHL All-Rookie First Team in 2008–09
- Won gold with Canada at the 2010 Olympics

CAREER HIGHLIGHTS

Doughty has an easy-going personality, but he is very serious when he plays hockey. Unlike many others who treat the puck as if it might explode, Doughty loves to handle the frozen rubber. He always shows great patience until it's time to quickly snap the puck to a teammate. Doughty has a high panic threshold and will spin around in whatever way he needs to when avoiding a check from the opposition. He was very impressive as a rookie with 27 points in 81 games in 2008–09, but even better in 2009–10 when he recorded 16 goals and 59 points, and was surprisingly named to Team Canada for the 2010 Winter Olympic Games at just 20 years old. Many believed he was too young for such a challenge, but he played very well and saw plenty of ice time for the Canadian side, which won the gold medal.

While Doughty's potential seems limitless, he will have to work on his conditioning to endure a long season and playoffs. The Kings made the post-season for the first time in eight years in 2010 and Doughty notched seven points in a six-game opening-round loss to the Vancouver Canucks, though he was a minus player in each of the final four games. At 6-foot-1 and 203 pounds, Doughty doesn't have imposing size and could stand to be a touch more aggressive. Still, there's little doubt he will continue to excel and help lead the Kings to many more playoff appearances.

Steve Downie is only 23 years of age, but he has experienced a lifetime of ups and downs already. It all started when he was almost nine years old and on the way to an early-morning practice with his father, John, driving. After hitting an ice patch, the vehicle went into a ditch and smacked into a couple of trees before a utility pole crashed through the windshield and struck John on top of the head. Steve was rescued from the crash with cuts and bruises as workers tried their best to free his father for 20 minutes. The boy saw his dad pass away at the scene and it was now up to his mother to raise Steve and his brother. If that was not to enough for a youngster to endure, Downie lost some of his hearing about four years later when bones around his eardrums began to harden. The hearing in one ear is worse than the other, but it seems to have stabilized. Through it all, Downie was still able to focus on hockey and eventually became a first round draft pick of the Philadelphia Flyers.

Downie did not put up the kind of numbers in junior that typically justify a first round selection and his demeanor left much to be desired. He played in three Ontario Hockey League cities (Windsor, Peterborough and Kitchener) and could be counted on for 20-plus goals a season and for getting into trouble. His first incident of notoriety came in Windsor when he had a vicious fight with a Spitfire teammate in practice. Later, just as he made his NHL debut with the Flyers, he was suspended 20 games for launching himself in a reckless and dangerous manner at Dean McAmmond of the Ottawa Senators in a preseason game. Downie was not getting the message and took another 20-game banishment when he was ruled to have deliberately slashed an AHL official with his stick. Even the Flyers had to be wondering what kind of player they drafted and when a chance presented itself to trade the 5-foot-11, 200-pound right winger, they did not hesitate to include Downie in the transaction that saw Philadelphia land defenseman Matt Carle from Tampa Bay. Downie finished the 2008–09 season by scoring three goals in 23 games for the Lightning and spent another 23 contests with Tampa's American Hockey League farm team in Norfolk, notching 25 points and racking up 107 penalty minutes.

Rick Tocchet was coach of the Lightning for the entire 2009–10 campaign and he was able to get more out of Downie by calming the wild winger at just the right moments. Tocchet played a similar game to Downie's when he was in the NHL and could sense when Downie might be in danger of losing his famous temper. Although he still racked up 208 penalty minutes, Downie managed to stay on the straight and narrow just enough to produce a 23-goal season. Naturally, it helped when he got put on a line with star center

Steven Stamkos and accomplished veteran Martin St-Louis, but it is also true both of those players benefited from having Downie do a great deal of the dirty work to get them more free ice.

Since he is not a large player, Downie relies on his great inner drive to compete at the NHL level. He can work very well along the boards and forechecks without fear. Downie can make a clever pass or let go a good shot, but his best work is done in front of the net, where he can show some surprisingly soft hands. If he learns not to over-handle the puck in certain spots on the ice and avoid turnovers, he can become an even more effective player. Most of all, Downie must learn to keep his penchant for volatility in check and realize he's of great value on the ice, where he can keep the opposition guessing. He nearly had a major lapse when he went out of his way to lock legs with Sidney Crosby late in the season, but seemed to let up just in time before the Penguins superstar would have suffered a major knee injury — a situation that would have been terrible for all concerned.

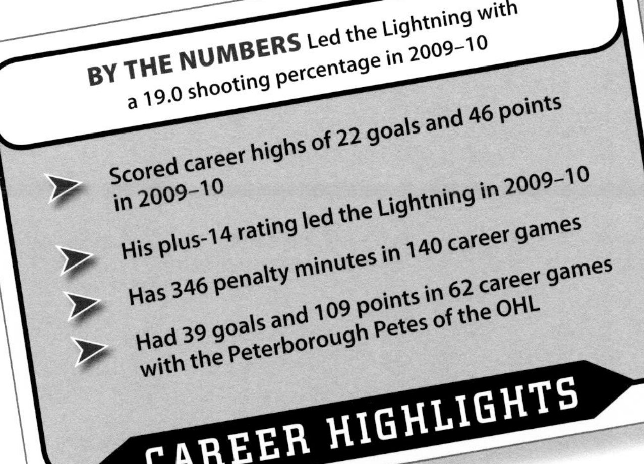
BY THE NUMBERS Led the Lightning with a 19.0 shooting percentage in 2009–10

- Scored career highs of 22 goals and 46 points in 2009–10
- His plus-14 rating led the Lightning in 2009–10
- Has 346 penalty minutes in 140 career games
- Had 39 goals and 109 points in 62 career games with the Peterborough Petes of the OHL

CAREER HIGHLIGHTS

Many have speculated that Downie's behavior is based on the fact he is resentful for what happened to his father that fateful morning in 1996. The young man insists that is not the case — at least, not anymore — and Stamkos has stated that while Downie initially appears to be a scary character, he is not that way at all. Developing a friendship with Stamkos is a great thing for Downie, who also needs to understand how a well-conditioned body will make him a better player, something that might endear him to new Lightning coach Guy Boucher for 2010–11. Even though he has a long way to go, Downie has made incredible strides for someone who was once was thought to be such a troubled person.

Matt Duchene was just four years old when he started playing hockey for his hometown Haliburton Huskies in Northern Ontario. He also benefited from his dad's decision to put up boards around the family's driveway, where he and his friends could hone their skills. Later on, some fishing line was used as mesh behind the net and young Matt made a makeshift goalie out of sheet metal and wood in shop class to give him a target to beat with his shot. His at-home "rink" was used in summer and winter, and he often worked out with childhood friend Cody Hodgson, a first round pick of the Vancouver Canucks in 2008. If the outdoor rink was not available, Duchene would go to the basement and practice his shot there. His father, Vince, was a quality goalie and was able to give his son good advice on how to beat the masked men. He also got sage words from his uncle, Newell Brown, a member of the Memorial Cup-champion Cornwall Royals in 1980 and an assistant coach with the Anaheim Ducks in 2009–10.

Duchene was also influenced in a positive way simply by being a childhood admirer of Colorado Avalanche center Joe Sakic. One of the NHL's all-time classy players, Sakic was a two-time Stanley Cup winner and will be a Hockey Hall of Fame member in the near future with 625 goals and 1,641 points to his credit. The Avalanche became Duchene's favorite team and he would practice drawing their logo and put Sakic's poster on his bedroom wall. He also liked the Montreal Canadiens and their illustrious history, deciding to wear sweater No. 9 in honor of Maurice 'Rocket' Richard. Like all young boys, Matt dreamed of one day wearing an NHL uniform and he started on the road to fulfilling that hope when he played major junior hockey for the Brampton Battalion of the Ontario Hockey League. He produced two great years in Brampton, where he just happened to play alongside Hodgson, his childhood buddy. Duchene scored 61 goals in 121 regular season games, but saved his best for the 2009 playoffs when he had 14 goals and 26 points in 21 post-season games, helping the Battalion to the OHL final that year. The timing of his impressive performance could not have been better since he was eligible for the NHL draft later that year.

It was thought the '09 draft was going to be a two-horse race, with the New York Islanders selecting John Tavares first overall and Victor Hedman going to Tampa Bay with the second choice. However, Duchene's play late in the season made him a real consideration for one of the top two selections, though he was ultimately very happy to be taken by the Avalanche with the third pick. Duchene is not the largest player at 5-foot-11, but he is a rather sturdy 200 pounds. In addition to having great offensive instincts and skill,

Duchene is also a very capable two-way player. His skating skills are exceptional and he can handle the puck with great dexterity. He is very good at taking a pass and gets a shot off quickly, while displaying a set of soft hands. The Avalanche were thrilled to land Duchene and he made the team as an 18 year old. He played 81 games as a rookie in 2009–10, netting 24 goals and 55 points en route to helping a young Colorado squad earn a very surprising playoff berth. Duchene helped secure a post-season spot for his team by scoring a shootout winner against the Vancouver Canucks with just three games to go in the season. He got his first taste of playoff action in a six-game opening round loss to San Jose and although he did not score, he contributed three assists.

Duchene's first NHL season also gave a highlight to Don Cherry and his 'Coach's Corner' segment on *Hockey Night in Canada*. It seems Duchene's grandfather was about to go and feed his cattle on a Saturday night, but there had been an ice storm and large chunks of ice and snow rested on the roof of the barn. The grandfather refused to go out until he had watched Cherry do his show and in the meantime the barn roof collapsed. If the grandfather had not been inside watching Cherry, there is a good chance he would have been under the debris that killed many animals. Cherry was flattered by the story and quipped that his moments on television are indeed very valuable.

BY THE NUMBERS Led the Avalanche with 10 power play goals in 2009–10

- Drafted third overall by Colorado in 2009
- Was a finalist for the 2010 Calder Trophy
- Third in team scoring in 2009–10
- Won a gold medal with Canada at the Under-18 World Championship in 2008

CAREER HIGHLIGHTS

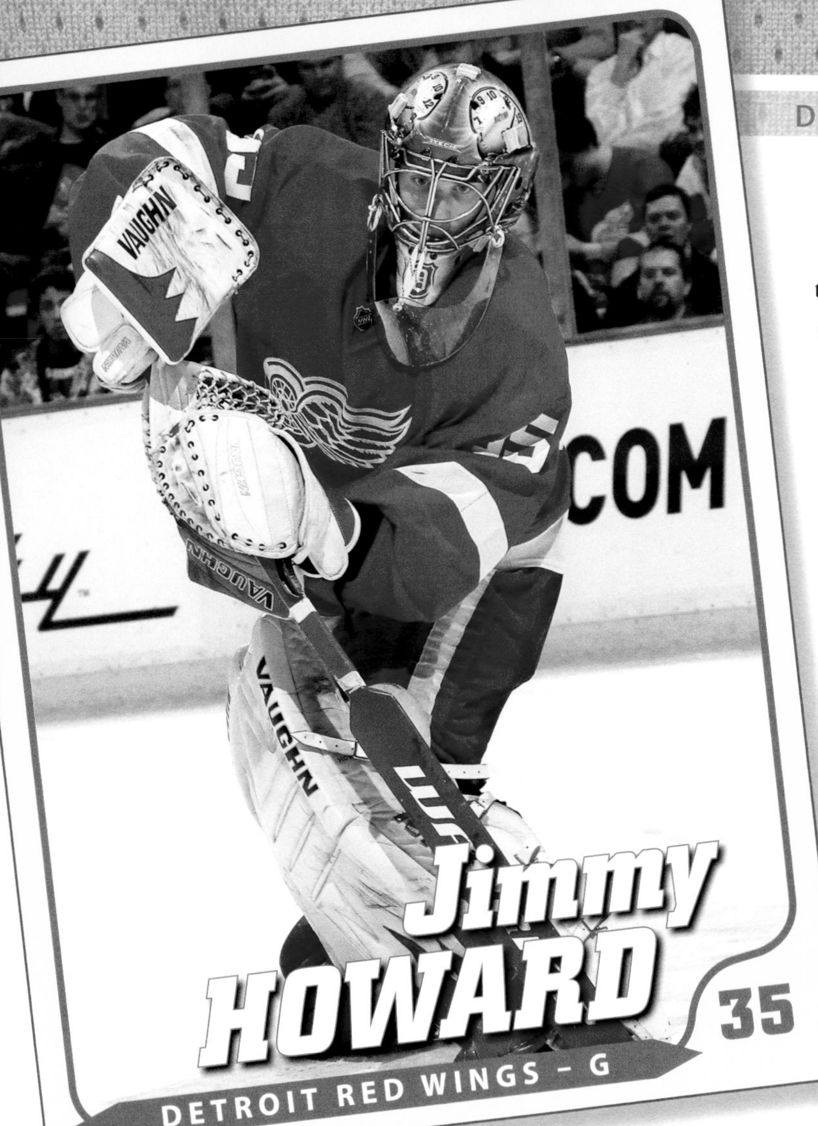

At the start of the 2009–10 season, rookie goaltender Jimmy Howard was considered the backup netminder to starter Chris Osgood. After all, Osgood had already won three Stanley Cups with the Detroit Red Wings and would have claimed a fourth if not for a close 2–1 Game 7 loss to the Pittsburgh Penguins in 2009. Detroit coach Mike Babcock was hoping to get Howard into a number of games, but did not see him as a potential No. 1 goalie. However, by late January, with the Red Wings struggling to get into playoff position, Babcock decided to hand the goaltending reins over to Howard. The rookie proved his coach made the right decision by winning 37 games in 63 total outings and guiding Detroit to a fifth-place finish in the Western Conference with 102 points.

One reason for Howard's success may have been that he was already 25 years old when the 2009–10 season began. Drafted 64th overall by the Red Wings in 2003, Howard was given every opportunity to develop his skills before being brought up to the NHL. In fact, Howard had only played in nine NHL games — posting an unimpressive 1–5 record — prior to joining Detroit on a full-time basis. The Red Wings were very patient with their young netminder, allowing him to play in the American Hockey League for four full seasons. He posted a quality, but unspectacular, record of 90–73–11 with the Grand Rapids Griffins and never went too deep into the playoffs. However, the Red Wings still liked what they saw of Howard and needed a backup who wouldn't be a big strain on their finances given they had devoted so many dollars to forwards and defensemen. Detroit had found great value in signing inexpensive backup Ty Conklin the year before, so there was a good precedent for Howard to follow.

Howard's main asset as a goalie is his ability to bounce back after he lets in a bad goal or has a tough game. He's not easily rattled and is able to focus on not surrendering another goal after one has already slipped by. He's able to anticipate the play and does a good job of maintaining proper position. Howard is a very flexible goalie and uses his athleticism to find a way to get a body part out to stop a shot. He moves from post to post very efficiently and gets back into position quickly when there is a rebound left out in front of his net. Like other goalies, Howard struggles when he ends up too far back in his net, but was doing a better job of living at the top of the crease as the season wore on. The biggest assistance Howard received during his first NHL season came from Osgood, who was nothing but supportive even though he lost his starting role and was hoping to push his career victory total to 400. The veteran recalled that others had been of great help to him when he first became a professional and he wanted to return the favor to

Howard. It also helped that the two had already known each other for the last five seasons, but Howard had to feel a little more pressure since Detroit had other good goaltending prospects already in its system.

A rough start to the season saw Howard cough up five goals to the St. Louis Blues, but he got better as the year wore on and ended up posting a .924 save percentage, while notching his first three career shutouts. Detroit played the upstart Phoenix Coyotes in the first round of the 2010 playoffs and Howard experienced some up and downs, just as he had in the regular season. However, he was in net for Detroit's Game 7 victory on the road and also picked up his first post-season shutout when he blanked the Coyotes 3–0 in the fourth game of the series. Detroit lost out in five games against San Jose in Round 2, but the playoff experience will only help Howard in his quest to one day bring another championship to the Red Wings.

BY THE NUMBERS

Was fifth in the NHL with a 2.26 GAA in 2009–10

- Drafted 64th overall by Detroit in 2003
- Was runner-up for the 2010 Calder Trophy
- Was fifth in the NHL with a .924 save percentage in 2009–10
- Is the only NHL goalie in history to face a penalty shot in each of his first two games
- Holds the NCAA record for GAA in a season with 1.19

CAREER HIGHLIGHTS

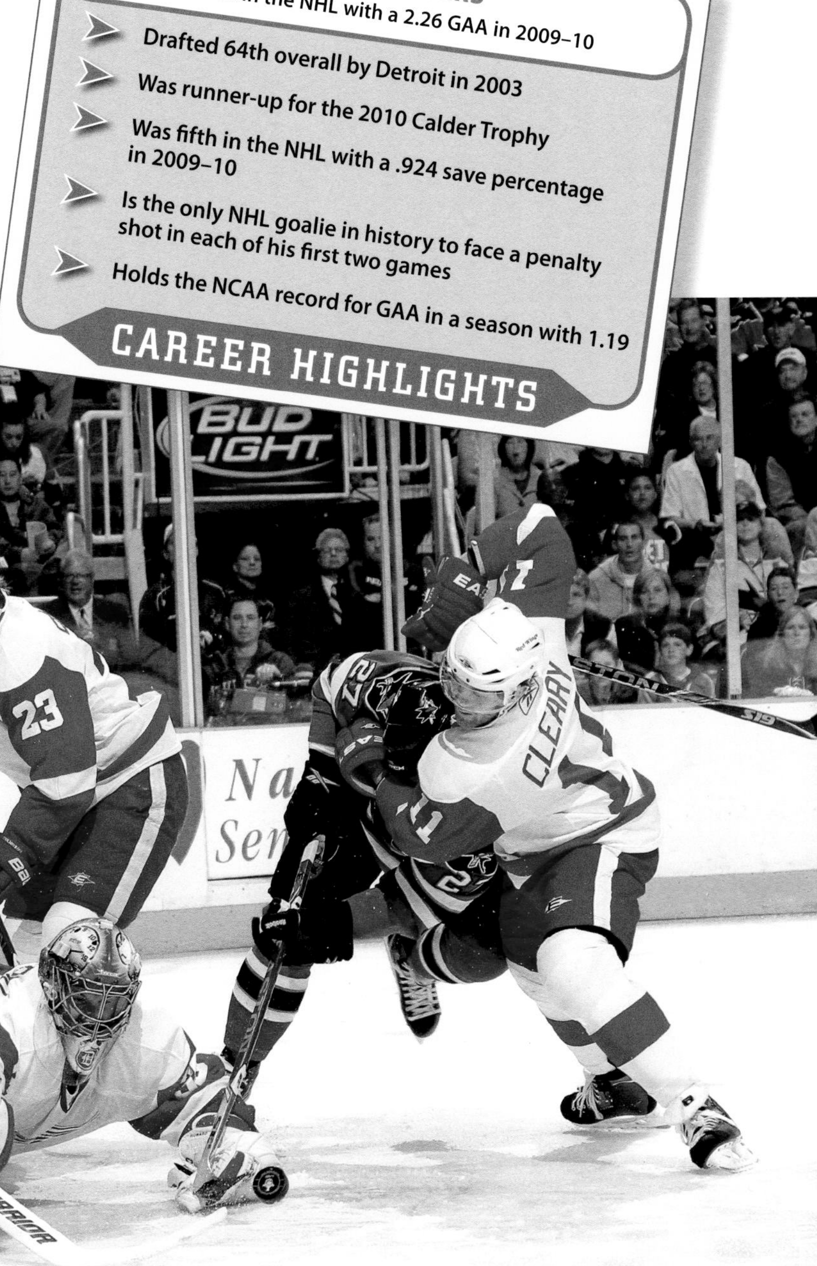

Evander Kane comes from a very athletic family. His father, Perry, was an amateur boxer and hockey player, while his mother, Sheri, was a pro volleyball player. He had an uncle who was an excellent ball hockey player and a cousin who played pro football in both Canada and the United States. Yet another cousin was a boxer who represented Canada at the 1992 Summer Olympics. Kane's father and grandfather were fans of heavyweight boxing champ Evander Holyfield, so much so that it inspired the name of Perry and Sheri's son, but only after mom gave her final approval. Perry still has a hand in training his son — mostly in the off-season — by getting Evander to work hard in the boxing ring, but the youngster will never be the champion Holyfield was in the 'sweet science.' It's just as well since Kane is a pretty good hockey player already at the tender age of 19.

Kane was born and raised in Vancouver and was a good all-around athlete who excelled in hockey, basketball, baseball and soccer. He was particularly adept at hockey and notched 140 points in just 66 games playing bantam hockey for the North Shore Winter Club. Kane then played midget for the Greater Vancouver Canadians and had 22 goals and 54 points in 30 games. He was eventually drafted by his hometown Vancouver Giants of the Western Hockey League and was with the team when they won the Memorial Cup in 2007. His first full year of junior saw him score 24 goals and that total jumped to 48 in his second season. Kane had grown to a solid 6-foot-1 and 180 pounds by this point and his good numbers caught the attention of all the NHL scouts. He was also a member of Team Canada at the World Junior Championship in 2009, though it was only through an injury that he made the final roster. But once he got into the lineup, the youngest player on the team showed he could play with the best juniors in the world, netting six points in six games.

Eligible for the 2009 NHL draft, Kane was very highly rated, but most of the attention went to John Tavares, Victor Hedman and Matt Duchene, who were ranked ahead of him and went in that order to the Islanders, Lightning and Avalanche, respectively. When Atlanta called Kane's name at No. 4, it was the highest any Giant has ever gone in the draft and also the earliest any black player has been selected on draft day. Kane made the Atlanta lineup to start the 2009–10 season and recorded an assist in his very first game. One game later, he scored his first career goal, a game-winner no less, against the St. Louis Blues and goalie Chris Mason in a 4–2 Atlanta victory. Kane had a bit of an up-and-down year, but managed to score 14 goals and total 26 points with three game-winning goals, despite missing 15 games with a foot injury and another with the flu.

Kane admitted to being a little star struck at first and it took a while to get acquainted with the NHL. He found that his veteran teammates were a big help, but his maturity and belief in his abilities were also factors in Kane's good performance. He has soft hands for a big man and is good from in close. He showed signs of being able to use his body effectively, but still needs to work on the power aspects of his game. Kane is not the type who goes looking for trouble, but he will not shy away from it at all. In the last game of the season, he was challenged by notorious pest Matt Cooke of the Pittsburgh Penguins. Kane's boxing background was on prominent and painful display as he dropped Cooke with a couple of hard blows.

The Thrashers are in need of a new franchise face since previous superstar Ilya Kovalchuk was traded away last season. Kane is the most likely player to fill that void and he may yet emerge as the best player to come out of the 2009 draft.

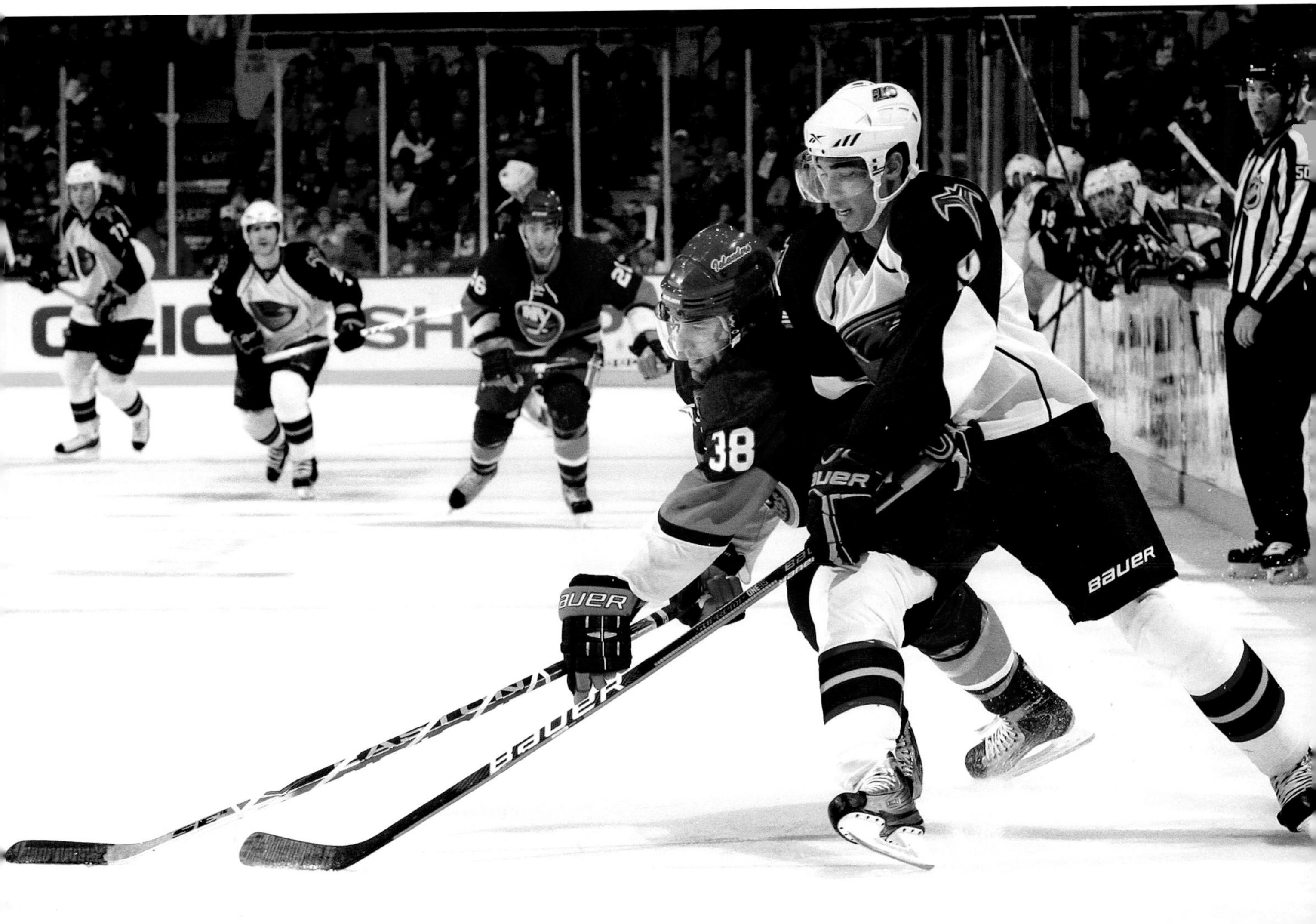

Anyone who reads Tyler Myers' résumé will notice a couple of facts about the defenseman that stand out. The first is he was born in Houston, Texas, hardly a hockey hotbed. His father, Paul, worked in the oil business in Houston, but when Tyler was 10 years old his father was transferred to Calgary, Alberta; the move allowed young Tyler to develop his athletic skills in a better hockey environment. If he had stayed south of the border, the now 6-foot-8, 220-pounder likely would have gravitated to basketball or football, sports more befitting of his size. His parents had a rule that his grades had to be high to play sports, so it was a good thing that Myers was a very good student. He attended the famous Athol Murray College of Notre Dame in Wilcox, Saskatchewan, when he was 15, but played his major junior hockey in British Columbia for the Kelowna Rockets of the Western Hockey League. Myers began his international hockey career playing for the United States, but when he acquired Canadian citizenship he decided to play for Team Canada. In 2009, he played for the Canadian side at the World Junior Championship held in Ottawa, Ontario, and was a big reason why Canada won the gold medal. In 2010, he represented his country at the World Championship.

Myers' size is the other noticeable item on his résumé; he's the second-tallest player in the NHL — only Boston's Zdeno Chara (6-foot-9) can look down on the young Sabre. Myers was rated as high as fourth overall among prospects for the 2008 NHL draft, but a knee injury and concerns about his mobility and offensive capabilities saw him fall to 12th, where the Buffalo Sabres traded up to take him. The Sabres felt they had a real gem on their hands, but were not sure when he would be ready to play in the NHL. Myers got a bit of a break when fellow Kelowna defenseman Luke Schenn (selected fifth overall in 2008) made the Toronto Maple Leafs out of training camp, leaving the top defenseman role with the Rockets to Myers. Kelowna had a great year in 2008–09, winning the WHL title. Myers posted a career-best nine goals and 42 points and was great in the post-season with five goals and 20 points in 22 contests, earning MVP honors for his play. Some observers felt Myers was a different player — more dominating — after returning from the World Junior tournament. Canadian coach Pat Quinn, a former NHL defenseman, had a great effect on Myers and it got him ready for the NHL.

Team management in Kelowna hoped Myers would return for one more year of junior in 2009–10, but the chances of that happening were slim. The Sabres liked what they saw in the young blueliner and were willing to keep him for at least nine games (a 10th appearance meant the first year of his NHL contract would

BY THE NUMBERS Led all rookie defensemen in scoring with 48 points in 2009–10

- Won gold with Canada at the 2009 World Junior Championship
- Played in all 82 games in his 2009–10 rookie season
- Led all Sabres in average ice-time with 23:44 in 2009–10
- Won the Calder Trophy in 2009–10

CAREER HIGHLIGHTS

kick in) before deciding to keep him for the entire season. Myers quickly showed he belonged, recording his first point in Game 2 versus Phoenix and his first goal in Game 5 against the New York Islanders, which was also his first two-point game. A few games later, on October 24, he scored a goal in a shootout to beat Tampa Bay. Myers' impressive early performance eliminated any doubt about returning him to Kelowna. He went on to lead all freshmen defensemen in scoring and finish third overall among all rookies with 11 goals and 48 points in 82 games. Most impressively, Myers won the Calder Trophy as the NHL's top first-year player.

Having a large body usually means it takes time before someone like Myers to grow accustomed to his frame, but he seems to have adjusted fine. Myers is a smooth skater who carries the puck with confidence, quarterbacks the power play with ease and has a hard, accurate shot to boot. Buffalo coach Lindy Ruff used Myers in every situation possible and the big teenager (he turned 20 in February) responded well to each challenge. Young defensemen are not supposed to be so good, but Myers registered a plus-13 rating despite all the ice time he was given. He was not overly aggressive with only 32 penalty minutes, but he will likely be more physical in the future. Any mistakes were errors of inexperience and they should become less frequent as he plays more NHL seasons.

The 2008 draft was loaded with highly sought-after defensemen and four were selected ahead of Myers (Drew Doughty at No. 2, Zach Bogosian third, Alex Pietrangelo No. 4 and Schenn fifth), but the Sabres might be the team that got the best all-around player.

Imagine the excitement of rookie James Neal as he waited for his Dallas Stars to hit the ice at the Air Canada Centre December 23, 2008, to face the Toronto Maple Leafs. Neal was born in Whitby, Ontario, a town just east of Toronto and was a passionate Leafs fan growing up. His family and friends were also Maple Leafs supporters and, although he was drafted by Dallas (33rd overall in 2005), he could not wait to make his debut against the team that defined his childhood memories. Every Toronto area youngster who comes back to play the hometown Maple Leafs is always ready to play their best game because it's in front of everyone he knew growing up and is on national television as well. Neal performed superbly. The large 6-foot-3, 206-pound left winger scored three times for his first NHL hat trick in an 8–2 Dallas victory. His first goal just 3:23 into the game was on a rebound, as was his second marker from right in front of the net. His third goal with just under 90 seconds to play was a wrist shot from the wing. Neal stayed with his family during the Christmas break and basked in the glow of a game he would never forget. The 2009–10 season saw Neal gain more recognition back home when he scored the overtime-winning goal October 28 against the visiting Leafs in a 4–3 Stars' victory. Neal must love playing against those blue and white sweaters.

For a player who was expected to need time to develop his skills to play in the NHL, Neal's rise to a permanent spot with the Stars was fairly quick. He played junior hockey with Plymouth of the Ontario Hockey League, but was never a prolific goal-scorer. Neal scored 27 times in 2006–07 while also posting 65 points, but was then sent to Iowa of the American Hockey League for some seasoning. He had respectable numbers of 18 goals and 19 assists in 62 games for the affiliate club and the apprenticeship seemed to get him ready to play in Dallas. Neal is one of those few players more suited to the NHL than the minor leagues. He played 77 games as a rookie for the Stars and scored 24 times while adding 13 assists. Neal played much of the 2009–10 campaign on the top line for the Stars featuring veteran Brad Richards and 25-year-old Loui Eriksson. The trio was one of the best in the league with Richards compiling 91 points and Eriksson netting 29 goals, while Neal scored 27 times and totaled 55 points.

The Dallas team was no longer relying on aging superstar Mike Modano and long-time netminder Marty Turco, who will not be back with the Stars in 2010–11. The team needed new leaders to emerge and the work done by the Richards unit was a very positive step in that direction. Neal is big, powerful and speedy with a soft pair of hands. He is a nice complement to the other two members of his line and it is quite possible that he will one day be a dominating player. His attitude

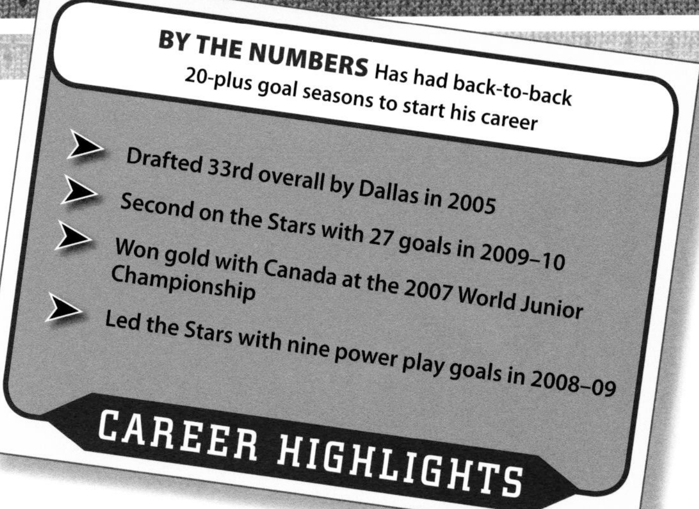

coming into his second year in the NHL was that he had to work harder than in his rookie year. There was no let up in his approach and the results were there for all to see. When teams call to discuss trades with the Stars, it is Neal's name that often comes up; GM Joe Nieuwendyk would be well advised not to listen to any offers for this rising star.

During the past season Neal and Eriksson lived together, but it was Richards who mentored both players. Neal has learned what it takes to be professional from Richards who had to calm the rather excitable youngster down at times when the up-and-down nature of big league hockey took its toll. Richards emphasized good habits and working on the details — especially when it comes to doing the right things in the defensive zone (Neal was only minus-5 in the 2009–10 season, not bad for a second-year player). Neal must learn to use his speed more effectively and work at controlling the puck in the other team's end. He still has some lessons to learn, but if recent history is any indication, it is certain Neal will adjust accordingly and continue to make an impact in the NHL.

BY THE NUMBERS Has had back-to-back 20-plus goal seasons to start his career

- Drafted 33rd overall by Dallas in 2005
- Second on the Stars with 27 goals in 2009–10
- Won gold with Canada at the 2007 World Junior Championship
- Led the Stars with nine power play goals in 2008–09

CAREER HIGHLIGHTS

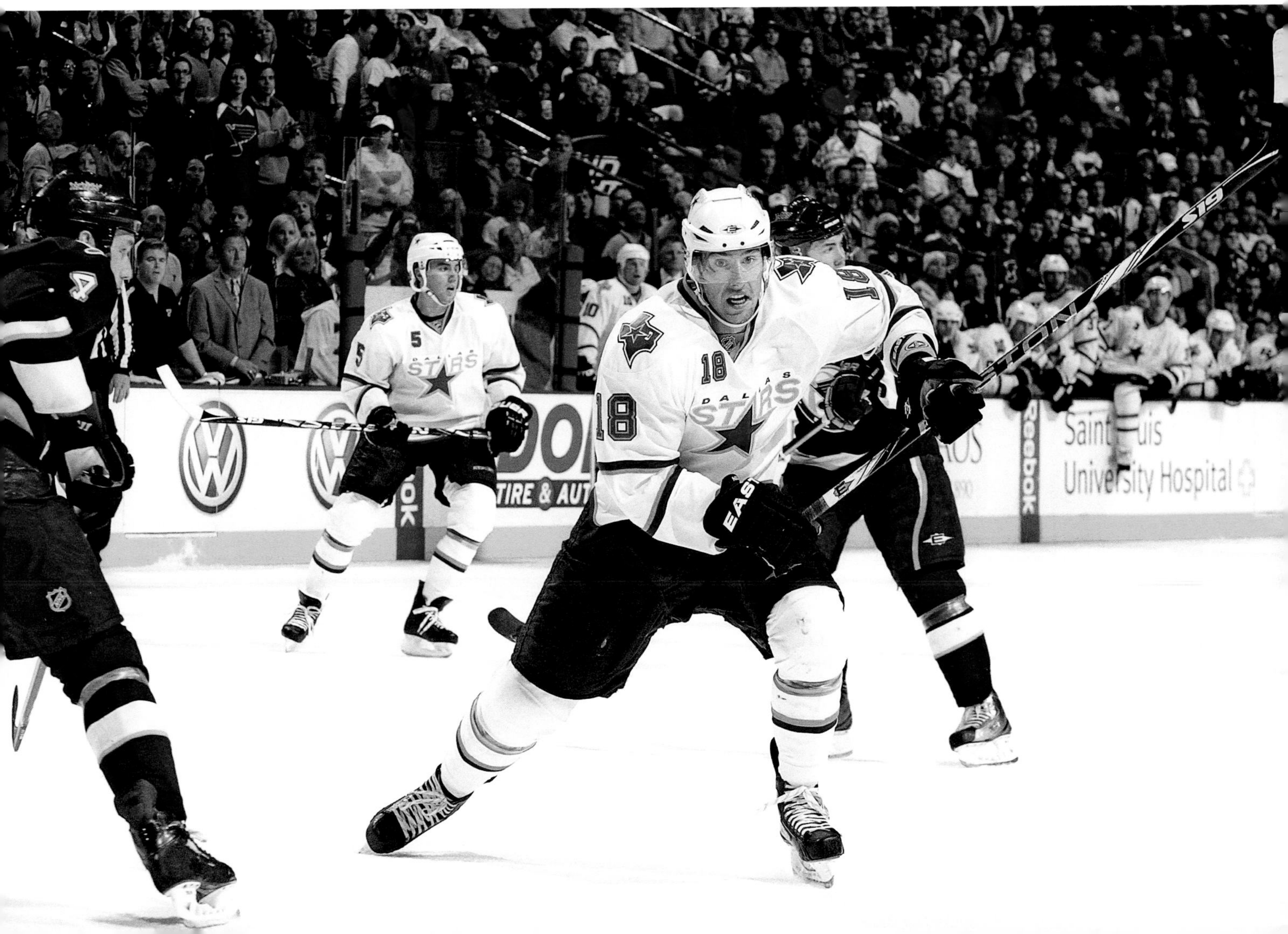

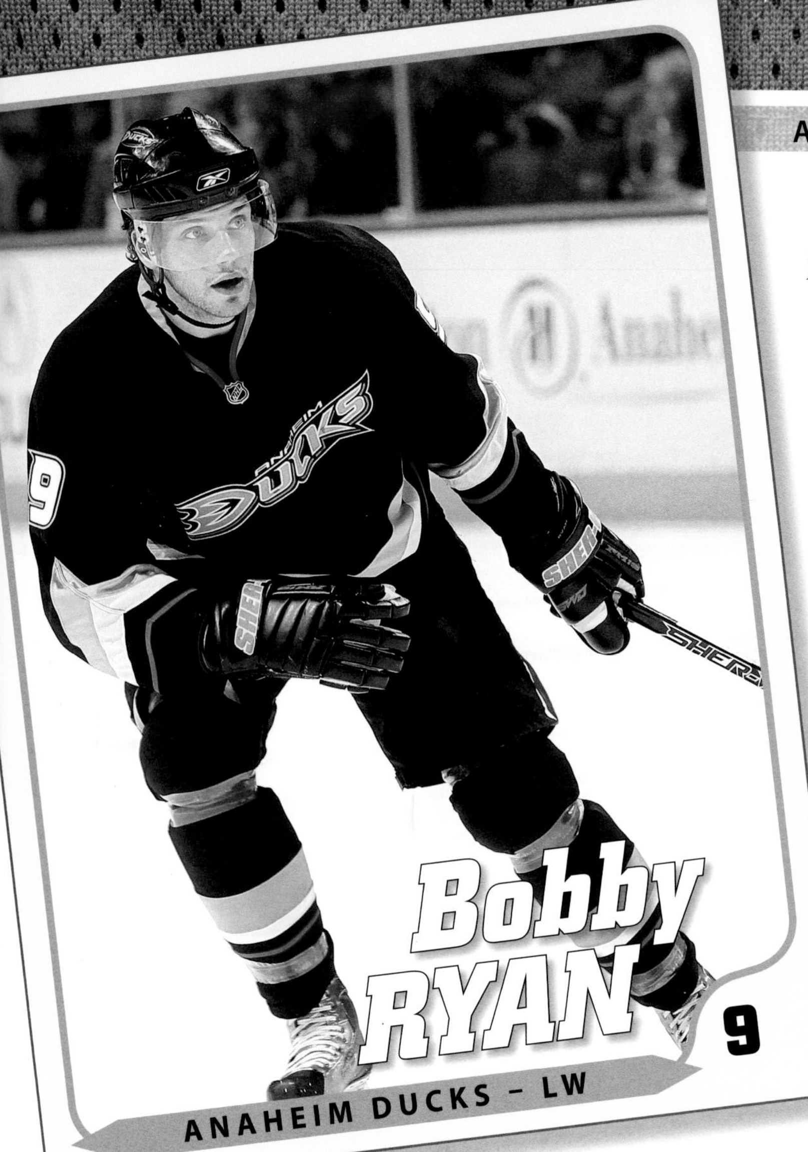

When a player is drafted second overall, he is often expected to help the team selecting him right away. Left winger Bobby Ryan was taken No. 2 in 2005 by the Anaheim Ducks, just after the Pittsburgh Penguins chose Sidney Crosby. The '05 draft was unusual in that, because of the NHL lockout the season before, there were no standings to work from; all the teams went into the draft lottery with weightings based on a blend of recent finishes. The second ball to come out the lottery drum belonged to the Ducks, but they were not as needy a club as some others. They selected the now 6-foot-2, 210-pound Ryan with the intention of having him go back to junior. When he arrived at the Anaheim training camp, it was pretty clear he was not in any kind of shape to compete for an NHL job. He was told to spend a good deal of time on the stationary bike instead of on the ice. Ryan did indeed return to junior and he played two great seasons for the Ontario Hockey League's Owen Sound Attack, recording 74 goals and 197 points in 122 games. At 20 years of age, it seemed Ryan was a sure bet to make the Ducks in 2007–08. But he played much of the season with Portland of the American Hockey League (21 goals and 49 points in 48 games) because of salary cap issues in Anaheim. However, his professional performance left no doubt he was ready for the NHL and he did get into 23 games for Anaheim in 2007–08, recording five goals and 10 points. Ryan was ready to arrive full-time.

It is something of a miracle that Ryan was playing hockey at all given what happened to his family when he was just 10 years old in 1997. After returning home from a Philadelphia Flyers hockey game, the native of Cherry Hill, New Jersey, went to sleep. His next memory is being at his grandfather's house and not knowing how he got there.

His father and mother, Bob and Melody Stevenson, had engaged in a domestic dispute that changed their lives forever that night. Bob Stevenson faced many charges as a result of the argument, even though his wife amazingly forgave him. The family left the state of New Jersey and moved to California to start a new life. Except for the mother, the family surname was changed to 'Ryan' and a good hockey program was found for the youngster to continue his development near Los Angeles. An only child, Bobby was told in very strict terms to always use his new surname (his father took it from the movie *Saving Private Ryan*) and say nothing about what happened in New Jersey. Strong, sincere and very determined, Ryan continued to play hockey (including a stay in Michigan) and eventually made his way to Owen Sound to play major junior hockey.

Ryan started the 2008–09 season in Iowa of the AHL and quickly put up 19 points in just 14 contests.

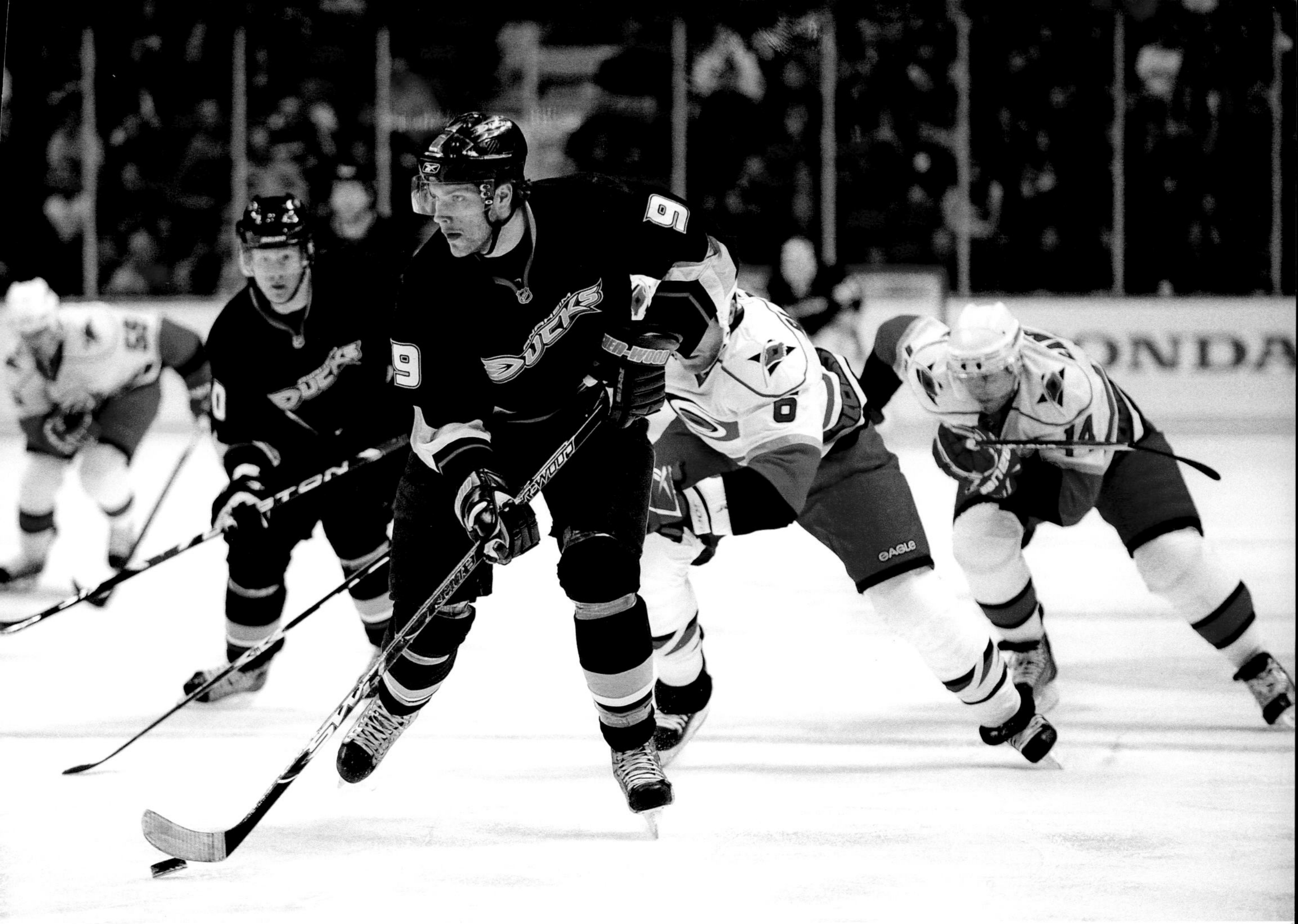

He was promoted to Anaheim and in 64 games, Ryan scored an impressive 31 goals while finishing second in the Calder Trophy race for top rookie. He then scored a team-leading 35 markers in 2009–10. Ryan has a very quick release and a move to left wing despite his right hand shot gives him a better shooting angle as he comes in on net. He uses his bulk very well and if he improves his skating a little, the sky is the limit for Ryan, who has amazed everyone already with his ability to overcome great odds and be a star in the NHL.

The U.S. Olympic Team selected Ryan for the 2010 Winter Games in Vancouver and he scored one goal and added one assist in six games. Ryan showed he has a good sense of humor by agreeing to appear in a video shown at the NHL Awards in Las Vegas where he gets teased about the American team getting the silver medal while his Anaheim teammate Ryan Getzlaf celebrates a gold medal for Canada.

As the summer of 2010 approached, Ryan was still without a signed contract even though the Ducks have put $25 million over five years on the table — a very generous offer considering his relative youth. Ryan's agent believes his client should be paid nothing less than teammates like Ryan Getzlaf and Corey Perry are earning. An offer sheet may come from another team or the Ducks might be forced to consider a trade. However it would likely be best for all concerned if Ryan continues to develop in Anaheim.

BY THE NUMBERS

- Led Anaheim with 35 goals in 2009–10
- Has had back-to-back seasons of at least 30 goals in 2008–09 and 2009–10
- Won silver with Team U.S.A. at the 2010 Winter Olympic Games
- Selected second overall by Anaheim in 2005
- Was a finalist for the Calder Trophy in 2009

CAREER HIGHLIGHTS

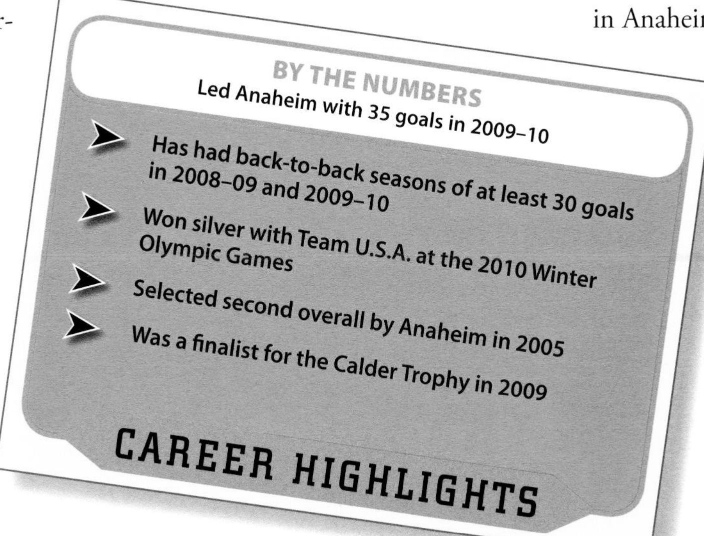

PROFILE INDEX

Alfredsson, Daniel 28
Anderson, Craig 74
Antropov, Nik 10

Backes, David 68
Backstrom, Nicklas 116
Backstrom, Niklas 60
Bergeron, Patrice 76
Boyle, Dan 78
Bozak, Tyler 156
Brodeur, Martin 22
Brown, Dustin 118
Bryzgalov, Ilya 64

Cammalleri, Mike 20
Carter, Jeff 120
Chara, Zdeno 12
Crosby, Sidney 32

Datsyuk, Pavel 122
Del Zotto, Michael 158
Doan, Shane 124
Doughty, Drew 160
Downie, Steve 162
Duchene, Matt 164

Fisher, Mike 80
Fleury, Marc-Andre 82

Gaborik, Marian 26
Getzlaf, Ryan 126
Giguère, Jean-Sebastien 84
Green, Mike 86

Halak, Jaroslav 88
Heatley, Dany 128
Hiller, Jonas 90
Howard, Jimmy 166

Iginla, Jarome 44
Kaberle, Tomas 130
Kane, Evander 168
Kane, Patrick 132
Keith, Duncan 92
Kessel, Phil 36
Kiprusoff, Miikka 134
Kopitar, Anze 58
Kovalchuk, Ilya 94

Lecavalier, Vincent 136
Lidstrom, Nicklas 54
Lucic, Milan 138
Lundqvist, Henrik 96
Luongo, Roberto 140

Malkin, Evgeni 142
Markov, Andrei 144
Miller, Ryan 14
Morrow, Brenden 52
Myers, Tyler 170

Nash, Rick 50
Neal, James 172

Ovechkin, Alex 38

Parise, Zach 146
Pavelski, Joe 98
Penner, Dustin 56
Perry, Corey 42
Phaneuf, Dion 100
Pronger, Chris 102

Rask, Tuukka 104
Richards, Brad 106
Richards, Mike 30
Ryan, Bobby 174

Seabrook, Brent 148
Sedin, Daniel 108
Sedin, Henrik 70
Spezza, Jason 150
Staal, Eric 16
Staal, Jordan 110
Stamkos, Steven 34
Stastny, Paul 48
St-Louis, Martin 112

Tavares, John 24
Thornton, Joe 66
Toews, Jonathan 46

Weber, Shea 62
Weiss, Stephen 18

Zetterberg, Henrik 152

ACKNOWLEDGMENTS

The author would like to thank the contributions of the following sources that were consulted while writing this book:

NEWSPAPERS

Toronto Star, The Globe and Mail, Toronto Sun, Calgary Sun, Ottawa Citizen, Ottawa Sun, Montreal Gazette, The Star-Ledger, National Post, The Tampa Tribune. Articles from the *Canadian Press*, the *Associated Press* and the *QMI Agency* appeared in some or all of these newspapers.

WEBSITES

Canoe.ca, HHOF.com, TheHockeyNews.com, TheFourthPeriod.com, Faceoff.com, CBCSports.ca, NBCSports.com, TSN.ca, Sportsnet.ca, Hockey-Reference.com, NHLPA.com, HockeyBuzz.com, HockeyDraft.ca, as well as NHL.com and its network of websites.

MAGAZINES

The Hockey News; *Sports Illustrated*; *ESPN the Magazine*; *McKeen's Hockey Yearbook,* 2009–10; *Maclean's*, *NHLPowerPlay*, *Hockey Now*, *Breakout*, *The Sports Forecaster*, 2009–10; *The Sporting News*, 2009–10 Toronto Maple Leafs programs.

RADIO

Interviews on the FAN 590 (Toronto), interviews and games on AM 640 (Toronto).

RECORD BOOKS

NHL Official Guide and Record Book 2009–10; *NHL Stanley Cup Playoff Guide*; *Total NHL*, *Total Hockey*, team media guides for all NHL clubs.

BOOKS

Home Ice: Hockey Canada's 2010 Roster by Lorna Schultz Nicholson.

TELEVISION

Regular season and playoff games on CBC's *Hockey Night in Canada*, The NHL on TSN, The NHL on Sportsnet, TSN's *That's Hockey*.

The author would also like to thank everyone at Firefly Books who helped in creating this book, especially Lionel Koffler, Michael Worek, Steve Cameron, Hartley Millson, Ashley Rayner and designer Kimberley Young.

Special thanks to my wife, Maria, and my son, David, for their support and understanding.